THE HISTORICAL BOOKS

L. THOMAS HOLDCROFT

WESTERN

Book

COMPANY

1618 FRANKLIN ST. • OAKLAND, CALIF. 94612

Manufactured in the United States of America

Western Book Company
1618 Franklin Street
Oakland, California 94612

TABLE OF CONTENTS

Maps and Illustrations   v

Chapter:

One: The Book of Joshua   1

Two: The Book of Judges   13

Three: The Book of Ruth   23

Four: The Book of 1 Samuel   27

Five: The Book of 2 Samuel   45

Six: The Book of 1 Kings   57

Seven: The Book of 2 Kings   75

Eight: The Books of Chronicles   93

Nine: The Book of Ezra   97

Ten: The Book of Nehemiah   103

Eleven: The Book of Esther   107

Bibliography   111

Appendices
One: False Deities of the Old Testament Era   113
Two: Questions and Projects   114

Index   116

All photographs used in this book were taken personally by
Professor Martin H. Heicksen of Levant Photo Service,
and it is through his courtesy that they appear.

MAPS AND ILLUSTRATIONS

Figure:

One: Israel's conquests west of the Jordan River 7
Two: The approximate settlement of the twelves tribes in the land 14
Three: Punitive invasions upon Israel in the time of the Judges 17
Four: Scenes from the life of Samuel 31
Five: Scenes from the life of Saul 35
Six: Events in David's life in the First Book of Samuel 43
Seven: David's empire at the time of his death 59
Eight: Solomon's temple as seen through Shushan Gate 63
Nine: Sites of events in First and Second Kings 73
Ten: Further sites and events in Second Kings 82
Eleven: Scene of the captivity of the ten tribes (Israel) 85
Twelve: Scene of the captivity of the Southern Kingdom (Judah) 90
Thirteen: Comparative chronology of the historical books 92
Fourteen: Palestine during the era of the Restoration 101

Photographic Illustrations

The Jordan adjacent to Zeretan vi
Excavations at Shiloh 11
The Valley of Lebonah 24
The fields and city of Bethlehem 26
The Judean wilderness seen from the cave of Adullam 37
The present-day mound at Beth-shan 51
Rocks at the site of Nob 55
Gibeon and the village of El-jib 65
An overall view of the site of Tirzah 69
The mound at Dothan 79
Ruins excavated at Megiddo 88
Jerusalem's hill of Ophel 99

The Jordan River as it appears in Palestine's central valley. This view, from a point adjacent to Zaretan (Zeredathah), looks north. It was near this site that Solomon's workers cast the bronze vessels for the temple: "In the plain of Jordan did the king cast them, in the clay ground between Succoth and Zeredathah" (2 Chron. 4:17).

1. THE BOOK OF JOSHUA

The book of Joshua, the sixth book of the Bible, continues the story of Israel where Moses left off. The Pentateuch recorded Israel's history up to the time when the nation was gathered in the Plains of Moab east of Jordan; it was left to Moses' successors to record the crossing of the Jordan and the possession of the land.

The Nature and Theme of the Book

Joshua is a militant book reporting Israel's victories in her efforts to subdue and possess the promised land. It has been compared to the book of Acts: each book describes an enlightened people pressing in to secure their inheritance and employ it in God's service. The first twelve chapters of Joshua report events of the conquest, the last twelve chapters pertain to the allotments of the tribes. The book consistently emphasizes that the victories and achievements of God's people are only effected through the guidance and empowering of God.

The Authorship of the Book

In the first verse of this book we are introduced to Joshua, the son of Nun. He is here set forth as "Moses' successor" and by inference it may be concluded that he is to be identified as the one who assembled and recorded the data contained in this book. Joshua, together with Caleb, was one of two men who was spared in the wilderness wanderings (Num. 14:30), and thus in point of years and experience he was an entire generation beyond his contemporaries. God had specifically declared that Joshua, as Moses' successor, should lead the Israelites into the promised land (Deut. 31:14-23). On both spiritual and practical grounds, Joshua was especially suited to serve as the spiritual and civil leader of his people at this stage of their history, and in the process almost surely to emulate his predecessor in maintaining a literary project.

It is characteristic of liberal interpreters to combine Joshua with the five books of the Pentateuch, and to refer to the whole as the "Hexateuch." Thus, by those who accept the documentary hypothesis, Joshua is assigned a composite authorship.

Evangelicals, generally, would reject this position. For those who will see them, significant differences between Joshua and the Pentateuch are clearly observable. For instance, the phrase "Jehovah the God of Israel" is found 14 times in Joshua, and only twice in the entire Pentateuch. It is obvious that because the Pentateuch and Joshua are the works of contemporaries, they may be expected to have similarities, but their differences are enough to indicate that the authorship of Joshua is distinctive.

Some relevant facts pertaining to the authorship of the book of Joshua are as follows:

1) Joshua is explicitly mentioned as the author of portions: e.g. "And Joshua wrote these words in the book of the law of God . . ." (24:26).

2) Incidents reporting details of personal communion between Joshua and the Lord are frequent in the book and these could plausibly have been known only by Joshua (e.g. 1:1, 3:7, 4:2, 5:2, 6:2, 7:10, 8:1, 10:8, and 20:1).

3) The descriptions frequently are so detailed and minute that they could only have been recorded by an eye witness.

4) The use of the personal pronouns "we" and "us" in 5:1,6 indicates that, at least this fragment, is a direct statement by Joshua.

5) Several statements of historical events indicate that the book was written prior to the monarchy in Israel and thus in Joshua's time rather than in a later era. (e.g. 9:23, 13:6, 15:63, and 16:10 are passages that describe events that necessarily precede David and Solomon.

6) The Talmud declares that Joshua wrote the whole of the book with the exception of the last five verses.

The foregoing data points strongly to Joshua's essential role in the preparation of the book. One important item of contrary evidence, however, is the fact that the expression "to this day" occurs 14 times in the book, but in only three places (22:3, 23:8, 23:9) would it fall within Joshua's lifetime. Keil takes note of these facts, and in the light of them suggests that we should ascribe the content of the book to Joshua, but recognize that Joshua's material must have been edited by someone (an elder) who outlived him. Since the book does not claim that Joshua was its author, the postulation of a later compiler-editor does not discount its authenticity. Most evangelical scholars probably are content to assign the authorship to Joshua, while at the same time recognizing that Joshua likely used other source materials (cf. the epic poem known as "The Book of Jasher" 10:13), and that others after his time to a greater or lesser degree modified the material that he had gathered.

Facts Concerning Joshua

Joshua had previously won Scriptural mention on such occasions as: his battle with Amalek at Rephidim (Ex. 17:9); his sojourn with Moses on Sinai (Ex. 24:13, 32:17, 33:11), his efforts to silence the prophets Eldad and Medad (Num. 11:26-30); his choice as one of the 12 spies (Num. 13:8); and his investiture as Moses' successor (Num. 27:18). In his personal background, Joshua was of the tribe of Ephraim of the house of Joseph. The name means "Jehovah is deliverance [salvation]" and it occurs in Scripture in a variety of forms including: Jeshua, Hoshea, Hosea, Jehoshua, Oshea. The name Jesus is the Greek form of this name.

Joshua was 80 years of age when he took office, and he was nominal head of the people until his death at 110. However, his active leadership was maintained only during the conquest, and it is believed that he was in semi-retirement for the last two decades of his life. Scripture nowhere makes a disparaging remark concerning Joshua, and he is portrayed rather as an ideal leader of the people of God. He succeeded most effectively in maintaining the theocracy: during his administration the real ruler of Israel was God.

The Scope of the Book

The book of Joshua represents about 30 years of Israel's history.

The Key Word and Key Verse

The key word is "inheritance." The key verse is 1:2, 3 "Arise, go over. . . unto the land which I shall give. . . Every place that the sole of your foot shall tread upon. . . have I given unto you."

The Authenticity of the Book

In the Hebrew Bible the book of Joshua is the first of the Former Prophets. (This is the group including: Joshua, Judges, Samuel, and Kings.) The book is joined to the Pentateuch by the common Hebrew conjunction translated "and"; hence its

connection with the preceding books is established. Some six books of the Bible either quote from Joshua or allude to its contents: 1 Chron. 2:7, 12:15; Psa. 44, 68, 78, 104; Isa. 28:21; Heb. 3:11-13; Acts 7:45; and Heb. 4:8, 9.

ANALYSIS AND EXPOSITION

I. The Invasion of Palestine (Chs. 1-5)

1. Joshua's Charge and Commission (Ch. 1)

The death of Moses was no surprise to God, for He had a Joshua ready to continue His work. Joshua was not strictly a successor to Moses, for no one except Jesus Christ may be thought of as succeeding Israel's great law giver, but Joshua was the one chosen to take Moses' place as earthly leader of the people. Whereas Moses had been a law giver, Joshua was to lead the people as their general. He was destined to be privileged to carry to completion the settlement of the nation in the land. The vision of the Israelites in their national home, which four centuries earlier Abraham had anticipated and that even the great Moses had not been privileged to see, was now to be fulfilled under Joshua's leadership.

God tempered His commission and challenge to Joshua by assuring him of divine help, and in what is known as the "two foot rule" (v. 3) made clear that the conquest of the land would be easily achieved. Though it was not until Solomon's time that all the land as here indicated was possessed, at least Joshua was sure of the divine support and enablement for the task before him. God's promise to Joshua may apply to all Bible believers: ". . . Be strong and of a good courage; be not afraid, neither be thou dismayed: for the Lord thy God is with thee . . ." (v. 9). An acquaintance with the newly completed "book of the law" (i.e. the Pentateuch) was declared to be the key to success: "This book of the law shall not depart out of thy mouth; but thou shalt meditate therein day and night, that thou mayest observe to do according to all that is written therein: for then thou shalt make thy way prosperous, and then thou shalt have good success." (v. 8) God from the beginning placed a premium on Bible knowledge.

The tribes of Reuben, Gad, and half-Manasseh were reminded of their promise to contribute armed forces to enable the other tribes to conquer the land. These two and one-half tribes had been granted territory east of Jordan, but only on the condition that they help the others in the conquest. Such an arrangement was a fair one since all of the tribes had achieved the overthrow of Sihon and Og to win the territory for the two and one-half tribes.

(See Num. 21:21-35; 32:1-42). Scripture notes that in this early period the people were so wholeheartedly committed to the leadership of Joshua that they voluntarily placed themselves under martial law in his command: "Whosoever . . . will not hearken unto thy words . . . he shall be put to death." (v. 18)

2. Rahab and the Two Spies (Ch. 2)

The city of Jericho was a formidable barrier to Israel's advance, and its subjugation was necessary before further conquest. Hence, one of Joshua's inaugural acts was the sending of the two spies to reconnoiter the city. When the presence of these agents was reported to the king of Jericho they stood to be captured except that Rahab offered them concealment and escape. At great personal risk, Rahab succeeded in diverting the pursuers of the spies, and eventually they were able to return to their own camp and make their report to Joshua. They declared: "Truly the Lord hath delivered into our hands all the land; for even all the inhabitants of the country do faint because of us." (v. 24)

The stalks of flax under which Rahab hid the spies would have been up to a yard long and an inch in diameter. A few bundles carefully placed would no doubt have been adequate to conceal the men. In so acting, Rahab was demonstrating faith in God and her commitment to Him in spite of the fact that Scripture specifically identifies her as a harlot. In an effort to reconcile this seeming contradiction of affairs, scholars since the time of Josephus in 90 A. D., have suggested that possibly the word "harlot" does not need to mean more than "innkeeper." They suggest that though Rahab opened her home to visitors, it does not necessarily follow that she lived an immoral life. Unfortunately, historical accounts of the customs of ancient times do not support this charitable interpretation. Scripture says, "By faith the harlot Rahab perished not . . ." (Heb. 11:31) and again "Likewise also was not Rahab the harlot justified by works, . . ." (Jas. 2:25).

Because Rahab offered them a refuge, the spies pledged that she and her family should be preserved in the forthcoming destruction of Jericho. The signal to indicate her favored status was to be the scarlet cord hanging from the window. Even so, Christ's shed blood provides deliverance from destruction for all who will avail themselves of its protection. On the basis of Matthew 1:5 "And Salmon begat Booz of Rachab; . . ." it is believed that Rahab became an ancestress of Christ.

3. The Jordan Crossed (Ch. 3)

The crossing of the Jordan was both pre-

ceded by and followed by thorough spiritual preparation and expression by the people. It is noted that this event took place just four days before the Passover. The priests carrying the ark led in the crossing with the entire company in procession behind them. The priests' lead was some 3,000 feet and this served not only to impress the people to remain a respectful distance from the sacred Ark, but also enabled all of the marchers clearly to view it. At the moment that the feet of the priests touched the water, the Jordan miraculously divided, and the people passed over on dry land. The language of Scripture seems to indicate that the people did not even see any water as they crossed the river bed.

The miracle of the crossing of the Jordan was all the greater because the event took place at the time of the spring floods. In the neighborhood of Jericho, the bed of the Jordan is less than 100 feet across, but at flood time the river has been known to swell to as much as a mile in width. (However in recent decades, flood control measures have been imposed.) Some students of Scripture consider that the drying up of the river was due to the collapse of overhanging clay banks a few miles to the north (Adam beside Zaretan is about 18 miles north of Jericho). The fact that in 1927 a 150 foot high cliff overhanging the Jordan collapsed and for 21 hours halted the flow of water in the lower river is cited as a proof of the feasibility of this proposal. However, most believers feel that it is more in the spirit of Scripture to conclude that God simply caused a congealing of the water in an instant apart from tangible means. Certainly, this entire episode must have constituted a great uplift to the faith of the Israelites regardless of the means by which it was accomplished.

4. The Memorial Cairns (Ch. 4)

To commemorate the crossing of the Jordan, two memorial cairns were erected, one in the bed of the river (v. 9), and the other at Gilgal (vv. 3, 20). Each consisted of twelve stones, and together, the cairns were to serve as memorials to remind latter day citizens of the power of the Lord in the realm of nature. Gilgal (meaning "a circle of stones") was the site of the first encampment west of the Jordan and it seems evident that it was here that the tabernacle was set up and remained for some time to come. The move of the tabernacle and national headquarters from Gilgal to Shiloh is described in Joshua 18. It is noted that, in fulfillment of their pledge, the two and one-half tribes sent a representation of 40,000 warriors across the Jordan to assist the remaining tribes in their settlement in the land.

Typically, the crossing of the Jordan has been compared with: 1) salvation -- from a barren wilderness to a new life; 2) death -- from pilgrimage to home; and 3) victory in spiritual crisis -- appropriating a promise to attain a new plane of Christian living. The outcome of these events was that the people developed a new appreciation and reverence for Joshua. "On that day the Lord magnified Joshua in the sight of all Israel; and they feared [i.e. reverenced] him, as they feared Moses, all the days of his life" (v. 14). God personally intervened to bestow upon Joshua personal status commensurate with his responsibility.

5. The First Passover in Canaan (Ch. 5)

This chapter reports great fear in the ranks of Israel's enemies so that ". . . their heart melted, neither was there spirit in them any more, . . . " (v. 1). Such a state of affairs was in fulfillment of God's promise: "This day will I begin to put the dread of thee and the fear of thee upon the nations . . . . " (Deut. 2:25). The miracle of the dividing of the Jordan especially impressed the kings of the Amorites and Canaanites, and it is thus evident that this event not only served the purpose of transporting the Israelites into the land but also achieved a favorable effect in what might be described as psychological warfare.

After the crossing, the Lord commanded the national circumcision of the people. Evidently this rite had been neglected during the years of wandering and the people had been counted out of communion with God. The renewal of circumcision was a sort of formal announcement that Israel was reinstated with God. At this time also, the people renewed the celebration of the Passover after a 39 year lapse (Num. 9:5). Four days after the Passover, the people ate of the food of the land, and the manna ceased. Thereby, the exodus was officially at an end.

The Man with the drawn sword was most certainly deity (He accepted worship from Joshua), and He is usually considered a preincarnate appearance of the Lord Jesus (one of several Old Testament Christophanies). His presence indicated the continuation of the divine leadership and concern for Israel, and impressed anew the fact of the holiness of God. Although Joshua was the human leader of the people, ultimately the triune God continued to maintain His divine leadership. Joshua's appointment did not constitute God's resignation.

II. The Conquest of Central Palestine (Chs. 6-8)

1. The Conquest of Jericho (Ch. 6)

In his efforts at conquest, Joshua's strategy was to drive due west. Such a course made it possible for Israel to drive a wedge into her enemies and separate the northern and southern tribes. The Canaanites were accustomed to attacks from the south but they had concluded that the Dead Sea and the Jordan offered a sure defence from the east. Hence they were comparatively easy victims for the conquering Israelites. Since the city of Jericho lay in the line of advance it became the next objective for conquest. This formidable "city of palm trees" was situated about 6 miles west of the Jordan at the head of three passes through the Mountains of Judea and on the main highways of ancient trade routes. To conquer it was to win a valuable prize.

Jericho is known to have been a walled city by about 3000 B.C., and according to the archaeologist, Garstang, the city which the Israelites captured was the fourth city on the same site. Jericho was only about 7 acres in area (some say about 13 acres), and it probably had a population of not more than 3,000, but in its day it was considered a great city and it compared favorably with other great cities of antiquity (e.g. Troy). Sir Charles Marston describes Jericho as follows:

> There had been two parallel walls fifteen feet apart, the outer six feet thick, and the inner one twelve feet. Both walls were thirty feet high, and across their tops houses had been built. The plan of the city was an oblong, the length being twice the breadth. At the northwest corner, facing the Judean hills, stood a tower or citadel.[1]

It is to be noted that there is some uncertainty concerning the dating of archaeological evidences at Jericho, and not everyone agrees that the Jericho that has been excavated is that of Joshua's day.

In the Lord's plan, the conquest of the city required a march about the city once each day for the first 6 days of the siege. The procession consisted of: the warriors, 7 priests blowing trumpets, the ark, and a rear guard. It is likely that the circuit would not have required more than about 20 minutes each day, or more than two and one-half hours on the seventh day. The great shout upon the conclusion of the seventh circuit on the seventh day seems to have been accompanied by a divinely caused earthquake that resulted in the utter collapse of the walls. Evidently the people of Jericho who survived the overthrow of the city were so cowered and terrified by events that they had no more will to fight.

---

[1]Charles Marston, The Bible Comes Alive (London: Eyre and Spottiswoode, 1937), p. 84.

God decreed that Jericho was to be destroyed utterly. As it were, the city was to be offered as a burnt offering to Jehovah. All people (except Rahab and her family) and all animals were to be slain, and any precious metals found were to be dedicated to the Lord. One has commented concerning the victory over Jericho and the destruction of the city: "If it did not typify, it certainly well illustrates the victories which the Gospel was to obtain over all the principalities and powers of earth and hell. No human force was used, nothing but the sound of the Gospel trumpet prevailed for the subversion of Satan's kingdom." There is a sense wherein it may be said the Israelites did not take Jericho, but God took it for them.

Although, as already noted, there are problems concerning the dating of Joshua's destruction of Jericho, in general it is agreed that archaeological findings impressively confirm the Biblical account. In what is usually identified with Joshua's destruction, it has been found that the inner wall of the city, as if from weak foundations, suddenly collapsed, and falling outward overturned the outer wall with it. In addition, there are evidences of a grievous fire, for the burnt strata there is three or four times thicker than in most cities that have been excavated. Even the scorched remains of foodstuffs have been found, and this would seem to accord with the Bible command to burn all, and not to take plunder.

Joshua pronounced a curse upon all who would try to rebuild Jericho (v. 26) but in the intervening centuries this curse has been successively defied. Thus, 1 Kings 16:34 reports the rebuilding by Hiel, the Bethelite, during the time of King Ahab. It was a prevailing heathen practice to seek to assure blessing upon a building venture by sealing a living child in an earthern vessel and burying it in the foundation. Hiel "laid the foundation thereof in Abiram his firstborn, and set up the gates thereof in his youngest son Segub" exactly as Joshua had predicted.

2. The Sin of Achan. Israel's Defeat at Ai (Ch. 7)

After the conquest of Jericho, Israel next sought to capture the city of Ai which was about 14 miles west and in the natural line of advance. The mountain pass in which Ai was located is now called Wady Kelt. On the basis of the size of army that Ai placed on the field, it has been estimated that the city represented a population of upwards of 12,000. However, another theory notes that the name "Ai" means "ruin," and it is suggested that Ai itself was only a military fortress-outpost maintained by the neighboring cities on the site of a previously destroyed city. At least one school of archaeology holds that excavations indicate that the city lay in ruins

from approximately 2000 B.C. to 1200 B.C. Regardless of the truth in these matters, what is plainly reported is that in the face of Ai's forces, Israel suffered an ignominious rout. Joshua and the elders were promptly driven to prayer in order to seek to discover the cause of their failure.

In this unique instance, God commanded Joshua to cease praying (v. 10), and instead take positive action to deal with sin in the camp. Joshua was divinely guided to find the culprit, Achan, of the tribe of Judah. By preserving the Babylonish garment, and silver and the gold, Achan had robbed God of due offerings, and a severe penalty was unquestionably merited. The actual value of the goods stolen by Achan was not great by contemporary standards, but to an Israelite it undoubtedly represented a vast sum. In addition, a sacred principle was violated. Achan was stoned, and although the language at this point is somewhat ambiguous, it may be inferred from the sudden termination of his genealogy in 1 Chronicles 2:7 that his family died with him.

A truly noteworthy lesson taught by the story of Achan is that the sin of one affects the entire body. In this case, God treated the nation, as He does His Church, as an organic whole. In later conquests, Israel would be allowed to retain the spoils, but Jericho was to be the firstfruits to be given to God as a burnt offering. For any citizen of the nation to retain what was properly and officially God's was indeed a grievous sin. In order that the lesson might not be lost to succeeding generations, the people erected a memorial consisting of "a great heap of stones" at the place of Achan's execution and burial. The site was appropriately named Achor (trouble). The defeat that the nation suffered due to Achan's sin led to the only recorded casualties (36 men) in all of the account of Israel's conquest of the land.

3. The Conquest of Ai (Ch. 8)

With due adjustment of sin in the camp, it was a simple matter for Israel to win a speedy and decisive victory over the people of Ai. Israel's strategy was to conceal some 5,000 soldiers at a distance from the city and then send the remainder of the army to attack. As the battle proceeded, the attackers feigned defeat and retreated, thus driving Ai's defenders out of the city. When the defending armies were far enough from the city gates, the 5,000 men in ambush swarmed forth and entering the city set it afire and destroyed any remaining defenders. When the burning city was seen by the retreating Israelites, they turned back to attack, and Ai's army caught between these attackers and the 5,000, was totally annihilated. This description of a successful ambush is the first Scriptural mention of such military strategy.

In conformity with the previous command of God (Deut. 27), Joshua next led the Israelites to the base of the mountains of Ebal and Gerizim that he might acquaint the new generation with God's Law. He first erected a simple stone altar, and after offering sacrifice, inscribed in the stones or a plaster surface, the ten commandments. These commandments, and the penalties for disobedience, Joshua read to all the people including: women, little children, and strangers. It may be visualized that for this reading Joshua with the priests and Levites stood in the valley between the mountains with half of the tribes standing upon the slopes of each in the manner of an audience in an amphitheatre. As the Levites read the curses, those on Mount Ebal responded with a chanted "Amen, " while as the blessings were read, those on Mount Gerizim responded similarly.

The cities captured by the Israelites appear to have been in each case the capital of a small city-state. Hence, by the conquest of the city, the victors came into possession of surrounding territories. Apparently, the conquest of Jericho and Ai were the two major steps in the conquest of Central Palestine. There is some archaeological evidence that the conquest of Ai actually included Bethel also, since the two cities were close together. There is evidence of a great destruction at Bethel in which it was burned by fire, and it has been suggested that this destruction took place during Israel's conquest under Joshua (but see Jud. 1:22-25). There is some indication that parts of the territories of Central Palestine were granted to Israel when the possessors simply conceded defeat and made the treaties with Israel (cf. Jud. 2:1-4). Also, in some instances, Israel did not at this time complete the conquest but by-passed certain occupied areas.

The Tel el Amarna tablets speak of the infiltration and the conquest of Palestine in what may be this very era by a people who were called the "Hebiru." The Hebiru are set forth as "trouble makers on the fringes of society." Scholars usually deny that they should be identified with the Israelites, for there is no real etymological relationship between "Hebiru" and "Hebrew." It would seem possible that the name "Hebiru" occasionally applied to the Hebrews and to any other wandering nomads, somewhat as the term "gypsy" is today used in a generic sense. The Hebiru are depicted in archaeological finds throughout western Asia in the era from 3000 to 1000 B.C. They seem not to have been a numerous people, nor does their role historically appear to have been particularly significant.

In achieving his conquest, Joshua showed sound military strategy by driving into the land at midpoint. He thus divided it into parts and was able to conquer each part in turn. There is evidence that the Canaanite nations at this time were weakened because of recent wars against Egypt. The Philistines were still a youthful nation with little national organization or spirit. Egypt had been greatly weakened through the plagues and disaster at the Red Sea, and was still recovering, while Assyria had not yet risen to be a world power. In addition to all these natural advantages, Joshua enjoyed divine intervention including: hailstones, the lengthened day, the collapsing walls, and fierce hornets!

III. The Conquest of Southern Palestine (Chs. 9-10)

1. The Covenant with Gibeon (Ch. 9)

The people of Gibeon no doubt realized that it was only a matter of time before Israel would attack and destroy them just as they had overthrown Jericho. Gibeon too, was situated in a mountain pass into the interior, and the city inevitably confronted the invader. It would appear that the crafty plot of the Gibeonites was motivated chiefly by a slavish fear, and not at all by a justifying faith as in the case of Rahab. The Gibeonite ambassadors evidenced their subtlety not only in their choice of clothing and equipment, but even in their conversation with Joshua and the elders. They vividly described past victories of Israel, but they made no mention of the crossing of the Jordan or of the victories in Palestine. Of these latter they undoubtedly were all too painfully aware!

Joshua and the elders demonstrated undue haste in their acceptance of the Gibeonites and their confirmation of a pact of non-aggression. Perhaps these leaders fell victim to the appeal of flattery in this attention from a supposedly distant city. Among Orientals, the acceptance of proffered food is the establishment of peace and friendship, and there is some evidence of such a symbolic act between the Gibeonites and Israel. Three days later when the truth of the situation came to light, Israel had no alternative but to spare the city. The Mosaic law (Deut. 20:10-20) specifically declares that an enemy taken without a battle and under agreement should be spared. Evidently the Gibeonites were content with their menial tasks if thereby they could be assured that their lives would be spared. God was greatly displeased when many decades later King Saul violated the covenant and attacked the Gibeonites. Hence, a severe divine penalty was imposed (2 Sam. 21:1-9).

2. The Southern Confederacy Defeated (Ch. 10)

The remainder of the kings of the southern cities, under the leadership of Adoni-zedek, King of Jerusalem, despised the Gibeonites for this apparent treachery and thus they prepared an armed attack. They constituted an alliance of five kings of city-states of southern Palestine and their union is usually known as the Southern Confederacy. The peoples of this region for the most part were Amorites, although there were also some Hivites and Jebusites. In the face of this threatening force, the Gibeonites sent a frantic message to Joshua pleading for help. By virtue of the covenant that had been made, Israel was obligated to respond, and with her Gibeonite allies do battle

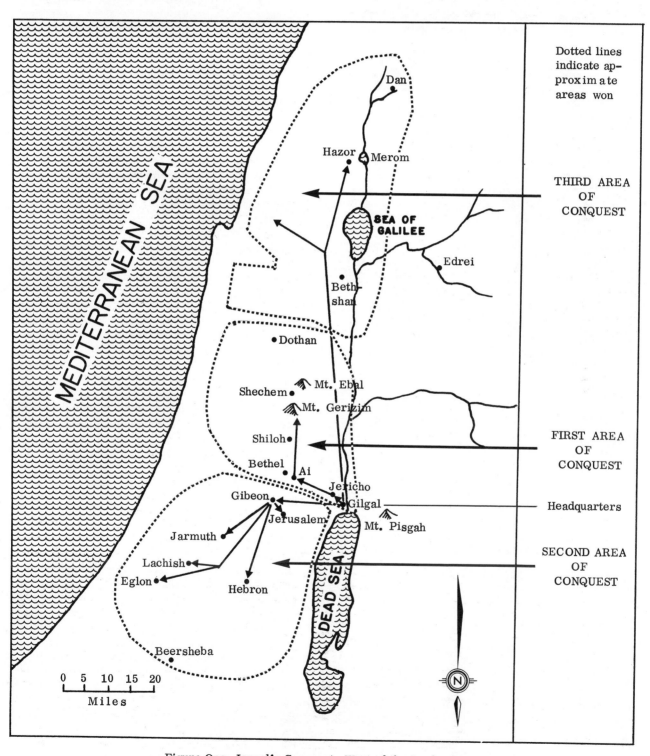

Figure One: Israel's Conquests West of the Jordan River

against the Southern Confederacy.

Joshua proceeded with vigor and confidence and after an all-night forced march covering some 26 miles his forces launched a surprise attack upon the enemy. God supported Israel's efforts, first by sending the deadly hailstones to destroy their enemies, and then by prolonging the day so that Israel might have sufficient time to complete the task of destruction. Hail is very rare in Palestine but not unknown and on those occasions when it has fallen it usually has wrought severe destruction. The long day of Joshua is perhaps the grandest in concept of all the Bible miracles, but it stands as a solemn record in the Word of God. No data on God's procedure is set forth, so that it is possible that the results were accomplished by a miracle of refraction rather than by the alteration of the motion of the stars and planets. The confirmation of the long day of Joshua is found in certain national traditions of Egypt, China, and India, and reportedly has been substantiated by findings of some modern astronomers.

The five kings of the Confederacy were captured and slain and their cities destroyed. The process whereby Joshua's captains put their feet upon the necks of the captured kings seems to have been an expression of victory rather than an inhuman barbarianism. The cave that had been the hiding place of these enemy kings was made their permanent tomb. Following this event, Joshua continued his conquest in southern Palestine and a number of other cities and their surrounding territory came into his possession. Although Scripture at this point reports "Joshua . . . left none remaining, but utterly destroyed all that breathed . . ." (v. 40), nevertheless some of the inhabitants of southern Palestine or their tribal groups then located elsewhere seem to have survived. Hence, Israel's problems with hostile tribesmen in the South continued to be manifested in her later history.

IV. The Conquest of Northern Palestine (Chs. 11-12)

1. The Northern Confederacy Defeated (Ch. 11)

The conquest of the northern area of Palestine likewise involved the defeat of a confederacy which is variously known as the Northern Confederacy or the Hazor Confederacy. According to Josephus, the forces of King Jabin of Hazor included 300,000 foot soldiers, 10,000 horsemen, and 20,000 chariots. It is estimated that at this time the city of Hazor alone boasted a population of 40,000 and it extended over nearly 200 acres. Humanly speaking, the fact that Joshua proceeded to the attack is evidence of the high morale of the Israelites at this time. Although the enemy possessed such advantages as

familiarity with the terrain, a fierce patriotism, and no restrictions on the basis of ethical scruples, Joshua's means to victory was the simple strategy of a surprise attack. The original indicates that Joshua's forces came upon the enemy "like a thunderbolt." The attack which began by the waters of Merom upon the massing enemy ended in the total routing of its troops throughout northern Palestine and a sweeping victory for Israel.

The houghing of horses (v. 9) consists of disabling the animals by severing the tarsal or heel tendon. This method of dealing with the horses was used because the heel tendon is the most vulnerable part. In some instances a horse so treated was allowed to live but was crippled to the degree that it was usable only for plodding agricultural purposes, and no longer could it run as a war-horse. The destruction of war-horses was equivalent to the destruction of unusable weapons of the enemy in modern warfare. It was the will of God that Israel dispose of all tokens of human strength and power, and in their place maintain confidence and trust in their divine protector. Humanly speaking, cavalry and chariots were an ominous threat to the foot soldiers of Israel, and it was to their advantage to destroy all that fell into their hands. Israel seems to have won a victory against these forces in northern Palestine because the battlefield was mainly mountainous. Jabin's horses and chariots were much less effective than they would have been on a level plain.

Joshua's "mopping up" activities included the subduing of the giant Anakims. These people dwelt in the mountain regions of the land, but after his campaign there were only a few survivors in the cities of the Philistines. Once again the Scriptural report: "So Joshua took the whole land" (v. 23), is subject to some modification. Neither on a regional basis, nor for the land as a whole, can it be said that Joshua conquered all portions in the sense of destroying or expelling the Canaanite peoples. Survivors of these tribes may have temporarily given obeisance to Joshua, but within a few years' time they were actually the cause of much trouble to Israel. It was not until David's time that the conquest and dispossession of usurping tribes was fully completed.

2. Thirty-three Defeated Kings (Ch. 12)

This account of the defeat of the two kings east of Jordan and the thirty-one west of Jordan represents victories over a seven year period. The kings appear to be enumerated in the order of their encounter with the Israelites. The majority of these kings would have about as large a constituency as the mayor of a small town today, but they would have had a great deal more authority. Although the king of Jerusalem was subdued at this time, his city was not permanently possessed until the time of David (see 15:63; 2 Sam. 5:6, 7). The Valley of Esdraelon for the time being was left in the hands of the Canaanites and the maritime plain continued to be peopled by the hostile Philistines. The failure to dispossess the Jebusites and Philistines has been noted as a major blunder in Joshua's strategy.

The general outlook of modern scholars is to emphasize the time span in Israel's conquest of Canaan, and to stress the diversity of her methods. Within limits, such views are not necessarily in conflict with the Bible account. The Bible has the barest record of the conquest of certain centers, and freely passes over most. It is not improbable that the conquest of Canaan was a combined effort of: military conquest, social absorption, religious proselyting, and legal treaty, all of which extended over a lengthy period.

The fact that a loving God should direct the Israelites to destroy and dispossess the Canaanites is a problem of perennial concern. However, it may be recognized that, in effect, the Israelites were achieving corrective surgery. It is considered that the Canaanites may be described as one of the most grossly depraved peoples of the ancient world. Their two chief perversions were: 1) their habit of burning alive their children as a sacrifice to Molech, 2) their practice of sex orgies in the name of worship to Baal. Sampey comments on Israel's role:

They were made the executioners of the wrath of God against people sunk in vice and corruption so great that there is no hope of reclaiming them . . . . Of course, no Christian nation could now treat a barbarous people thus without raising a storm of protest from the civilized world. . . . In the days of Moses and Joshua . . . the nations . . . recognized the right of peoples to devote their enemies to destructions in a holy war. . . . Hence, it was possible to use the Israelites in that early time as executioners of the just wrath of God . . . . Instead of employing pestilence or earthquake, Jehovah saw fit to destroy them by the sword of Israel. [2]

V. The Division of the Land. Residence in Canaan (Chs. 13-22)

1. The Boundaries of the Land. The tribes East of Jordan (Ch. 13)

---

[2]John Sampey, The Heart of the Old Testament (Nashville: Broadman Press, 1922), pp. 75, 76.

At this point, Scripture describes Joshua as "old and stricken in years." He was probably from ninety to one hundred years of age, and evidently his days of active leadership were over. The boundaries that the Lord proceeded to describe were not actually to become a part of Israel until the time of Solomon, some 500 years later. Even in Solomon's time they were to be possessed for only a brief period and never actually colonized by Israel. Thus the challenge which God set forth was indeed appropriate: ". . . there remaineth yet very much land to be possessed."

The divine intervention in securing the land and specific instructions for its apportionment reveal that the settlement of the tribes was something of a sacred matter. The family and tribal inheritances were valued as a spiritual legacy as well as for their own sake. On this occasion God specifically confirmed the action of Moses in granting the territory east of Jordan to the two and one-half tribes: Reuben, Gad, and half-Manasseh. Some of the events in the conquest are reviewed, including the slaying of the treacherous Balaam (v. 22, cf. Num. 31:8).

2. The Possession of Caleb (Ch. 14)

God's procedure in settling the tribes was to direct the inheritance of the general area by lot, and then to leave to Joshua and the ten chieftains the determination of the exact boundaries by mediation. The actual implementation of the lot-drawing was not until later, after the removal of the tabernacle to Shiloh (see chs. 18,19). Once again it is pointed out that the Levites received no territorial inheritance as such, but rather a number of cities (actually 48) with their suburbs. The basic support of the Levites was to be by means of their share of the sacrifices brought by the people. The total of 12 tribes was maintained by the division of the tribe of Joseph into two sections: Ephraim and Manasseh.

Caleb had supported Joshua on the occasion of the report of the 12 spies (Num. 13), and at that time, which was some 45 years previously, Moses had promised that Caleb should be rewarded for his faithfulness. He came now, also, as the representative of the tribe of Judah, and therefore particularly merited the grant of a portion of the tribal territory. Though Caleb requested his particular inheritance, he did not unfairly take advantage of his position to ask to be especially favored. Mt. Hebron, to which he was assigned, although in the tribal territory, was at that time overrun by the vicious sons of Anak. Caleb's effort to conquer his possession is related in the next chapter, and also in Judges chapter one.

3. The Possession of Judah. Caleb's Conquest. (Ch. 15)

Although Caleb succeeded in achieving victories by his own hand in the conquest of his territory, he also appealed for help from others, and he offered the hand of his daughter to anyone who achieved victory. The contest was won by Othniel, a nephew of Caleb. This fine young man became doubly related through the marriage that rewarded his military success. The descendants of this union constituted most of the aristocracy of Judah. In total area, Judah received nearly one-third of the whole country, though by no means was all of the land usable. The territory included: the southern wilderness, the fertile lowlands, and the rugged hill country. This chapter mentions some twenty-nine cities within the area.

The city which Othniel captured was known as Kirjath-sepher--"the city of records." Probably it was a cultural center with a library housing important records of the day. A significant statement in v. 63 declares: "As for the Jebusites, the inhabitants of Jerusalem, the children of Judah could not drive them out." The conquest of the Jebusites and of the city of Jerusalem was a project of first priority when David assumed the throne of the united Kingdom (2 Sam. 5:6-9).

4. The Tribal Possessions of Ephraim and Manasseh (Chs. 16, 17)

The tribes of Ephraim and Manasseh each received a generous grant of land, for their large populations required ample space. Nevertheless, they expressed disappointment that their allotments had not been larger: "The hill is not enough for us . . ." (17:16). Joshua's advice was that they should drive out the Canaanites and thereby win the additional space they needed. Historically, the tribes ignored this suggestion: ". . . when the children of Israel were waxen strong . . . they put the Canaanites to tribute; but they did not utterly drive them out" (17:13, cf. 16:10).

Scripture makes special mention of the fact that because Zelophehad had no sons, the family property inheritance was vested in his five daughters (17:3). Also in chapter 17 the city of Beth-shean is mentioned (vv. 11, 16), and Israel's fear of her iron chariots noted. Because the city possessed such superior military resources, Israel chose not to molest it. At a later time the city became a stronghold of pagan temples and Finegan describes two that have been excavated: ". . . the Southern temple may have been the Temple of Dagon of 1 Chron. 10:10, and the Northern temple may have been the House of Ashtoroth of 1 Sam. 31:10. Serpents played an important part in the cult . . . plaques with serpents and shrine-houses with serpents on them were found in the temples."[3] It is the opinion of archaeologists that the "iron chariots" of the time were actually wooden vehicles shod with a hoop of iron about the wheels.

5. The Tabernacle. The Seven Remaining Tribes. (Chs. 18, 19)

The removal of the tabernacle and the national headquarters from Gilgal to Shiloh was an arrangement that was to be in effect for more than three centuries--until the time of the death of the prophet Eli and the beginning of the monarchy. Shiloh has been investigated by archaeologists, and it has been revealed to be a purely Hebrew city, apparently founded and built by their own efforts. The city contrasts with contemporary cities in being rather crude and primitive, and with houses of stones set together without mortar.

It was at Shiloh that most of the land divisions were decided. Representatives of the seven tribes appeared there and drew lots to determine the tribal portions (19:51). Undoubtedly the choice by lot involved a liberal measure of providential guidance. Descriptions of the allotted portions begin as follows: Benjamin (18:11), Simeon (19:1), Zebulun (19:10), Issachar (19:17), Asher (19:24), Naphtali (19:32) and Dan (19:40). Only after the tribes had selected their inheritances did Joshua choose his own (19:49, 50). In view of the insignificance of Timnath-serah in Mt. Ephraim which Joshua claimed for himself, it has been said, "He dispensed a kingdom, but for himself was content with a petty inheritance."

6. The Cities of Refuge (Ch. 20)

The provision of the cities of refuge had already been set forth in Numbers 35. The appointment of three cities east of Jordan is described in Deuteronomy 4:41-43. Now, an additional three to serve west of Jordan are reported. The cities were so distributed that no citizen would be too far from at least one of them. (About fifty miles was the greatest distance.) The roads to the cities were kept clear so that nothing could hinder the flight of the manslayer, and signposts were placed at the crossroads to guide to the city of refuge. If an unintentional slayer took refuge in such a city, he was guaranteed immunity from the prevailing law of blood revenge until such time as a fair trial could be held. In case of proved innocence, the slayer could enjoy indefinite refuge in the city. Law pro-

---

[3]Jack Finegan, Light from the Ancient Past (Princeton: Princeton University Press, 1946), p. 142.

Excavations at the site of ancient Shiloh have revealed remains of numerous structures, including water storage cisterns as pictured here. Shiloh was Israel's headquarters during the formative years of national life.

vided the cities of refuge to protect the people from family feuds, while at the same time giving full place and dignity to due legal process.

7. The Portion of the Levites (Ch. 21)

Inasmuch as the tribes were at this time being settled in their permanent inheritances, the Levites also felt that their promised cities should be provided. Hence, a delegation of family heads approached the leaders to request their portion. The division of the cities to the various Levitical groups was by lot, with a total of forty-eight being provided. These cities included the cities of refuge and extended throughout the land. The suburbs of the cities were part of the grant, no doubt to provide grazing land for the flocks and herds of the Levites.

8. Reuben, Gad, and Half-Manasseh (Ch. 22)

Since the need for warfare ceased when the tribes became settled, Joshua felt that it was now a fit time to dismiss the armed men of the eastern tribes. He is described as sending them away with a statement of commendation and appreciation, a charge to continued godliness, and liberal riches which were the tribal share of the military plunder by Israel's armies. In so disposing of the army of eastern tribes, Joshua emphasized that this action, and their expected future conduct, were all in conformity with their past covenants with Moses.

The eastern warriors were no sooner on their own soil, however, then they proceeded to erect their own altar. This act appeared as a move of secession, and it was seemingly a violation of the law that required offerings to be only at the place that the Lord should choose. Jumping to conclusions and reacting hastily, the western tribes immediately prepared for civil war. Open hostilities were averted, however, when the two and one-half tribes adopted an attitude of humility and sincerity, and carefully explained that they had built the altar only as a memorial to teach godliness to all future generations. The westerners were satisfied, and the tribes returned to their homes in peace.

VI. Joshua's Farewell (Chs. 23, 24)

1. Joshua's Address to the Elders and Tribal Heads (Ch. 23)

The events of these chapters took place thirteen or fourteen years after the completion of the conquest of Canaan. Joshua had spent the intervening time in retirement. It may be assumed that Joshua called the national leaders to his residence in Timnath-serah (19:50). His address consisted of a review of the mighty works of God in their midst and a consideration of God's promises for the future. The nation could expect to prosper in temporal things in proportion as they served God in spiritual things. Joshua warned the leaders not to be content with less than complete victory over the Canaanites, and he warned that if these people survived they would be: "snares and traps unto you, and scourges in your sides, and thorns in your eyes until ye perish from off this good land" (23:13).

As an encouragement in their task, Joshua promised: "One man of you shall chase a thousand: for the Lord your God, he it is that fighteth for you" (23:10). He emphasized that God's provision was complete and that the only restriction was the measure of human appropriation. The Scriptural report notes the classes of leaders in Joshua's audience: These included: the elders who comprised a governing body, the heads who were the representatives of the tribes and families, the judges who interpreted the Law of God, and the officers who enforced the decisions of the judges. It was on this occasion that Joshua described his impending death in the frequently quoted words: "I am going the way of all the earth" (v. 14).

2. Joshua's Address to all the People (Ch. 24:1-28)

For his final address to the nation, Joshua chose the city of Shechem, and there he called for a national assembly. His sermon was partly historical, for he reviewed the past history of the nation, but as well, he called for general obedience and dedication to God. A noteworthy declaration by Joshua is found in the latter part of v. 15--"but as for me and my house, we will serve the Lord." Inasmuch as it was Israel's covenant with Jehovah that was the one great unifying factor in the nation, it remained absolutely vital that the people persist in obedience to that covenant. For national Israel,

spiritual dedication had vital political and patriotic outcomes.

Although Joshua had presented God's message in a challenging and forthright manner, it in no wise deterred Israel's firm and confident response. Three times the people pledged faithfulness to God and unswerving obedience to His voice. To confirm this covenant, Joshua erected a stone memorial at the site. This place, Shechem, had been the scene of Abram's first altar in the land of Canaan (Gen. 12: 6,7). A pledge of this nature made God the Chief Ruler of the nation, and Israel may thereby be described as a "theocratic republic."

3. The Death of Joshua (24:29-33, cf. Judges 2:8)

After his farewell speeches, Joshua apparently returned to his retirement and nothing again brought him forth. He died when he was 110 and was buried in his home city. Joshua's epitaph was brief but eloquent, "Joshua the son of Nun, the servant of the Lord" (v. 29). Scripture indicates that Joshua, in serving God both under Moses, and as a leader in his own right, was a man under orders. He is magnified and honored, not according to his person, but by his accomplishments. Actually, his personality is not seen as brilliantly shining forth, but consistently he is set forth as a man greatly pleasing to God and a man who fulfilled the task to which he was commissioned.

The bones of Joseph which had been preserved throughout the wanderings were also buried on the occasion of Joshua's funeral. In this connection, John Elder notes:

> . . . For centuries there was a tomb at Shechem reverenced as the tomb of Joseph. A few years ago the tomb was opened. It was found to contain a body mummified according to the Egyptian custom, and in the tomb, among other things, was a sword of the kind worn by Egyptian officials.[4]

The book of Joshua also closes with the death of Eleazar the priest. As someone has remarked: "the book of Joshua both begins and ends with death."

---

[4]John Elder, Prophets, Idols and Diggers (New York: Bobbs-Merrill, 1960), p. 54.

2. THE BOOK OF JUDGES

The story of the people of Israel and their life in the promised land is here continued. However, the conquest and victories of Joshua are replaced by accounts of oppressions and defeats. The book of Judges is not so much a chronological historical account, but rather, a topical presentation of selected events. This era has been called: "The Dark Ages of Israel's History," and the book itself has been called: "The Book of Failure." Israel failed to enjoy the peace and prosperity that God desired for them because they failed to walk in obedience to the divine precepts.

The Nature and Theme of the Book

Israel's leaders during this era are called "Judges" since this is the word that was chosen as a translation of the title found in the Septuagint version. The book is considered to have been appropriately named, inasmuch as it is a record of the leadership of some fourteen judges who ruled and delivered Israel.[1] In virtually every case, the rule of the judge is linked to Israel's periodic departures from the revealed plan of God. These cycles proceeded: 1) a Godly generation, 2) spiritually indifferent descendants, 3) open apostasy, 4) God's punishment, 5) national repentance and a new era of piety, and 6) a deliverer (judge) provided by God.

The punishment that the Lord permitted in the case of each cycle of apostasy was manifested in an oppressive invasion by Israel's Canaanite neighbors. Seven complete cycles are recorded in the book of Judges. However, the book is essentially topical in nature, and therefore historical facts are selected not for their own sake but for their value in setting forth the theme: Disobedience to God can only result in suffering and sorrow. It is estimated that Israel was in a state of apostasy only about one-fourth of

this period, although the book's concern for these matters might give the impression of a higher ratio. The recurring refrain "every man did that which was right in his own eyes," illustrates the inherent sinfulness of man. In repeated instances, for the people of Israel to do what was right in their own eyes was to do what was not right in God's eyes.

The Authorship and Chronology of the Book

According to Jewish tradition, Samuel was the author of this book. Internal evidence confirms the date to about Samuel's time, and the data and insights reported are clearly those that Samuel could have known. The particular posts held by Samuel in his adult life would have given him both opportunity and inclination to have prepared this record. It was apparently written some time in the reign of Saul or David, but before the latter conquered Jerusalem. (cf. 1:12; 2 Sam. 5:6-8, 18:31)

The number of years accounted for by various judgeships and intervals totals 410. However, in the comparative Bible dating given in 1 Kings 6:1, the total interval between the exodus and the fourth year of Solomon's reign is said to be 480 years. This interval would not allow a full 410 years for the era of the judges only, for too many events before and after are included. Thus, it is assumed that not all of the judgeships and rest periods are a consecutive series for the nation as a whole. More than one judge may each have been ruling a particular region in the same era. Thus, the chronology is considered to be compressed, and the traditional duration of the era of the judges has been fixed at 300 years. Some modern scholars would limit it to as little as 180 years. Inasmuch as the ancients had much less concern for chronological records than scholars today, it is likely that these matters will continue to remain uncertain.

The Office of Judge

The title "judge" (Hebrew shophet) connotes one whose role was to "bring into right relationship with." Primarily, these leaders fulfilled three functions: military leadership, administration, and the

---

[1]There were thirteen administrations under the judges, for Deborah and Barak administered jointly. However, since Abimelech was a usurper, only twelve of the administrations were legitimate, and only in nine instances does the Bible specifically declare that a given individual "judged Israel."

Figure Two: The approximate settlement of the twelve tribes in the Land.

settlement of disputes. They were men and women raised up by God to organize and rally the people to meet their oppressors, and to lead Israel into the state of virtue that the Lord desired. Although the judges were the only human administrators that the nation possessed in this era, the authority accorded them was limited, and there is little or no record of their activities in arbitrating or pronouncing sentence in legal matters. They were neither absolute, nor were they permanent in their own rule, nor did they found hereditary dynasties. In theory, through-out this era, God was to remain the true ruler of the nation.

Israel's political and organizational structure during this time has been identified by the term 'amphictyony.' This word connotes an association of neighboring tribes or clans who come together in order to protect and promote a common religious center. The term usually is used to apply to certain Greek states, but it applies equally well to Israel. It is noted that the individual judges were each associated primarily with only one portion of the nation, and some related specifically to a single tribe. Six of the judges (Shamgar, Tola, Jair, Ibzan, Elon, and Abdon) may be considered minor; the remainder are thought of as major.

The Value and Authenticity of the Book

The era of the judges was almost as extended in time as the era of Israel's monarchy, and that portion of Scripture which gives scholars insight into this period is of abiding importance. The Book is a vital part of the Bible canon, and its events are referred to frequently in other books.[2] The common critical theory that claims that Israel's conquest of Palestine was by infiltration during several centuries of time is clearly opposed by this portrayal of actual conditions.

In achieving the purposes for which it was written, the book of Judges unfolds a great deal of valuable historical data. However, as already noted, the events of the book are not necessarily in chronological order. It is generally agreed that material in the last four chapters should follow 2:13, and that the book should begin with 2:6-9 preceding the first chapter. In general, the book depicts Israel beginning in humble dependence upon God (1:1 - 2:5), and then sinking to greater and greater depths, culminating in the horrors of the last four chapters.

ANALYSIS AND EXPOSITION

I. The Preface to the Book (1:1-3:4)

1. The Incomplete Victory of the Tribe of Judah
(Ch. 1)

At the outset, the book reveals Judah taking the initiative in subduing certain tribes of the Canaanites and Perizzites. The leader of these enemies was Adoni-bezek whom Israel captured, and according to the custom of the time, mutilated, by cutting off his thumbs and great toes. Since Caleb's inheritance was included with that of Judah, his part and that of Othniel in conquering Kirjath-sepher is here once more related (cf. Josh. 15:13-19). A 'nether' spring is simply one located in the lower part of the land. The 'children of the Kenite' (the name Kenite means smith) of 1:16 are identified by some scholars with the inhabitants of Jerusalem known as the Jebusites (cf. Josh. 15:63; 2 Sam. 5:6, 7).

According to 1:19, Judah was deterred in

achieving a complete victory because of her fear of the chariots of iron of the Canaanites. An archaeological corroboration of this report is an inscription by Thothmes III of Egypt telling of an invasion of Canaan and the capture of 900 chariots of iron. It is usually pointed out, however, that Judah's real deterrent was her lack of faith. Comments Douglas:

The disastrous result of disobedience to the command of God was the existence of a compact and powerful mass of heathenism in the heart of Israel, which no doubt contributed to the ruin of the first king of Israel . . . and continued increasingly to work mischief until the people were carried captives by invaders who entered Palestine along the road which lust of gain had left or thrown open.[3]

Among the tribes who failed to complete the conquest of their territory were: Manasseh (v. 27), Ephraim (v. 29), Zebulun (v. 30), Asher (v. 31), Naphtali (v. 33), and Dan (v. 34).

This chapter relates the story of the conquest of Bethel (vv. 22-26). It has been suggested that this conquest may have taken place as an aftermath of that of Ai (cf. Josh. 8:17 et al), and that this report is simply an added detail. Israel's forces are here identified as "the house of Joseph," which probably would be the combined armies of Ephraim and Manasseh. The word 'descry' in v. 23 means 'to spy out.' The agreement to spare the unnamed citizen of Bethel in return for his help to the spies is, of course, similar to that extended to Rahab. He probably showed the spies which portions of the city were weakest and easiest to breach to permit the entrance of their forces. After Israel's conquest, this man sought to perpetuate the memory of his native city by applying the original name 'Luz' to his new community in the land of the Hittites.

2. The Visit of the Angel (2:1-5)

This brief section reports the appearance of an angel of the Lord in order to communicate the mind of God. The nature of the angel's message would suggest that he was actually a person of the Godhead, and if so, the event is described as a theophany. The divine messenger chided the people for their disobedience, and he announced impending judgment. This judgment was temporarily postponed when the people displayed genuine repentance and thus won divine forgiveness.

---

[2]References to people and events from the book of Judges include: 1 Sam. 12:9-11, 2 Sam. 11:21, Psa. 78:61-64, 83:11, Isa. 9:4, 10:24, Acts 13:20, Heb. 11:32.

[3]George C. Douglas, The Book of Judges (Edinburgh: T. & T. Clark, n.d.), p. 15.

3. A Summary of Events (2:6-3:4)

This section presents a general survey in retrospect of the flow of historical events in Israel. It is not so much a historical report, but rather a sort of philosophical statement of the underlying nature of the history of Israel. There came a time when God no longer fully forgave and restored the people in their repeated apostasies. Thus, He allowed the survival of certain troublesome alien nations in order to teach an enduring lesson to Israel. In 3:3-5, a total of eight gentile nations is named, each of which on one occasion or another, chastened Israel. It is noted that the first Bible mention of Ashtaroth occurs here (2:13).

II. Israel's Apostasies, Captivities, and Deliverances (3:5 - 16:31)

The contents of this section may best be considered topically rather than chapter-by-chapter.

1. Othniel, the Anointed Judge (3:5-11)

Even prior to the time that he rose to be a judge, Othniel was already a familiar figure in Israel (cf. Josh. 15:13-19, Jud. 1:12-15). At that time Othniel had distinguished himself by capturing the town of Kirjath-sepher (later called Debir), and as a reward he had received Achsah, Caleb's daughter and his cousin, as his wife. It is noted that Achsah became immediately a loyal wife who proceeded to win from her father, Caleb, a plot of land with upper and lower springs. Othniel was of the tribe of Judah, and his name means 'lion of God.'

The election of Othniel to the post of judge was God's response to the prayers of the people. These prayers had been accompanied by the people's repentance of their intermarriage with their pagan neighbors, and their rejection of the worship of Baal. The oppression from which Othniel delivered the people was Israel's first since their settlement in the land. The oppressor was Chushan-rishathaim who is described as "King of Mesopotamia" and by this name judged to have been either an Amorite or an Aramaean. His name means "Chushan of double wickedness," and he was responsible for eight years of oppression upon Israel. With the Spirit of the Lord to empower him (v. 10), Othniel achieve decisive victory and forty years of peace.

2. Ehud, the Left-handed Judge (3:12-30)

Ehud was of the tribe of Benjamin, and although described as left-handed, is thought of on the basis of the original, either as ambidextrous or as crippled in his right hand. Such a peculiarity was common among the Benjamites (cf. 20:16). Ehud assumed the role of deliverer or judge only after Israel had suffered eighteen years under Eglon, king of Moab. In their oppression of Israel, the Moabites entered into a coalition with the Ammonites and the Amalekites, and they placed one of the chief cities (probably Jericho) of Israel under occupation. There is evidence from archaeology that Eglon was one of the most powerful of Moab's rulers, and Josephus declares that he built a palace at Jericho. It would appear that the troop garrison that he maintained in Israel numbered 10,000 soldiers.

Ehud's strategy began with the presentation to Eglon of a generous gift, probably the year's tribute payment. When the gift had been delivered, he dismissed his company, and after a short time returned alone to the king. He claimed to have a secret divine message for Eglon, and thus secured a private audience. When they were alone, Ehud drove his dagger into Eglon's abdomen, thus assassinating him. Scripture notes that the dagger was a cubit long (i.e. 18 inches), but owing to Eglon's size, it was barely long enough. The dagger was necessarily homemade because the conquerors had prohibited the manufacture of arms in Israel. The "quarries" that are twice mentioned (3:19, 26) as figuring in this episode are considered by some scholars to be references to the carved stone idols that the Moabites had erected in the land.

Ehud contrived to make his exit without revealing the murder, and it was some time before the body of his victim was found. This period of time was sufficient for the Israelite to make his way to Mount Ephraim (apparently a highland within the borders of the tribe of Benjamin). There he sounded the rallying trumpet, and soon led forth an army sufficient to annihilate the now leaderless enemy force of 10,000 men. Israel's procedure in this accomplishment was simply to man the fords of the Jordan, and as the Moabites streamed by seeking their own borders, methodically to destroy them. After this episode, Israel had peace for 80 years.

3. Shamgar, the Ox Goad Judge (3:31)

The total Biblical information concerning Shamgar is limited to one verse: "And after him was Shamgar the son of Anath, which slew of the Philistines six hundred men with an ox goad: and he also delivered Israel." It is likely that this oppression by the Philistines was limited and local in nature. An ox goad consisted of a sharpened pole upwards of ten feet in length. Shamgar would be reduced to fighting with an ox goad because the occupying Philistines permitted no military weapons. He serves to illustrate the worker who is poorly equipped, but nevertheless achieves victory with what he has.

4. Deborah and Barak, the Associate Judges
(4:1-5:31)

The Lord raised up Deborah in response to the prayers of the people after twenty years of oppression at the hands of the Canaanites. Deborah is the first woman of recorded history to lead a nation (or at least a coalition of tribes), although it should be noted that she was also a wife and probably a mother (4:4, 5:7). Her unique position has led to references to her as the "Hebrew Boadicea"; while the meaning of her name (Deborah means bee) has led to her being called "the Queen Bee of the Hive of Israel." The only other female head of state mentioned in Scripture is the usurper, Athaliah.

The center of power of the oppressing Canaanites was the city of Hazor, and it was the tribes adjacent to this city that particularly suffered. Archaeologists report that Hazor was a great Canaanite city constituting a formidable fortress. Although the city had been destroyed by Joshua a century or so earlier (Josh. 11:11), apparently it had been promptly rebuilt. Jabin, who ruled at this time, would be either a descendent of the original Jabin, or the name 'Jabin' was a generic name for all the Canaanite rulers of this era. In actuality, Jabin's oppression did not represent an external attack, but simply an uprising of a minority group within Israel's borders. Since Israel seems not to have maintained a standing army until new leadership could be secured to rally recruits, she was at the mercy of her attackers.

Deborah enlisted the assistance of Barak (Barak means lightning), who presumably was of the tribe of Naphtali, and she assigned him the task of military leadership. Barak, either through fear, or out of respect for Deborah, refused to proceed without the personal presence of the prophetess. Eventually, Deborah agreed to accompany him, although she chided Barak for demanding such an arrangement and pointed out that it would cost him the loss of face. With the issue of leadership settled, Deborah and Barak proceeded to Mount Tabor and there they gathered a military force numbering 10,000. These recruits were primarily from the tribes of Naphtali and Zebulon, although Issachar also seems to have been involved.

When news of the massing Israelite army reached Sisera, the captain of the Canaanites, he speedily attacked. Although Barak's forces forsook their vantage point on Mount Tabor and descended to the valley to do combat, God intervened to give them a prompt victory. According to Josephus, there was a sudden desert storm that flooded Esdraelon and left it muddy and impassable for Sisera's chariots. Hail and sleet chilled and incapac-

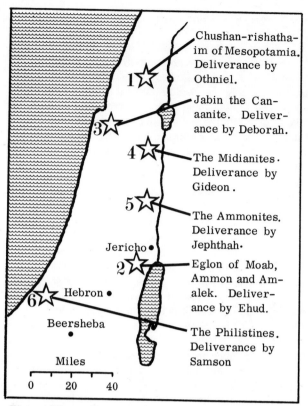

Figure Three: Punitive invasions upon Israel in the time of the Judges (numbers indicate the order).

itated his warriors. Thus, Israel's foot soldiers easily overcame the chariots and mounted forces of Sisera; the Canaanite army was utterly routed and destroyed, and General Sisera fled for his life. In the tent of Jael the Kenite, where he took refuge, Sisera also met his doom. Jael coolly murdered him by driving a nail into his temple. Scripture commends the faith of Jael, but not her treachery.

Whereas a prose account of Deborah's victory is given in Chapter 4, the same event is described in poetic form in Chapter 5. The differences are simply those appropriate to the different literary media. This martial poem known as "Deborah's Song" is the only poetic composition in the book of Judges. Culler describes it as "a wild and passionate war ballad," and he notes that "the description of the battle is couched in short incisive sentences dealing successively with the kings, horses, the river, and the stars." Booth declares "The orderly division into stanzas, the skillful use of parallelism to build up to a crescendo--all stamp this as the work of a literary genius." The poem is in three and four beats, which is the most popular Hebrew meter. The reference to the queen mother was characteristic of an era in which a man might have many wives, but only one mother. Deborah described the extent of the oppression under the Canaanites, and she especially rebuked the tribes of Israel who had not cooperated in the battle. Since Judah is not mentioned, it is inferred that this tribe had not been expected to participate.

The first Scriptural mention of the professional scribe is found in this story. ". . . and out of Zebulun they that handle the pen of the writer" (5:14). It is noted that Barak is mentioned elsewhere in Scripture, and in Hebrews 11:32 he is cited as an example of faith. Following events at this time, Israel enjoyed forty years of freedom and peace.

5. Gideon, the Fleece Judge (6:1-8:35)

Although the Midianites had been largely destroyed in the time of the conquest two centuries earlier (Num. 31:1-18), apparently the nation had now recovered its strength. The oppression at this time was one of the most severe that Israel suffered. The people were reduced to abject poverty by the continued Midianitish raids, and they were forced to live in dens and caves and to perform their harvest at odd times and places. It was for this reason that Gideon was found threshing wheat by the winepress. It is probable that the grain so harvested would be stored in underground granaries or grain pits similar to those that have been excavated at Kirjath-sepher. God expressed His concern for the people in their oppression by sending to them an unnamed prophet to assure them of the divine power to deliver. At the same time, the prophet rebuked them in the Lord's name because "ye have not obeyed my voice." It is noted that even these measures of divine intervention did not occur until after seven years of Midianitish oppression.

In proceeding to implement His promises to deliver the people, God extended His choice and call to Gideon ("the cutter down"), the eldest son of Joash of the tribe of Manasseh. The perseverance, courage, and faith exemplified in Gideon in threshing by the winepress was exactly that caliber of character that the Lord sought. The angel challenged Gideon: "Go in this thy might, and thou shalt save Israel" (6:14). The heavenly visitor confirmed his word to Gideon by a supernatural sign in accepting the broth, the flesh, and the unleavened cakes that Gideon offered. Says Lang of this "angel of the Lord":

> . . . the words used concerning Him, while implying distinction from Jehovah, imply also a mysterious unity with Jehovah. Was He the Word who in the beginning was with God, and was God, and who, in the fulness of the time was made flesh? So said the Christian fathers of the earlier centuries. [4]

---

[4]John M. Lang, Gideon and the Judges (New York: Fleming Revell Co., n.d.), p. 96.

Says Matthew Henry of Gideon's call: "from threshing corn, he is fetched to thresh the Midianites." Gideon manifested due humility in the face of such an extraordinary honor.

The first act of the newly commissioned and empowered leader was to throw down the altar of Baal, and to build an altar to God. Upon this altar he offered his father's second bullock; presumably because the first had been confiscated by the Midianites. Gideon's fellow citizens were at first horrified by the young leader's irreverence toward Baal, but they accepted the plea of Gideon's father that if Baal were truly God he would have protected himself. Gideon next began gathering an army, but he paused to be reassured by God on the occasion of the well known fleece episode. Gideon's army at first numbered 32,000, but God chose to reduce its size so that the people might see that the forthcoming victory was wrought by the hand of God. After the two prescribed tests, only 300 warriors remained.

The tiny army, outnumbered 450 to 1, was "armed" with lamps, pitchers, and trumpets. Clearly, they were to fight a battle of faith in which numbers and human resources as ordinarily measured were irrelevant. In the divine strategy, Gideon's army came upon the enemy by night, and at the appointed time they smashed the pitchers, held aloft the lamps, shouted, and blew the trumpets. The terrified Midianites, who already had been made fearful by a dream, fled in utter confusion. Gideon's army, suddenly enlarged by a host of recruits, pursued and destroyed freely. It was no doubt particularly this classic episode in Gideon's life that led to his inclusion in the catalog of the heroes of faith who ". . . subdued kingdoms, wrought righteousness, obtained promises" (Heb. 11:32, 33).

6. Abimelech, the Usurping Judge-King (9:1-57)

Abimelech was the son of Gideon, but he appears to have inherited none of his father's virtues. His mother was a Shechemite maidservant, and his allegiances tended to remain much closer to the Shechemites than to his father's family. Abimelech secured his position as judge by arranging for the murder of his seventy brothers, and only Jotham, the youngest, managed to escape. The hired assassins for this brutal crime were paid with money that Abimelech had received from the people of Shechem, and they in turn had obtained it from the temple of Baal.

The excessive enthusiasm of the people of Shechem on behalf of Abimelech led them to crown him king. "And all the men of Shechem gathered together . . . and made Abimelech king" (v. 6). However, this coronation was not at all recognized by God, and was merely a local gesture confined to the city of Shechem. It is evident that the alliance was based on no principles other than the idolatrous worship of Baal and a sense of partnership in crime. It is an irony that this illegitimate coronation took place at the historic site that enshrined Jacob's venerable oak and Joshua's stone of witness (Josh. 24: 26). It is assumed that the house of Millo was the fortress area of the city of Shechem.

At this juncture, the young Jotham appeared upon Mount Gerizim and in the form of a fable[5] he rebuked the murderous, self-styled king. This pronouncement that has been called "The Fable of the Trees" is the most ancient fable known to literature. The fable is poetic in form and it constitutes a dramatic expression of the age-long problem of recruiting good men for public office. The fable made the point that good trees choose to occupy themselves in producing fruit. It is the bramble that could not seemingly make any one better by its living that, nevertheless, counts itself worthy of a place of honor. By thus ridiculing the coronation of Abimelech, Jotham denounced the abortive monarchical institution, and as it were, pronounced a divine curse upon such a state of affairs.

After a three-year interval, many citizens of Shechem began to resent the despotic rule of Abimelech. The spokesman and leader of these rebels was Gaal, the son of Ebed. Zebul, Abimelech's deputy ruler of the city, remained loyal to his master and hence worked against Gaal. After contriving to delay and divert Gaal's efforts at insurrection as long as possible, he proceeded to expel the troublemaker from the city. Nevertheless, Abimelech evidently ignored such loyalty, and he proceeded totally to destroy the city. It may be assumed that Zebul perished in this destruction. By sowing this land with salt, Abimelech practiced that type of total warfare which would render a fertile land into a state of arrid desert.

From Shechem, Abimelech proceeded to Thebez, and he sought to set fire to the stronghold tower of this city, just as he had done previously. However, while he was making preparation for this deed, a woman in the tower dropped a piece of millstone on his head and shattered his skull. In his last conscious moments, Abimelech's thought was only for his reputation, and thus he ordered his armor-bearer to thrust him through that he might not go down in history as one slain by a woman.

---

[5]This literary piece is correctly a fable rather than a parable because it deals with imaginative situations rather than real events. A parable concerns events that actually have occurred, or may occur, in human experience.

These events fulfilled Jotham's prophecy that had foretold both the destruction of Abimelech and also the destruction of the city of Shechem. With Abimelech's death, the nation returned to a period of peace.

7. Tola, the Issacharite Judge (10:1, 2)

Little is known of Tola, but Scripture reports that he judged Israel twenty-three years. He was of the tribe of Issachar, he was Abimelech's paternal uncle, and he lived and died in the city, still not located, of Shamir. The name Tola means "to save."

8. Jair, the Gileadite Judge (10:3-5)

The outstanding fact about this man was that he had thirty sons and that each rode a colt and governed a "city" (probably a village by modern standards). In the original, there is a play on the words "city" and "colt." Jair was associated with the land of Gilead. He judged Israel twenty-two years.

9. Jephthah, the Judge Who Covenanted (10:6-12:7)

Jephthah was the son of a harlot, and thus, early in life he was cast out of his father's home by his jealous step-brothers. He spent his youth in the remote region of Tob, and there he headed a party of freebooters who pillaged Syrian and Ammonitish tribes. He has been somewhat romantically described as Israel's "Robin Hood." Jephthah's family turned to him for leadership and help out of urgent necessity after they had suffered oppression for eighteen years at the hand of the combined forces of the Philistines and Ammonites. Jephthah agreed to become the national leader only after his brethren agreed to restore him fully to family relationships.

After seeking to negotiate diplomatically with the Ammonites and suffering a rebuff, Jephthah prepared to make war upon the enemy. It may be noted that Jephthah's message to Ammon mentioned that Israel had dwelt in Canaan for "300 years." (11:26) This incidental reference indicates the duration of the era of the judges up to this time. Before setting forth to battle, Jephthah made his memorable vow to God: "If thou shalt without fail deliever the children of Ammon into mine hands, Then it shall be, that whatsoever cometh forth of the doors of my house to meet me, when I return in peace . . . shall surely be the Lord's and I will offer it up for a burnt offering (11:30, 31).

In the ensuing war, Jephthah was granted an abundant victory so that twenty cities of the Ammonites fell into his hands and the enemy was totally subdued. He returned to fulfill his vow. To the dismay of Jephthah, the first creature to come to meet him was his daughter, his only child. After two month's delay, and with many misgivings, he "did with her according to his vow which he had vowed" (11:39).

The fate of Jephthah's daughter has long been a problem for Bible scholars. If Jephthah slew his daughter as an offering to Jehovah, then he actually committed a crime under the delusion of a loyal pledge. If he merely committed his daughter to perpetual virginity, then the language and implications of Scripture seem excessive. Says Douglas:

> The prevalent opinion in the Christian Church, the Fathers agreeing in this with Josephus and with other ancient Jewish authorities, has been that Jephthah made a vow to sacrifice to Jehovah whatever first came out of his house, leaving it to Providence to determine whether this should be an animal or his daughter; hoping that it would not be she, yet prepared to give her up in death if she was the first one to come out.[6]

It should be noted that the general outlook at this time sanctioned human sacrifice, and the temptation to offer children to Molech seems constantly to have been an enticement to Israel.

On the other hand, it is considered that Jephthah would have been equally grieved at the enforced perpetual virginity as at the outright loss of his daughter, for in either case he would have been denied posterity. Nowhere does Scripture definitely say that he put his daughter to death, and twice it speaks of the maiden's virginity being lamented. Not all commentators are so dogmatic as Douglas who says: "It is some lifelong surrender of his only child to the service of Jehovah which alone explains the words of the chapter."[7] It would seem more consistent with literal Scripture to consider that Jephthah actually offered his daughter as a human sacrifice, but it is more appealing to New Testament Christians to consider that he simply dedicated her to perpetual virginity.

Once again the Ephraimites were jealous because they had not been invited to take part (cf. the story of Gideon), but this time they were punished harshly for their hostility. When they threatened to burn the house of Jephthah, they so stirred his anger, that he rallied an army that eventually slew 42,000 Ephraimites. Those who escaped from the battlefield were later identified because of the tribal habit of dropping "h's" so that they could not pronounce the word "Shibboleth." Booth notes that for a man of Ephraim to commit this error of pronunciation "in each case proved to be the last mistake that Ephraimite ever made." After these events, Israel enjoyed six years of peace.

10. Ibzan, the Bethlehemite Judge (12:8-10)

Ibzan, just as Jair, had thirty sons, but Scripture also notes that this judge was favored with thirty daughters as well. He was a native of Bethlehem, and he judged Israel seven years.

11. Elon, the Zebulonite Judge (12:11, 12)

Elon was of the tribe of Zebulun, and he held office for ten years.

12. Abdon, the Family Judge (12:13-15)

This judge had 40 sons and 30 nephews, each with his own ass colt. Such large families were the outcome, of course, of plural marriages. The fact that each young man possessed a colt would indicate a measure of prosperity. Abdon judged eight years and was identified with the tribe of Ephraim.

13. Samson, the Mighty Judge (13:1-16:30)

It is Samson's distinction to be the only judge whose entire biography from birth to death is reported in Scripture. His father was Manoah, but his mother remains unnamed. The birth of this chosen leader was announced by the "angel of the Lord" who is usually considered a theophany of Jesus Christ. The strict requirements of the pledge of the Nazarite were to be imposed upon both the mother and her expected son. As a child, Samson enjoyed a special blessing of God: ". . . the child grew, and the Lord blessed him. And the Spirit of the Lord began to move him at times" (13:24, 25). The name Samson means "little son" or "sonny."

Samson's first experience in courtship involved conflicts and contradictions sufficient to doom the ensuing marriage to failure. Although the young Samson was the vessel for the moving of the Spirit of the Lord (13:25), he nevertheless defied his parents in seeking the hand of a woman of Philistia. To his parents' pleas he responded: "Get her for me: for she pleases me well." On the other hand, Scripture notes that even Samson's attachment was "of the Lord" (14:4).

The marriage between Samson and the woman of Philistia eventually turned to tragedy, not because of Samson and his kinfolk, but because of the racial prejudices of the Philistines. Apparently the marriage ended almost as soon as the seven-day festiv-

---

[6]Douglas, op. cit., p. 63.

[7]Ibid., p. 66.

ities that celebrated the marriage concluded, and Samson's bride was given instead to his companion. Samson contrived a dramatic protest by means of the three hundred foxes (actually jackals), but in this he achieved merely the wanton destruction of property. The outcome was the murder of Samson's wife and her father by the enraged Philistines. Although Samson seems genuinely to have been attached to the maiden, her willingness to betray her husband to her own people would indicate that the affection was not truly mutual.

A further series of acts of violence ensued, and Scripture reports that Samson "smote them hip and thigh with a great slaughter" (15:8), and that he then withdrew from Philistia and took up residence in Judah upon the rock Etam. The expression "hip and thigh" is a proverbial way of indicating great slaughter. In the next round in Samson's conflict with the Philistines, his own people bound him and delivered him to the enemy, but he readily freed himself. It was at this time that he secured the jawbone and slaughtered 1000 Philistines. Scholars have suggested that the refreshing water obtained by Samson after this episode, came not from the jawbone, but from the region "Lehi" which means "jaw." The final truth in this matter awaits more conclusive evidence concerning the exact intention of the original text.

For the next twenty years Samson judged Israel, and comparative peace and prosperity prevailed. It was after this period that he met Delilah, and, falling victim to her enticements, he divulged the secret of his strength. Samson erred in considering that his associations with Delilah were a launching into greater freedom; actually they led him into greater bondage. It has been said: "As soon as a man steps aside from the path of righteousness, he begins to dress his soul in chains." By confiding his secret to Delilah, Samson broke down the protective barrier of spiritual separation that was his real protection from the Philistines. He became truly a victim of the Valley of Sorek (Sorek means "snare"). The cutting of Samson's hair was only an outward confirmation of the breakdown of separation that already existed. Scripture reports pathetically: "And he wist not that the Lord was departed from him" (16:20). Thus, the outcome was his capture by the Philistines, the cruel putting out of his eyes, and the commitment to grind at the mill.

Samson's death achieved his revenge upon the Philistines. When brought in mockery into the temple of Dagon, he attained his former strength anew, and pulled down the building upon his enemies and upon himself. In many ways, Samson's greatest victory was in death, for in that hour he slew more Philistines than in life. It is pointed out that had he died to self at the beginning of his career instead of at the close, his life would have been vastly different. Although Samson's life is not to be imitated, it stands as an illustration of the power of faith. Booth remarks: "The Israelites were serving the Philistines when he started public life: they were serving the Philistines when he finished it. But he left some wonderful stories which will last forever."[8] In spite of Samson's record of the abuse and loss of the power of God, he nevertheless succeeded in preparing the people for the final blow against Philistia under Samuel. It is impossible to predict how much more strikingly successful this life would have been had Samson not been prey to a slavish subjection to his passions.

The expression in 14:18 "If you had not plowed with my heifer" seems to have been a local idiom meaning, "If you had not had the aid of my bride." The person "used as his friend" (14:20) was probably the groomsman at the wedding. The "with" mentioned in 16:7 is a cane from any growing shrub or tree. In 16:13,14 the reference is to the web of a weaving loom, including its parts constituting a pin and a beam. Some scholars have suggested that it was perhaps the story of Samson, carried to Greece by Phoenician traders, that became the basis of the myth of Hercules.

III. Anarchy in Israel (Chs. 17-21)

This section of Scripture describes a period of confusion in Israel, but two main events stand forth:

1. The Tribe of Dan Founds the City of Dan
(17:1-18:31)

The story of the founding of Dan involves two streams of action that eventually merge. At the outset, there is the story of the misguided Micah and his mother. This pair seem to have had a desire to worship and honor God, but their zeal was not according to knowledge. Clearly, the mother indulged her son in material substance, but she failed to impart worthy qualities of character and personal integrity. From money that Micah had stolen from his own mother, idolatrous images were constructed, and a worship shrine established. Eventually, Micah's son, the temporary priest of the shrine, was replaced by the hired services of a migrating Levite. In flagrant ignorance of divine values, Micah declared: "Now . . . the Lord will do me good, seeing I have a Levite to my priest" (17:13).

---

[8]Osborne Booth, The Chosen People (St. Louis: The Bethany Press, 1959), p. 83.

In the meantime, the tribe of Dan had failed to dispossess the Amorites who held their tribal grant, and they wrongly determined that they ought to seek a new home. Watts comments about God's attitude towards this project:

> This fact appears as a probable explanation of the omission of Dan from the list of tribes of Israel in Revelation 7:4-8. Dan's disregard for the sacredness of his inheritance is thus judged as causing him to fail to have a full portion among the tribes of Israel participating in the kingdom of Christ.[9]

It happened that the tribal spies commissioned to find a suitable new home came upon Micah's center of worship and also the city of Laish. And thus, when the tribesmen began their migration, with a corps of fighting men leading the way, one of their first acts was to pillage the home of Micah, appropriate his equipment for worship, and virtually kidnap the hired Levite. The city of Laish which they subsequently conquered became the northern city of Dan.

Teraphim in 17:5 and 18:17 are believed to have been small images of men used as good luck charms. They were not worshipped as idols, but were held rather to be a visible or tangible token that spoke of man's influence in the control of his own affairs. The expression "until the day of the captivity of the land" (18:30) designates the duration of Micah's false priesthood. It probably refers to the time of the Chaldean invasion, but it might be a more limited period ending in the destruction of Shiloh by the Philistines.

2. The Fate of the Benjamites (19:1 - 21:35)

These chapters relate the sordid story of the deed of the Benjamites who by cruel physical abuse caused the death of a concubine of a visiting Levite. All Israel was shocked by such a crime, and an avenging army was quickly recruited. Comments Lang: "The response to the appeal is an evidence of ill-balanced and excessive zeal." In the resulting war, the Benjamites eventually fell victim to the shrewd strategy of their attackers, and the final outcome was that only six hundred Benjamites survived. This punitive action cost the tribes no less than 40,000 fatal casualties in the first two days of battle.

In the mellowing influence of elapsed time, the tribes began to repent for their treatment of the Benjamites, particularly of their vow to refuse marriage between any tribal maiden and the surviving Benjamites. A face-saving opportunity arose when the tribes saw the need of punishing the uncooperative people of Jabesh-gilead. With uncompromising severity, they destroyed all people of the city except unmarried females. These, numbering four hundred, were provided as wives for the Benjamites. The remaining two hundred Benjamites were provided wives by granting them official permission to kidnap maidens of Israel who were engaged in ceremonial religious dances at Shiloh in the valley of Lebonah. These dances took place on the occasion of certain of the annual feasts. There is evidence that other ancient peoples frequently practiced marriage by capture, so that this provision for the Benjamites may not have seemed so startlingly strange.

The outcome of all of these events was that the tribe of Benjamin achieved some degree of normalcy once more, but never again did it, as a tribe, attain to any noteworthy status. Some three centuries later, Saul the Benjamite said to Samuel: "Am I not a Benjamite, of the smallest of the tribes of Israel?" (1 Sam. 9:21). In later history, the tribe of Benjamin appears largely to have been absorbed by Judah, although tribal identities quite evidently were maintained to make possible St. Paul's account: ". . . of the stock of Israel, of the tribe of Benjamin, an Hebrew of the Hebrews" (Phil. 3:5). It is clear that events during the era of the judges established tribal strengths and balances of power that were perpetuated in later history. In an era when "there was no king in Israel: every man did that which was right in his own eyes" (21:25), men and tribes found their respective levels, and their characteristic traits assumed their permanent form.

---

[9]Wash J. Watts, A Survey of Old Testament Teaching, Volume I (Nashville: Broadman Press, 1947), p. 242.

3. THE BOOK OF RUTH

The events described in the Book of Ruth took place during the era of the judges, so that the two books are linked with the connective "now." The story avoids reference to strife and war, and is concerned instead with normal human experiences and basic human emotions. It becomes clear that even though the era of the judges was one of much warfare and chaos, yet in many communities there were long periods when life continued peacefully and normally. Lang says of this book:

> . . . It relieves the gloom left by the chronicles of these days, full as they are of depressions and servitudes, of apostasies from Covenant standing with all the bitter fruits of such apostasies, of evil in the sight of Jehovah, and of a confusion which degenerates into violence and lawlessness.[1]

The Nature and Theme of the Book

The book appears to have been written for the purpose of accounting for the genealogy of David since no such information is given in the books of Samuel. Hence, the book leads up to the concluding genealogy with "David" being the last word recorded. Inasmuch as Ruth was the grandmother of David, she also was an ancestress of the Messiah. Ruth is one of four women mentioned in our Lord's genealogy in Matthew chapter one.

The book of Ruth is a love story, not so much between a young man and a young woman, but between a young woman and her mother-in-law. Writes Culler:

> Goethe speaks of the story of Ruth as the "loveliest little idyl"--a characterization on which every discerning reader will set his seal. In answer to the question why he did not write a poem on it a poet replied, "I dare not lest I mar that which is already perfect."[2]

Newell has an interesting comment: "This is the Book of Ruth, but less than nine verses comprise all she says in it." It is sometimes claimed that this book is a propaganda piece favoring mixed marriages; clearly this is false, for the book is simply the story of the ancestry of King David.

The course of events that led Ruth to become an ancestress of David went hand in hand with her search after rest. In her day, as an unmarried woman, she had neither respect nor security. Naomi twice referred to Ruth's search after rest--"the Lord grant that ye may find rest, each of you in the house of her husband" (1:9). "Then Naomi her mother-in-law said unto her, My daughter, shall I not seek rest for thee, that it may be well with thee?" (3:1). This desired rest was only truly possible through redemption and union, and thus it was not attained until Ruth married Boaz. Ruth's search for rest constitutes a dramatic theme that for most readers tends to overshadow the prosaic account of genealogical relationships.

Special Associations of this Book

The Book of Ruth is assigned in the Hebrew Bible to the "Writings" (Heb. Kethubbim, or Gk. Hagiographa). Devout Jews read Ruth annually at the Feast of Pentecost, the harvest festival. Lee tells an interesting story about this book:

> The great literary authority of the eighteenth century, Dr. Samuel Johnson, introduced and read . . . [the book of Ruth] to his friends in a London Club, a pastoral which he said he had lately met with, and which they imagined had only just been composed; and when they were loud in their praises of its simple and pathetic beauty, he informed them that it was only the story of Ruth which he had read them from a book they all despised--the Bible.[3]

[1]John M. Lang, Gideon and the Judges (New York: Fleming H. Revell Company, n.d.) p. 32.

[2]Arthur J. Culler, Creative Religious Literature (New York: Macmillian Company, 1930), p. 66.

[3]Robert Lee, The Outlined Bible (London: Pickering and Inglis, n.d.), p. 8.

The Valley of Lebonah about three miles northwest of Shiloh. The village of Lebonah, visible at the left center in the distance, supplied the oil for the tabernacle, and later the temple. The valley is also known as the "Valley of the Dancing Maidens" for it is the site where the men of Benjamin captured brides (cf. Judges 21:19-23).

The Authorship of the Book

Jewish tradition assigns the authorship to Samuel, and an analysis of the literary style appears to confirm this claim.

The Occasion of Writing and the Scope

The book was probably written after David became king, for only then would there be sufficient interest in David's genealogical background to record this homey romance. The fact that the custom of the removal of a man's shoe to confirm a transaction had been forgotten (4:7), is evidence of the later writing of the book. It was written about 150 years after the events it records. According to 1:4, the book covers a period of a little more than ten years. There is some evidence that these years were during the time of Gideon.

The Key Word and Key Verse

The key word of the book of Ruth is "rest." It is considered that 1:9 is the key verse: "The Lord grant that ye may find rest, each of you in the house of her husband." These words were, of course, spoken by Naomi.

The Value of the Book

The book of Ruth is especially valuable for its typical teachings and practical lessons. Some noteworthy truths to be gleaned include:

1) Just as Boaz redeemed Ruth, so Christ, the great Kinsman-Redeemer, at infinite cost, has redeemed the Church and made her to be His bride.

2) The state of hopelessness of Ruth the gentile represents all sinner-outsiders who in themselves are without hope. Ruth was brought from the land of exile and given a place of great honor.

3) This story teaches that even in the worst surroundings there may be pure noble souls. Politically, these events occurred during dark days in the land of Judah.

4) The providences of God are effectively demonstrated. While it may have been considered Ruth's "hap" to light upon the field of Boaz, yet this event was directly in the express purpose of God.

5) In this book the exceeding forcefulness and far-ranging consequences of specific choices are revealed. The final estate of Ruth and Orpah came to be vastly different due to their choices along the way. Ruth found happiness and rest in Judah; Orpah passed into obscurity in Moab.

Analysis and Exposition

1. Ruth's Choice (Ch. 1)

The famine that led to Elimelech's migration may have been due to the ravages of the Midianites during the time of Gideon. Typically, a famine in Bible times would be understood as God's judgment upon a disobedient people. For Elimelech and his family to leave Bethlehem ("the house of bread") and proceed to the alien land of Moab clearly seems to portray the child of God who lives beneath his profession. Elimelech erred in believing that deliverance lay in Moab, for in fact, the sojourn there turned to tragedy with his death and the death of his two sons. The name "Mahlon" means "sick"; the name "Chilion" means "pining." In having married Moabite maidens, the sons showed spiritual indifference, for their wives were legally excluded from the family of Israel. "An Ammonite or a Moabite shall not enter into the congregation of the Lord; . . . for ever" (Deut. 23:3). Thus, the fact that Moab became a place of graves may partly have been a stroke of divine judgment.

Naomi's decision to return to Canaan probably had spiritual motivations, for one's Gods were often thought of geographically; turning to Jehovah would call for a return to the land of Judah. Ruth's decision to accompany Naomi has often been seen as a decision between heaven and hell. Her course of action would be especially remarkable in her day when women were allowed only limited freedom to choose. Ruth proceeded in spite of her mother-in-law's advice and her sister-in-law's example, and she thus renounced all of her past associations for a virtually unknown future. Ruth's words "if ought but death part thee and me" (1:17) are said to be the basis of the clause "till death do us part" in the traditional marriage ceremony. Ruth's unswerving decision stands in stark contrast to that of Orpah who returned to the darkness of heathen idolatry and is never mentioned in Scripture or history again. It is evident that the ten-year interval in Moab, and the tragedy there, left Naomi scarcely recognizable when she returned to Judah (1:19-22).

2. Ruth Sets Forth to Glean (Ch. 2)

The women arrived in Judah at the beginning of the harvest, and Ruth promptly secured her mother-in-law's permission to become a gleaner. Although gleaning was a menial task, it was one of the few means of livelihood open to a single woman in Ruth's day. The Law of Moses had prescribed: "And when ye reap the harvest of your land, thou shalt not wholly reap the corners of thy field, neither shalt thou gather the gleanings of thy harvest" (Lev. 19:9). Ruth also qualified for special consid-

eration as a stranger in the land. "And if a stranger sojourn with thee in your land, ye shall not vex him. But . . . thou shalt love him as thyself" (Lev. 19:33, 34). Scripture indicates that Ruth set out to glean simply at random, and it was seemingly by chance that she happened to choose the field of Boaz. Centuries later shepherds tended their flocks upon these same fields, and it was here that the angels first announced Jesus' birth.

The kind treatment that Ruth received in the field of Boaz was not merely the result of mere chance, however; he had heard of her unselfish life and he admired her for it. (cf. 2:11, 12). Boaz gave Ruth the privilege of gleaning throughout the harvest season and of drinking from his water supply. It is clear that at this time Boaz' motives were simply his practice of genuine godliness. Boaz instructed his reapers to let fall "some handfuls of purpose for her" and thus he deliberately provided extra portions, though without openly appearing to do so. The ephah which Ruth gleaned on her first day was a little more than a bushel, and it was a remarkable amount for a single day of gleaning. Bodie comments concerning this achievement: "Not so much which her diligence has secured, but that which his love has freely given." The Christian enjoys God's "handfuls of purpose" in all of the special providences and divine gifts which especially favor his life.

3. Ruth Presses Her Claim Upon Boaz (Ch. 3)

The Law of Moses had included the levirate law which provided for the marriage of a widow by her brother-in-law (Deut. 25:5-10). The purpose of such a procedure was to preserve families from extinction by providing sons who would maintain the name and possess the inheritance of the first husband. The levirate law appears to have been practiced widely in the ancient world, and cuneiform tablets from elsewhere in the Middle East made reference to it. In the Jewish system, a brother-in-law had the right to refuse his deceased brother's wife if circumstances were unfavorable. Although Naomi actually was the widow entitled to remarriage under this system, she unselfishly relinquished her rights in favor of Ruth. Apparently she understood that the immediate next of kin, entitled and perhaps somewhat obligated to act under levirate law, was Boaz (2:3). That this claim was in error was a later discovery.

By today's standards, Naomi clearly was a matchmaker who sent Ruth to the threshingfloor for the express purpose of arranging a marriage. However, she was merely acting within her legal rights, and in conformity with the customs of the day. Similarly, the method used by Ruth to secure the interest and attention of Boaz, though bizarre and dramatic by today's standards, would not be thought so in their society. Eastern culture provided that a position crosswise at the master's feet was not improper, since such people did not ordinarily undress for bed. When Boaz discovered Ruth, and realized the significance of her visit, he declared himself as considering her in high favor. However, he pointed out that there was a nearer relative. The gift of six measures of barley served as a seal or pledge assuring the fulfillment of Boaz' promises. The expression "to spread a skirt" symbolically implies "to extend protection."

4. The Marriage of Ruth and Boaz (Ch. 4)

On the day following, Boaz met with the near relative at the gate of the city so that there might be witnesses to any transactions. This near relative was called by Boaz "such a one"; but preachers have sometimes designated him "Mr. Barefoot." At first "such a one" agreed to redeem the land of the deceased Elimelech, for he assumed it was simply a matter of the redemption of a property inheritance as the Law prescribed (cf. Lev. 25:24, 25). Boaz' description: "Naomi . . . selleth a parcel of land" is more accurately rendered: "Naomi . . . hath sold away a parcel of ground" (i. e. lost by default). When "such a one" learned that he who redeemed the land must also take Ruth the Moabitess to wife, he was quite willing to step aside. According to Rabbinical tradition, the near kinsman did not choose to marry Ruth because he was already married and had two sons. Since she was a gentile by birth, it may have been his impression that to marry her would mar his inheritance. Any children born of the marriage to Ruth would have competed with his other children for a share of the family inheritance.

The Mosaic provision of the loosed shoe was somewhat modified (cf. Deut. 25:5-9) so as to be a symbol of the confirmation of a transaction; it was equivalent to a marriage license for Boaz rather than an action against a man who had rejected his brother's widow. The sense of shame and unworthiness for failing to redeem the widow seems not to have prevailed by this era in Israel's history. Typically, the inability of "such a one" may be seen to represent the Law which likewise was unable to redeem. Boaz' was permitted to redeem the lost inheritance by paying Naomi's debts, and to recover the lost relationship by taking Ruth in marriage. No doubt Boaz paid in silver, for this was the usual symbol of redemption, and thus, by his generosity, Ruth was transformed from poverty to riches. The gathered witnesses were pleased with the outcome of the transaction, and they pronounced blessings upon the happy pair. The baby son that was born into this home was Obed, and eventually he became the grandfather of David. Such events brought great joy to Naomi who no doubt had largely abandoned the hope of male heirs in the family. The book of Ruth closes without introducing a single character who was wicked, evil, or cruel.

The city of Bethlehem with the fields of Bethlehem in the foreground. This view looks west across the traditional property of Boaz.

4. THE BOOK OF 1 SAMUEL

This portion of Scripture has several titles, but the one best known is that of the Authorized version which is based upon the original Hebrew. The Septuagint calls First and Second Samuel the First and Second Books of the Kingdom; in the Vulgate this latter word is rendered "Kings." In the judgment of many, it is wholly valid that Samuel, who is either the principal actor, or the one anointing the principal actor, be given due recognition in the title of the book.

The Nature and Theme of the Book

While the book of 1 Samuel is basically a historical account, it is history written with an emphasis upon the fundamental need of genuine spirituality to assure material well-being. The primary emphasis of the book is the spiritual status of the leaders and their people. Although legalism and conformity to the Law are assumed, there is no actual mention of the Law in either book of Samuel, and there are only two references to the Levites. The progress of the nation from the disorganization of the era of the judges to an established orderly monarchy is described in terms of its spiritual motivation and background. The greatness of the prominent men, Samuel, Saul, and David, was precisely proportionate to the measure of their spiritual interest.

The Authorship of the Book

The crediting of the authorship to Samuel is a rabbinical tradition, and it has the endorsement of the Old Testament and of Christ. "Now the acts of David the king, first and last, behold they are written in the book of Samuel the seer" (1 Chron. 29:29). Jesus accepted the canonicity and authenticity of this book when He used it to defend the action of his disciples in plucking corn on the Sabbath. "But he said unto them, Have ye not read what David did, when he was an hungered" (Mt. 12:3). The book gives specific evidence of having been written by an eyewitness. Writes Manley:

The book contains a picture so primitive, vivid, and detailed as to force the conclusion that the author lived near to the events. The geographical facts are scrupulously exact.[1]

It is usually assumed that the latter section of the book, beginning with the report of the death of Samuel in 25:1, was written by the prophets Nathan and Gad. It is also possible, of course, that these scholars had some hand in the total manuscript; it is not implausible to think that they would make limited editorial changes in the light of more recent information available to them.

The Occasion of Writing and the Scope

The book was probably written in the later years of Samuel, at the time that David was preparing to assume the throne. It was evidently a time when the nation lacked a central temple, and therefore the writing of the book must have been within the generation involved in the events that the book describes. Inasmuch as Jewish history from the birth of Samuel through the reign of David is depicted, it may be concluded that 1 Samuel covers a little more than one century of national history.

The Key Word and the Key Verse

The key word of 1 Samuel is taken to be "pray" (or "prayer," or "prayed") with the thought that this is a book which stresses the need of a spiritual emphasis first of all. A suitable key verse is 12:23a "Moreover as for me, God forbid that I should sin against the Lord in ceasing to pray for you."

The Value of the Book

First Samuel is the sole record of the events in Israel that led to the establishment of the kingdom and the choice of the recognized ruling family. Samuel, who anointed both Saul and David, has been called the "Kingmaker." The consequences of the decision to adopt a monarchal rule constitute the central

---

[1]G. T. Manley, The New Bible Handbook (Chicago: Inter-Varsity Christian Fellowship, 1948), p. 168.

theme of the balance of the Old Testament story of the nation of Israel.

Analysis and Exposition

I. The Story of Samuel (Chs. 1-7)

1. The Birth of Samuel (Ch. 1)

For a Hebrew wife, such as Hannah, to be childless was counted a form of divine chastening. Hannah's sorrow was appeased neither by the fact that she was blessed with a truly pious husband, Elkanah, nor by the fact that he expressed his affection by bestowing upon her a worthy (i.e. double) portion. Hannah's burden of prayer led her to Shiloh, for it was there that the tabernacle had been somewhat permanently installed since the time of Joshua (cf. Josh. 18:1). Eli's misunderstanding of the fervency of her prayer might indicate both his own lack of spiritual insight, and that he rather commonly encountered people who were drunk. Nevertheless, Eli was able to reassure Hannah, on the basis of his overall knowledge and experience, that God would do right, and thus she went to her home with her burden lifted. In Hebrew, the name "Hannah" means "grace."

Little Samuel (which means "asked of God") was probably three years of age when he was presented at the tabernacle, since this was a common age for such dedications. Hannah considered that by this act she was fulfilling her vow to God, and inasmuch as the law of vows required a husband's approval (cf. 30:3-8), Elkanah must have concurred in the vow. The gift that she brought consisted of a bullock, flour, and wine, and these gifts served as a burnt and meal offering, and also a drink offering to God. Although the lad, Samuel, was a Levite (1 Chron. 6: 33, 34), it does not appear that he was a descendant of Aaron, and therefore he was not primarily among the select group of Levites who also served as priests. The name "Shemuel" is an alternate form of Samuel.

It is evident that in this period government by judges had merged into government by priests. The background of Eli is obscure, but Hebrew tradition says that he was of the tribe of Ithamar. If this is so, it would indicate that there had been a change from the original high priestly line of Eleazar. The inadequacy of the spiritual leadership provided by Eli and his house resulted in an overall weakening of the national spiritual vitality. The members of the family of Elkanah who worshipped the "Lord of Hosts" (an expression not occurring previously in Scripture, but hereafter used freely for a total of 281 references) were in refreshing contrast to the majority of their peers. In the light of these conditions, Hannah's

loan of her son to such a priestly family was indeed an outstanding sacrifice.

2. Hannah's Prayer and the Warning to Eli (Ch. 2)

The Song of Hannah in the first ten verses of this chapter constitutes her prayer of thanksgiving as she dedicated her little son. It is a forerunner of Mary's Magnificat (Lk. 1:46-55). Hannah expressed thanksgiving to the Giver, rather than permitting herself to be concerned solely with the gift. The expression "my horn is exalted in the Lord" was Hannah's way of saying that God had honored her and that He had given her strength, dignity, and status. But above all, her rejoicing was in all that God was to her. Writes Deane:

> She saw beyond the immediate present, and in the mercy displayed in her own case, she recognized the Divine economy in the government of the world, and a promise of future blessing not on individuals only but on her nation also.[2]

The customs recorded in this chapter (vv. 12-17) were far from the divine ideal. The priests had become exceedingly greedy and demanding, and instead of participating with the worshippers in the joyous feast of the peace offering, they were taking advantage of the devout by making such offerings a time to demand generous portions of the meat as gifts. Not only did they require that which properly belonged to the offerer, but in some cases they also appropriated the Lord's portion. One of the particular outcomes of such reprehensible actions of the part of the priests was the engendering of public contempt for the temple sacrifices. Thus "men abhorred the offering of the Lord" (v. 17).

The portrait of the child, Samuel, dressed in his priestly ephod or robe, ministering before the Lord, is of tender appeal. In the forthcoming night visitation, the mention of the lamps may suggest one of Samuel's chores was to maintain the various temple lights. The coat brought to him each year by his mother may have been in the fashion of a priestly coat, for this also was part of their garments. Eli's appreciation of Hannah and Samuel at this point serves somewhat as a redeeming aspect of an otherwise misguided life. Eli apparently appreciated virtue, but not enough to impose its stern requirements above the sentimental indulgences of an elderly father's affection.

Eli's inclination to honor his sons above God (v. 29) permitted their sins of rapacious greediness

---

2William Deane, Samuel and Saul (New York: Fleming Revell Company, n.d.), p. 15.

and flagrant violation of divine law even to the point of openly committing acts of fornication. At best, Eli had only mild rebukes for his sons, Hophni and Phinehas, and for the most part under the rule of their father, their evil continued unchecked. Nevertheless, God chose to intervene by sending an unnamed prophet, called simply "man of God," that Eli might be duly warned. This messenger declared that the line of Eli would be cut off in favor of one who would serve God in truth and piety. In this pronouncement to Eli, the messenger affirmed the standard spiritual principle "them that honour me [i.e. God] I will honour, and they that despise me shall be lightly esteemed" (v. 30).

3. The Night Visitation to Samuel (Ch. 3)

The occasion of the Lord's night visit to Samuel was at a time when there was no genuine prophet in Israel and knowledge of the Lord was most limited. It is supposed that Samuel was a boy of about twelve at this time, and that as a youthful temple worker he would be housed in quarters immediately adjacent to those of the high priest. Samuel three times mistook the call of the Lord for the voice of Eli, and only on the fourth call did he answer acceptably: "Speak; for thy servant heareth" (v. 10). The gist of the Lord's message was an announcement of His unswerving intention to bestow perpetual judgment upon the house of Eli. This message to Samuel clearly intimated his own call to service, even though it was verbally limited to an account of the doom of the incumbent.

The next morning, Eli questioned Samuel concerning the nature of the divine communication. Eli's response to Samuel's account was simply an abject resignation to the will of God: "It is the Lord: let him do what seemeth him good" (v. 18). The rejection of the house of Eli meant that God was transferring the priesthood from the line of Aaron's younger son, Ithamar, to the line of the older son, Eleazar. While Eli's sad plight invokes sympathy and pity, his helpless indifference to God's standards could expect no other outcome. Divine justice was forced to act.

The chapter concludes with a statement of approval upon the person and ministry of Samuel: "and all Israel from Dan to Beersheba knew that Samuel was established to be a prophet of the Lord" (v. 20). In Samuel, God found a man of adequate caliber that He might launch the order of the prophets. Samuel's spiritual successors served Israel in succeeding centuries, and they represented His voice and His message for the chosen people of each generation. About half of the prophets named in the Scriptures left writings which now comprise the Bible. As the first of the prophets, Samuel was re-

sponsible for upgrading the status of Shiloh to make it indeed a center where the pious might come to meet with their God and be directed in His will.

4. The Loss of Israel's Ark to the Philistines (Ch. 4)

The war with Philistia recorded in this chapter probably took place while Samuel was still too young to have assumed public leadership. As the battle progressed, Israel became hard pressed, and in their desperation with 4000 of their men slain, they proceeded to bring the ark of God to the field of battle in the vain hope that thus they might achieve victory. When Hophni and Phinehas arrived on the battlefield with the ark, the Israelites cheered so loudly that the Philistines were temporarily intimidated. The invaders soon rallied, however, and to the cry, "Be strong, and quit yourselves like men, O ye Philistines" they achieved a crushing victory over Israel. Hophni and Phinehas and 30,000 Israelitish soldiers were slain, and the ark of God was captured. Israel's use of the ark had been, of course, superstitious and irreverent, and God simply permitted matters to take their course.

The messenger who brought to Eli the tragic news of the battle losses is identified in Jewish tradition as Saul who was to become king (cf. v. 12). Eli, who was now 98 years of age, was so shocked and stunned by the news, particularly that the ark of God had been lost, that he collapsed and suffered a fall that resulted in his death. This tragedy, together with the untimely death of both of his sons, was clearly the promised divine judgment that had finally struck (2:31, 34). It was in this fateful hour that a child was born and given the name "Ichabod"--"the glory is departed." On the basis of incidental scriptural references, plus archaeological research, it is believed that the Philistines at this time pressed their advantage and proceeded to pillage and destroy Israel's national capital at Shiloh. (cf. Jer. 7:12, 26:6-9, Psa. 78:60-64). Thus, it would have been on this occasion that the empty tabernacle was transferred to Nob where it appears to have been in the time of Saul (1 Sam. 21:1-9).

5. The Ark in Philistia (Ch. 5)

The Philistines proceeded to carry the ark to Ashdod. However, in that place it proved to be a curse to them, for God displayed His displeasure by destroying Dagon and imposing a plague upon many of the people. Philistia's national god, Dagon, is believed to have been an idol which was represented by the head and trunk of a man and the body of a fish. Relief sculptures, believed to represent Dagon, depict him wearing a crown. The concept of a god as a merman was no doubt appropriate to the Philistines who were ardent fishermen. On this occasion they learned that though they might conquer Israel, they would be unable to conquer the God of Israel.

In Ashdod, and then in Gath and Ekron, the presence of the ark resulted in a serious plague. The word "emerods" is an old form of the word "hemorrhoids" (piles) which is a condition of aggravated swelling of the tissues at the bowel opening. It has been suggested that this condition may have been related to the bubonic plague which is associated with flea-carrying rodents and involves an enlargement of glands in the pubic area. In the presence of so much suffering and death, the Philistines proceeded to plead with their leaders to send the ark out of Philistia. The Philistine leaders are called "lords" because, typically, they would have been invested and crowned, even though the extent of their domain might be only a village or a small city and the lands immediately adjacent.

6. The Return of the Ark (Ch. 6)

When seven months had elapsed, the Philistines determined that they had suffered sufficiently and they prepared to return the ark to Israel. Their diviners or religious leaders showed commendable insight into the necessary spiritual steps, but since all pagan religions ultimately derive from worship to Jehovah, it is not wholly surprising that they might have retained some true insights. Further, they were immediate neighbors to Israel, and it may have been that they had taken opportunity to acquaint themselves with Israel's worship. The golden objects that they sent with the ark to be a trespass offering may have been actual sculptures of the afflicted body parts and the mice, or they may have been mere symbols. These objects are later called "the jewels of gold" (v. 15). It is clear that they represented considerable wealth in gold. Milk cattle (in Old English "milch") are cows that recently have given birth to a calf and hence are producing milk. The mother instinct of such a cow would incline her to want to stay with her calf rather than to proceed to the land of Israel.

The cattle with the ark arrived in the Israelitish city of Beth-shemesh during the time of summer harvest (June and July) and thus was widely witnessed by the field workers who freely rejoiced. The Levites who came to officiate led in a special service of thanksgiving, using the milk cows as sacrifice, and the wood of the cart as kindling. The joyful occasion, however, was sadly marred by the curiosity of the town folk who irreverently looked inside the ark. Some 50,070 of the people of Beth-shemesh were smitten by God "with a great slaughter." As the outcome of such a tragedy, the people of Beth-shemish, just as the people of the Philistine cities, pleaded that the ark be taken elsewhere. Thus,

their messengers brought their appeal to the neighboring city of Kirjath-jearim.

7. Samuel Leads Israel in Spiritual Revival. The Philistines are Defeated (Ch. 7)

In response to the plea from Beth-shemesh, the men of Kirjath-jearim accepted custody of the ark. This city was the next large town on the road toward Shiloh. Further, it was well inside the boundaries of Israel's territory. Accommodations for the ark were provided by Abinadab whose name, appropriately, means "father of generosity." As a supposed temporary expedient the citizens of the community appointed Eleazar, the son of Abinadab, as keeper of the ark. Inasmuch as this appointment did not seem displeasing to God, it is assumed that this Eleazar was of the priestly line. For the next twenty years the ark remained at Kirjath-jearim under these arrangements (cf. 7:2, 2 Sam. 6:3), but it is apparent that so long a stay was an evidence of general national indifference.

During the interval in which the ark was in Kirjath-jearim, the people became weary of their oppression under the Philistines. Thus, they responded to the exhortation of Samuel to return to the worship of Jehovah instead of worshipping Baal and Ashtaroth, the pagan deities of Canaan. The measure of penitence was so genuine and widespread that it led to a national gathering at Mizpeh. There the people worshipped devoutly, while they prayed and confessed their sins. Because Israel was a subject people, dominated by the Philistines, this gathering was interpreted as a move to achieve national independence. Very promptly, therefore, the Philistines proceeded to amass an army and launch an attack. No doubt because the prayers of Samuel had preceded the whole project, the outcome was a resounding victory for Israel and the complete rout of the Philistines. God gave divine aid in the battle by means of a great thunder that "discomfited" (i.e. confused and scattered) the Philistines. A victory of this sort had already been won by Samuel on his knees.

To mark their regained freedom, the Israelites named the place of victory "Ebenezer" and erected there a stone memorial. The implication of the name was "hitherto hath the Lord helped us." Although Samuel was not blind to the temporary ups and downs that the nation had experienced, he primarily looked to the overall spiritual stability that God's people had enjoyed. In Samuel's own life God had been consistently faithful, and not again during the prophet's lifetime did the Philistines dominate Israel. Further, the sacred record during this period has no report of any incidents of war with other Canaanite tribes (or Amorites) who were neighbors to Israel and who might have been hostile.

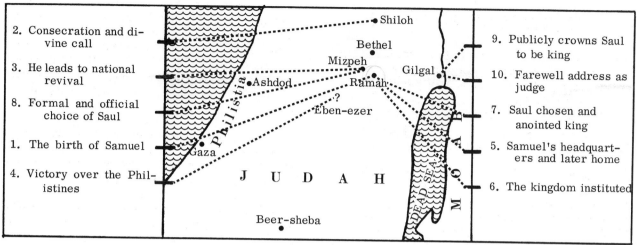

2. Consecration and divine call

3. He leads to national revival

8. Formal and official choice of Saul

1. The birth of Samuel

4. Victory over the Philistines

Shiloh

Bethel

Mizpeh

Ashdod

Gilgal

Ramah

?

Eben-ezer

Gaza

J U D A H

Beer-sheba

PHILISTIA

DEAD SEA

MOAB

9. Publicly crowns Saul to be king

10. Farewell address as judge

7. Saul chosen and anointed king

5. Samuel's headquarters and later home

6. The kingdom instituted

Figure Four: Scenes from the life of Samuel

With peace prevailing, plus a genuine sense of spiritual interest, Samuel found that his person and ministry were freely in demand. He established Ramah as a center, and each year toured in a circuit ministry to Bethel, Gilgal, and Mizpeh. At this time, Samuel was not associated either with Shiloh, the earlier national capital and home of the tabernacle, or with Nob, which later became the national center of worship (cf. 1 Sam. 21:1-9). Perhaps in his day neither center was functioning, for Scripture notes that Samuel erected an altar at Ramah. It is concluded that during this era, Samuel founded the first school of the prophets and began recruiting and training young men to succeed him in the prophetic ministry.

II. The Story of Saul (Chs. 8-15)

1. Israel's Demand for a King (Ch. 8)

When Samuel approached the age of retirement, it became evident that his sons were unsuitable to succeed him. They had failed to maintain the high order of Godliness which their names affirmed: Joel means "Jehovah is God"; Abiah means "Jehovah is my father." Their leadership gave no evidence of true virtue, and rather, they were clearly guilty of accepting bribes and perverting judgments. The elders of Israel boldly approached Samuel, and on the basis of such a state of affairs requested that they be allowed to establish a monarchy. Samuel reacted to this disappointing personal rejection by turning to God in prayer.

Apart from the objection to Samuel's sons, Israel's desire for a king was of long standing. A nationwide political movement in this direction had been gaining momentum throughout the period of the later judges (12th century B.C.). While various factors seemed to justify the establishment of a kingdom, the fact remained that the plan ran counter to the Lord's preference for the people. As a theocracy, Israel was much more sensitive to the direct intervention of God, and dependent upon Him; also, the theocracy was a simpler and less costly form of government and much more suited to the people of God during their earthly sojourn. At best, it can be said that Israel's demand for a king was directed to God's permissive will rather than His direct will.

In his reply to the elders, Samuel proceeded to arrange for a national assembly. There, he presented to the gathered citizenry a vivid and faithful description of conditions in a monarchy. He warned of the endless demands and ceremonialism of an oriental court, and stressed the despotism that would be imposed. His words, however, fell on unheeding ears, for these were some of the very factors that seemed so attractive to the Israelites. They continued their demands for a king, and eagerly anticipated the day when he should judge their disputes, lead their armies, and increase their prestige abroad. Although they did not resort to force of arms, these public agitators on behalf of the monarchy, otherwise brought to bear all of the moral pressures possible.

Samuel reluctantly carried the answer of the people to the Lord, but there he found a gracious reception, notwithstanding the circumstances. The Lord comforted Samuel and told him to comply with the wish of the people. Thus, it was by divine command that Samuel chose, anointed, elected, and crowned Saul; although, as already noted, the entire project was God's permissive and not His direct will. Writes Blaikie:

The people had shown themselves unworthy of the high privilege of having God as their king. When men show themselves incapable of appreciating a high privilege, it is meet they should suffer the loss of it, or at least a diminution of it.[3]

A possible redeeming feature in Israel's demand for a king was a difference in their attitudes from those of their pagan neighbors. At no time did the Israelites seriously copy the pagan pattern and specifically consider their king also their priest and their god.

2. Saul Chosen to be King (Ch. 9)

Saul is first introduced in Scripture in the story of the search for his father's lost asses. Scripture conveys a most favorable impression of the appearance and character of this young man: "Saul, a choice young man and goodly: and there was not among the children of Israel a goodlier person that he: from his shoulders and upward he was higher than any of the people" (v. 2). It is clear that physical appearance was an important qualification in winning public approval. Although Saul, the son of Kish, was from the tribe of Benjamin (just as the eminent Saul of the New Testament) which was the smallest of the tribes, it appears that his family was one of some prominence (cf. 1 Sam. 14:51; 1 Chron. 8:33, 9:39).

In his quest for the asses, Saul eventually came to Samuel to enlist divine aid in the search. Whether Samuel was at Ramah, his headquarters, or further south near to Bethlehem (cf. 10:2) is not recorded, but the former is assumed. Samuel had been prepared by the Lord for the visitor, so that he not only knew Saul when he saw him, but he proceeded to invite the youth to a public dinner in his honor. Remarks Blaikie: "The meeting between Samuel and Saul was preceded by previous meetings between Samuel and God." Thirty guests attended the dinner, and Saul, both in the serving and the seating of the guests, was singularly honored. However, Samuel carefully refrained from announcing the true nature of the occasion. The prophet preferred to wait until the two men were alone before he would reveal the Lord's appointment for the life of Saul.

3. The Private Anointing and Later Public Choice of Saul (Ch. 10)

When Saul left Samuel's home after the public dinner, the prophet accompanied him. When they were alone outside the city, Samuel proceeded to anoint him with oil, thus signifying his special calling. Saul went forth with the promise of several signs to be fulfilled as confirmations of his call, and one by one these came to pass. One of the most noteworthy of the signs was that Saul should

become endued with the power to prophesy. The fulfillment of this promise is recorded in verse ten. The prophetic ministry manifested in Saul so impressed the people that they coined the proverb: "Is Saul also among the prophets?" Evidently, Saul had not previously been noted for his spiritual attainments, but his new responsibility and status now led him to spiritual pursuits.

In keeping with the customs of the day, and because worship was not centralized at the tabernacle while the ark was absent, Jehovah evidently permitted worship in various centers throughout the land called "high places." Samuel is described as going to a "high place" to worship (9:12); the worshipping prophets were returning from a "high place" (10:5). The name "Ramah" itself means "high place," and Gibeah, which was Saul's home, is also called "the hill of God" (v. 5). In later centuries, worship in high places was almost always idolatrous, and in general, God required centralized worship in the temple. It is interesting to note that the prophets who worshipped in this era freely used musical instruments in their worship (v. 5).

In order that all the nation might be informed of God's choice for their king, Samuel next proceeded to call for a general assembly at Mizpeh. There, he briefly rehearsed the nature of God's dealings with the people, and then proceeded to make a public selection of the candidate for king. The inquiry finally pointed to Saul, but he was only publicly acclaimed after he had been brought out of his hiding place in a storehouse. Saul, of course, had known the outcome of the divine choice, and out of modesty, had hidden himself. He was promptly accepted by most of the nation, and even a voluntary bodyguard attached themselves to him. However, there were the "children of Belial" who remained opposed to his candidacy, and who considered him unworthy.

4. Saul's First Victory (Ch. 11)

For a time, Saul returned to tending the flock of his father in spite of the fact that he had been acclaimed king. All of the machinery of Israel's monarchal government had yet to be established. According to Josephus, it was a month later that Saul had opportunity to display his merit in the incident of Jabesh-gilead. This city suffered oppression at the hands of the Ammonites. True to their reputation of "revolting cruelty and unbridled rapacity," the Ammonites demanded the privilege of putting out the right eye of every citizen of the city. Saul was greatly stirred at the report of this threat, and he undertook to recruit an army. Since the nation was now for the first time united under a king, the enthusiastic response promptly led to the enrolling of 330,000 volunteers.

---

[3]W. G. Blaikie, _A Manual of Bible History_ (New York: Thomas Nelson and Sons, n. d.), p. 115.

On the following day, when Saul launched his battle, the Ammonites were wholly taken off guard. Apparently, they had believed the deliberately misleading report that on that day the people of Jabesh-gilead would surrender. Saul's strategy involved not only the surprise attack, but the division of his forces into three armies to attack simultaneously on three fronts. Following the battle with the Ammonites, Saul proceeded diplomatically to forgive all of his recent critics, and to ascribe his victory to the intervention of God. Such actions assured widespread popularity, so that the people proceeded enthusiastically to Gilgal, and there with Samuel officiating, crowned Saul their king. The peace offering at that time would have been sacrifices of thanksgiving.

While the events of chapters nine and ten seem to have taken place while Saul was young (e.g. "And he had a son, whose name was Saul, a choice young man"), it would appear that the events culminating in the crowning of 11:15 were somewhat later. This would be inferred because Scripture reports that after Saul had reigned only two years (13:1) Jonathan, his son, was a fully grown man and a captain in the army (13:3, 22). However, the many possible variants in personal chronologies discourage dogmatic conclusions in this regard.

5. The Kingdom Proclaimed. The Abdication of Samuel (Ch. 12)

Samuel apparently delivered his farewell address to an assembly of the entire nation. The mechanics of such a procedure are not explained, but perhaps he spoke in an area adjacent to the tabernacle during one of the three annual feast days. In his address, Samuel reviewed God's gracious dealings with the nation, and then exhorted them to spiritual faithfulness under their new ruler. Samuel's claim to scrupulous honesty throughout his rule as judge went wholly uncontested by his peers; rulers of such integrity were rare in Samuel's day. The Lord confirmed the message by sending a supernatural sign of thunder and rain at a most unusual time. Further confirmation of Samuel's life and ministry is found throughout Scripture. Thus: "Moses and Aaron among his priests, and Samuel among them that call upon his name; they called upon the Lord, and he answered them" (Psa. 99:6).

The official surrender of civil government into the hands of Saul freed Samuel from his duties as judge and gave him the necessary time to exercise his prophetic ministry. In his role as prophet, he extended his influence even more effectively than he had as judge. When king Saul chose to reject Samuel and his message, the prophet directed himself toward the youthful David. Samuel filled an important role in preparing David for his office, and sowing the seeds of true godliness. The imprint of Samuel remained evident in the kingdom long after his death. The name "Bedan" in verse 11 is thought to be another form of "Balak."

6. The First Pronouncement of the Divine Rejection of Saul (Ch. 13)

Saul apparently began his rule while continuing to reside in his family home in Gibeah (10:26, 13:26, 15:34). It appears that by this time Israel was once more under the domination of Philistia and not truly independent. Thus, Saul's organization of an army of 3,000 men with 1,000 in the command of Jonathan was in itself a defiant move. Matters were compounded when Jonathan impatiently proceeded to engage in overcoming a small garrison (some translators render the word "monument") of Philistines on the frontier. This skirmish naturally antagonized the Philistines so that they gathered a vast army numbering 30,000 chariots, 6,000 horsemen, and foot soldiers as "the sand which is on the sea shore." In the face of so great a threat, Saul's fighters suffered demoralizing fear that drove most of them to flee and hide. Thus, Saul arrived at Gilgal, the supposed rallying point for the Israelites, with only a small band of frightened followers.

Saul had made a prior arrangement with Samuel (1 Sam. 10:8) that the prophet should meet him at Gilgal and conduct a service of worship and make offerings to God. However, as the days passed, and Samuel did not come, Israel's position became increasingly perilous and Saul's impatience mounted. Hence, on the seventh day, Saul proceeded himself to officiate at the offering of sacrifices. Doubtlessly, both he and his helpers knew that for one who was not a priest to officiate at the sacrifice in this manner was an act of flagrant disobedience and rebellion against God.

When Samuel arrived, just as the sacrifice was completed, he was gravely displeased with Saul's actions. To have thus intruded into the priesthood gave evidence that the king neither respected Samuel's office, nor did he genuinely trust the promise of divine aid. Both in the outward consequences of the act, and in the motivation that had led to it, Saul demonstrated that his heart was not right toward God. It was the desire of the Lord to find "a man after his own heart" (v. 14), and it was now clear that He must seek another rather than continue to hope in Saul. At this time, Samuel proceeded to pronounce the forthcoming divine judgment, and the fact that Saul would lose his kingdom.

Israel's subjection to Philistia throughout this period is specifically reported. In particular, the Philistines determined that the Israelites should possess no armaments, and thus they denied them the tools to work with iron. There is some uncertainty whether the Hebrew word "pim" is properly translated "file," or whether it refers to a unit of coinage. Thus, a possible rendering of v. 21: "And the price was a pim [2/3 shekel] for the mattocks and for the coulters, and 1/3 shekel for the axes and the sharpening of the goads." The share and the coulter are parts of a plow, and the mattock is a type of a pickaxe. This period of Israel's subjection to Philistia is called the "captivity of the land" (Jud. 18:30).

7. Jonathan's Strategic Defeat of the Philistines (Ch. 14)

For some time, the armies of Israel and Philistia lay encamped on opposite hillsides with a densely wooded valley between that prevented any casual engagements. The youthful Jonathan, becoming restless at the inactivity, proceeded to slip out of camp, and with only his armour bearer accompanying him, to scale the heights that he might confront the enemy. Jonathan's remarkable boldness so impressed the Philistines that they refrained from attack. Jonathan and his armour bearer entrenched themselves on what seems to have been a ledge, and there proceeded by hand-to-hand combat to slay a larger number of Philistines. A severe earthquake that occurred at that moment added to the confusion, and the outcome was that the entire army of the Philistines was routed and put to flight. In this venture, Jonathan seems to have acted in genuine faith in God rather than in mere youthful foolhardiness. It is a matter of interest that in World War I, General Edmund Allenby captured the city of Michmash from the Turks by using a strategy worked out through reading the Bible account of Jonathan's victory.

In the face of these events, it appears that Saul first thought to call for a worship service to investigate the divine will (cf. v. 18). It was probably in this connection that he issued his decree requiring all Israelites to fast throughout the day(v. 24). However, even before the worship service was underway, the sounds of confusion and disorder in the ranks of the Philistines increased (v. 19), and Saul apparently decided that the course of action was already evident. Israel was responsible to attack immediately. In following such a course, the Israelites completed the rout of the Philistines that Jonathan had begun, and even Hebrew defectors and captives once more returned to their ranks.

Jonathan had been battling the Philistines at the time that Saul proclaimed the fast day, and thus in ignorance, he ate wild honey in the woods. Saul is hardly to be justified in imposing fasting during a time of warfare, but this did not invalidate the oath before God. To break it was to incur divine displeasure in spite of the circumstances, and therefore, Jonathan deserved to be judged. In his newfound piety, Saul would have been willing actually to slay Jonathan for his violation of the restriction, but even Saul gave way before the weight of popular opinion responding to the hero of the day. Such a strange course of events is partly a commentary upon the harsh standards of the times, and partly an insight into the instability of mind and character of King Saul.

It may be assumed that the time when the people began to eat ravenously of their spoil was at sundown on the day of battle, for in Jewish time, sundown marked the end of a calendar day. Saul showed wisdom in erecting an altar for the use of the people as a place of sacrifice at this time. The spoil had included meat animals, and the people were neglecting the proper legal procedure in dressing these for food. The laws required that all such animals slain by the Israelites be ceremonially bled and dedicated to the Lord. In their haste to satisfy their hunger, the people were committing wrong in failing to heed this requirement.

Saul continued the victories that began at this time, and in turn he subdued each of the surrounding kingdoms. He provided that the borders of Israel were comparatively secure, and that for the most part, the nation was free from foreign oppression. Saul's family is here identified, including both his wife and sons. In addition to the three sons mentioned here, a fourth, Ish-bosheth (also called Ish-baal and Esh-baal) was destined to fill an important place in later history (cf. 2 Sam. 2:8). The son called Ishui here, is elsewhere called Abinadab. Only two daughters are named, Merab and Michal, and this latter was destined to become the wife of David. Scripture names only Ahinoam as the true wife of Saul, although it also mentions Rizpah, a concubine (2 Sam. 3:7).

8. The Second Pronouncement of Saul's Rejection (Ch. 15)

Saul's next activity was an attack upon the Amalekites as an act of long postponed reprisal upon the oppressors of his people during the wilderness wanderings (cf. Ex. 17:8-16). God commanded: "now go and smite Amalek, and utterly destroy all that they have, and spare them not; but slay both man and woman, infant and suckling, ox and sheep, camel and ass" (v. 3). Such severity constituted the judgment of God upon a people who for four centuries had resisted Him, and had oppressed His people. The Lord gave Israel an overwhelming victory in the battle, but Saul disobeyed God by sparing Agag the king. He also brought back with him the best of the livestock. Evidently, Saul not only desired popular applause, but also he yielded himself to the promptings of carnal greed.

Samuel was informed directly by God of the fact of Saul's disobedience. Scripture reports: "It grieved Samuel; and he cried unto the Lord all night" (v. 11). As it were, Saul had totally conquered the armies of the Amalekites, but in turn he had been conquered by a few sheep and oxen. In the face of Samuel's charges, Saul twice excused himself. He first blamed the men of his army for saving the livestock, and he further sought to affirm

that actually he had saved them for sacrifice. Samuel's response included the classic principle "Behold, to obey is better than sacrifice, and to hearken than the fat of rams. For rebellion is as the sin of witchcraft, and stubbornness is as iniquity and idolatry" (vv. 22, 23). Samuel thus clearly discerned, even in Old Testament times, the fundamental necessity of the surrender of the heart to God.

On this occasion, Saul once more confessed that he had been wrong (cf. v. 24). However, even though Saul confessed "I have sinned" more frequently than any other character of the Bible, neither on this occasion, nor on similar occasions, was his

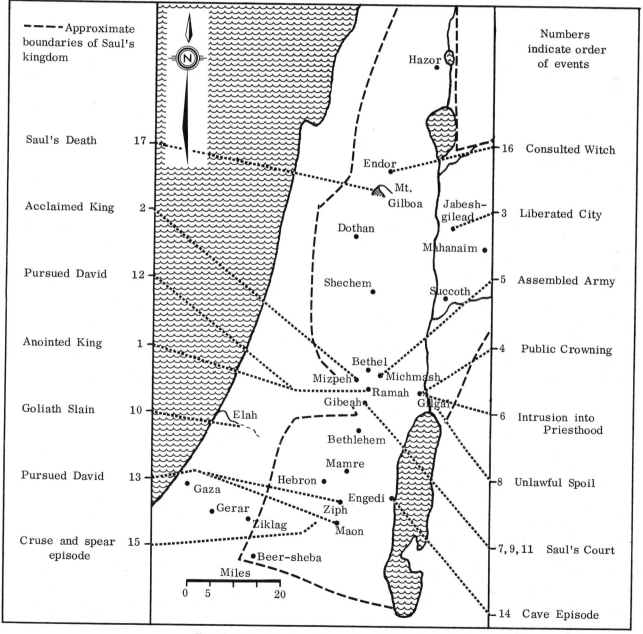

Saul's Death	17		16	Consulted Witch
Acclaimed King	2		3	Liberated City
Pursued David	12		5	Assembled Army
Anointed King	1		4	Public Crowning
Goliath Slain	10		6	Intrusion into Priesthood
Pursued David	13		8	Unlawful Spoil
Cruse and spear episode	15		7, 9, 11	Saul's Court
			14	Cave Episode

- - - - - Approximate boundaries of Saul's kingdom

Numbers indicate order of events

Hazor
Endor
Mt. Gilboa
Jabesh-gilead
Dothan
Mahanaim
Shechem
Succoth
Bethel
Mizpeh
Michmash
Ramah
Gibeah
Gilgal
Elah
Bethlehem
Mamre
Hebron
Gaza
Engedi
Gerar
Ziph
Ziklag
Maon
Beer-sheba

Miles
0   5   20

Figure Five: Scenes from the life of Saul

confession accompanied by true penitence. Whereas, previously, God had rejected the family of Saul as Israel's ruling house, He now pronounced the personal rejection of Saul himself. Saul's claim that his unwise action had been "because I feared the people" (v. 24), appears to be a mere rationalized excuse. Even on this occasion, Samuel allowed Saul to "save face" before the elders and the people by leading them in worship. Whether Samuel was right in this act is a matter of dispute, and some have criticized him for it. Thus:

> Samuel speaks brave words to the foolish king; but finally, in a moment of weakness, he consents to offer sacrifice with Saul standing beside him as king. Saul has outwitted the good man. He can now say that Samuel's conduct does not square with his words . . . . Samuel's inconsistency gave Saul the advantage and encouraged him to pay no attention to the decree of rejection.[4]

God's act of rejecting Saul is described as an occasion of divine repentance (v. 11). From time to time elsewhere in Scripture (cf. Gen. 6:6, 32:14), God found it necessary to reverse His intention for mankind because, in turn, humans had disqualified themselves in particular covenant relationships. The change is exclusively in man and not in God, and this fact is reaffirmed: "the Strength of Israel will not lie nor repent" (v. 29). The immutable God, by the very requirements of His nature, maintains without change those policies that He has determined. Man chooses whether to relate to these policies with blessing and prosperity or with destruction and condemnation. A brief note in this paragraph (v. 33) describes Samuel as fulfilling the stroke of divine justice upon Agag in the place of disobedient King Saul. Apparently, Agag precipitated the stroke of justice by his own flippancy and presumptuousness.

III. The Story of David (Chs. 16-31)

1. David Anointed King (Ch. 16)

With the rejection of Saul an accomplished fact, God commissioned Samuel to anoint the chosen successor. Since it was an act of treason to appoint a new king while one still reigned, Samuel acted in secrecy. He proceeded to Bethlehem at the Lord's suggestion, on the pretext of making sacrifice. At that city, Samuel directed himself to the house of Jesse, and there set about to select one of Jesse's sons as the new king. However, even Samuel was

---

[4]John R. Sampey, The Heart of the Old Testament (Nashville: Broadman Press, 1922), p. 102.

mistaken as to the exact candidate, and once more the Lord declared a basic principle of His economy: "The Lord seeth not as man seeth; for man looketh on the outward appearance, but the Lord looketh on the heart" (v. 7). On the basis of this principle, God indicated that His choice was the youth, David. Apparently the anointing of David was kept secret, or at least generally minimized, although clearly Jesse and David knew the purpose of the anointing.

The choice of young David as the future king is a remarkable illustration of the grace of God. At the time that Samuel came, David had been assigned to tend the family sheep, and he was not even considered to be a possible candidate. In later years, David remembered that God had chosen him out of his place of obscurity and he referred to himself as a "dead dog," and "flea" (24:14). David is described as the youngest (v. 11) of eight brothers (17:12), but elsewhere he is described as the seventh son (2 Chron. 2:15). It is conjectured that one of the sons of Jesse may have died before reaching maturity. For David to have been "ruddy" (v. 12) implies that he had hair of a reddish color. Such a characteristic was considered a mark of attractiveness among the dark-haired Hebrews.

It was about at this time that Saul became oppressed by an evil spirit, so that a clever harpist was sought out to comfort him. Someone recommended David, and before long this anointed and talented young man found himself in the royal court. This choice of David as harpist appears to have been apart from any knowledge or consideration of his later destiny. David was chosen apparently because he possessed musical skills, but no doubt also because he exhibited a pleasing and cheering personality. Also, by this time he may have achieved some limited local fame, or at least respect, because of his destruction of the lion and the bear which he later reported (cf. 17:34-36). For Saul to conscript a fine young man in this manner was just the sort of situation that Samuel predicted would be the outcome if the people insisted upon a king (cf. 8:11).

The statement in 16:14 is puzzling: "But the Spirit of the Lord departed from Saul, and an evil spirit from the Lord troubled him." Saul's behaviour would probably have appeared as a manic-depressive psychosis, but clearly it was no mere mental illness but rather, possession by a spiritual higher power. It is possible that this evil spirit was actually God's convicting Spirit which is evil to a man who himself is evil; but more probably it was a satanic spirit, and it was from the Lord only in the sense that it oppressed Saul according to God's permissive will. In this latter case, God would have been involved inasmuch as it was sent by Him as a punishment.

A view of the Judean Wilderness out of the main entrance of the Cave of Adullam. Saul conducted his interview with David from these slopes.

2. David's Victory Over Goliath (Ch. 17)

There is uncertainty concerning the exact chronology of the story of David: it is possible that the events of this chapter constituted an incident during David's court residence described in the previous chapter. David may have been temporarily dismissed by Saul and thus have gone back to his shepherd activities. It is clear that when David came to the field of battle with provisions for his brothers, he came as a young shepherd lad. Had he been age twenty or older at this time, he would have been in Saul's army and would not have been free to remain at home. It appears that his victory over Goliath at this time meant the end of his shepherd life, and from that time onward he became a permanent resident in the royal household. The fact that David must come from home with provisions for his brothers in the army is evidence of the very informal fashion of military organization at this time.

Scripture reports that Goliath was over nine

and one-half feet tall, that his coat of mail weighed over 150 pounds, and that the head of his spear weighed 18 pounds. It has been suggested that Goliath may have been a survivor of the race of Anakim giants (Num. 13:33). For David, as a virtually unarmed young lad, to attack such a seasoned Philistine warrior must be judged to have been an expression of genuine faith. David testified "The Lord that delivered me out of the paw of the lion, and out of the paw of the bear, he will deliver me out of the hand of this Philistine" (v. 37). David's continual assertion of courage and faith led to the audience with Saul, and to the commission to challenge Goliath in the name of the army of Israel. So personally reassuring was David's faith, that his victory was clearly no surprise to him even though it seems to have been to all who witnessed the event. In the rout of the Philistines which followed the slaying of Goliath, Israel is reported by Josephus to have slain 30,000 of the enemy. The Israelites pursued the Philistines from the valley of the battle far back into their own territory and even to the gate of the city of Ekron.

Saul's enquiries concerning the identity of David's father (vv. 56, 58) may not have been for the purpose of gaining knowledge, but rather to compliment Jesse, David's father. The social custom in some societies extends a compliment, not to the man who achieves, but to the man who fathered him; Saul's procedure may reflect such a practice. A second possibility is that Saul previously knew David only as a young harpist in his court, and that he had paid no heed to the family relationships. Now that David had attained a measure of eminence in his own right, Saul wished to broaden his acquaintance with David and David's family. A third possibility is that the chronology of events is such that this actually was Saul's first meeting with David: the events of chapter sixteen may have followed rather than preceded this incident. Scripture passes over the fact that the riches and marriage to the king's daughter (v. 25) that was promised to the one who slew Goliath appears not to have been bestowed upon David.

3. David in Saul's Court (Ch. 18)

One of the gratifying outcomes of David's residence in the court of Saul was his friendship with Jonathan. Deane points out: "The friendship there begun never wavered, was never darkened for a moment; it continued unimpaired by envy or jealousy till the last." White discusses the covenant between David and Jonathan:

> This covenant evidences one of the finest friendships in history. All through the centuries the love of Jonathan and David has symbolized that unselfish fraternal

feeling that should characterize the true relations of man with an exalted, common purpose in life, and their relation became the foundation for many of the best known fraternal organizations.[5]

His friendship with Jonathan became to David a sustaining bulwark to help him through many difficult days. Jonathan's gifts of his personal effects to David including his robe, his armor, and his weapons, were clearly expressions of a profound and sincere friendship.

While David's friendship with Jonathan was growing, so was Saul's jealousy and his open hostility against David. Saul clearly saw that David's popularity and his hold upon the people were steadily increasing. David's feat on the battlefield in the slaying of Goliath, and other apparently unrecorded public exploits, came to be celebrated above Saul's victories. The hatred that Saul came to feel for David went hand-in-hand with the king's submission to the sway of a supernatural evil spirit. While on the one hand, the spirit gave him prophetic powers, on the other it goaded him to commit violent, irrational acts in fits of blind fury. Saul's procedure in appointing David army captain was probably merely a strategy planned with the hope that David would be destroyed in warfare. Certainly, the rather bizarre requirement of tokens of the death of 100 Philistines as a dowry payment for the hand of Michal, Saul's daughter, reveals such an intention. However, David took the challenge seriously, and when he had slain double the quota, Saul had no alternative but to surrender Michal. In a subsequent attempt by the Philistines to avenge the slaying of their two hundred associates, David's military skill and courage won him further popular approval.

4. David's Flight From the Court (Ch. 19)

As the breach between Saul and David widened, Jonathan did what he could to repair it, but he succeeded in effecting only a temporary reconciliation. When David won fresh victories and new acclaim, the enraged Saul hurled his javelin at David in a deliberate murder attempt. David's only recourse was to take flight and thereby begin a series of wanderings that extended through several years. His escape was aided by his wife, Michal, who by means of a dummy in David's bed, deceived Saul's messengers until David was out of reach. The dummy appears to have been partly devised by use of a teraph (pl. teraphim). These were apparently doll-like figures used by the Israelites in Old Testament times as household gods

---

[5]Wilbert W. White, _Old Testament Records, Poems and Addresses_ (New York: Young Men's Christian Association, 1900), p. 166.

and not necessarily considered idolatrous. This occasion of the flight of David is associated with the composition of Psalm 59.

In his fugitive life, David went first to Samuel at Ramah, and together the king-elect and the prophet took up residence in Naioth. This community is believed to have been the section of Ramah which comprised the dwelling place of the students of Samuel's prophetic school. At this time it was Samuel who offered leadership to the school of the prophets, just as Elijah and Elisha were to do in a later era. Saul chose to disregard the sacredness of David's refuge, and thus he sent three successive contingents of messengers, and finally came in person with the expressed purpose of slaying David. On each occasion, those with murderous intentions were so moved in such spiritual surroundings that they forgot their evil purpose and instead remained to worship. It is ironical that in spite of this spiritual blessing, Saul remained the same wicked sinner; he was entranced, but he was not transformed.

5. David's Covenant with Jonathan (Ch. 20)

In his quest for information and counsel concerning his relationship to Saul, David called upon his friend, Jonathan. The friends agreed that David, with an adequate excuse, should be conspicuously absent from the royal table at the feast of the new moon. It was the custom at this time that each male Israelite should observe the beginning of a new month by participating in a feast, and naturally the royal court make provision for such occasions. Saul's reaction to the absence of David from the monthly feast was to be communicated to the latter by Jonathan's procedures at target practice. As matters transpired, Saul made very clear his intention to kill David, and Jonathan sadly made known this fact to David. At the risk of their lives, the two friends enjoyed a final meeting and then departed with a benediction of peace.

The covenant between Jonathan and David (vv. 15-17) would assure that neither royal house would destroy the other. Such a covenant was needed in a day when policies of total extermination, in the case of a change in the ruling family, were often standard practice. The sacrifice in Bethlehem that Jonathan described (vv. 28, 29) would have been legitimate in this era because there was actually no official worship center. The ark remained in the house of Abinadab, and the empty tabernacle, although last reported at Shiloh, from events in the next chapter now appears to have been moved to the priestly city of Nob (See Josh. 18:1; 1 Sam. 1:3, and discussion of 1 Sam. 4:19-22). Noteworthy texts in this chapter include: "there is but a step between me and death" (v. 3), and "thou shalt be missed, be-

cause thy seat will be empty." (v. 18).

6. David's Visit to Nob (Ch. 21)

Upon leaving Jonathan, David proceeded to the priestly city of Nob (also called Nobeh) and there he visited Ahimelech, the priest. David quite unjustifiably led this man of God to false conclusions about his flight and circumstances. Thus, under false premises, David obtained a portion of the shewbread for food and the sword of Goliath for a weapon. Our Lord mentioned the incident of David and the shewbread (Mt. 12:3, 4), not so much to justify David's deceit, but to explain the true nature of the Law. Jesus sought to emphasize that along with all its rigors, the ultimate concern of the Law was for human welfare. It has been suggested that David avoided the truth, either as a misguided attempt to shield Ahimelech, or because he was suspicious of the observer, Doeg (v. 7). This man later proved to be a treacherous betrayer.

After leaving Nob, David travelled southwest to Gath, the headquarters of the Philistines. There, he took refuge with king Achish, hoping to remain incognito. However, the servants of Achish recognized David and they called him "king" (v. 11), probably out of respect for his military achievements, or possibly because they knew the story of David's anointing by Samuel. In response to such information, Achish proceeded to imprison David, and he probably would have destroyed him. However, David met the situation by very convincingly feigning insanity. Achish, who according to tradition, had seen both his wife and daughter become insane, only too gladly released the supposedly mad David. It is believed that David wrote Psalm 34 during his imprisonment, and Psalm 56 to celebrate his deliverance.

7. David at Adullam. The Massacre of the Priests
(Ch. 22)

From Gath, David continued southward to the Cave of Adullam. This cavern, he made his headquarters, and it was there that he gathered about himself many of those who were later to be his associates in ruling the land. At this time, they were economic and social outcasts, perhaps in part, because of the despotic nature of the rule of king Saul. The choice of such persons: the debtor, the distressed, and the discontented is consistent with divine providence and grace. Although David and his 400 followers would have comprised a nuisance threat to King Saul, they definitely did not appear as a serious military threat. It was while he was at Adullam that David wrote Psalm 142.

David next sought a safe refuge for his parents, and hence he journeyed to Mizpeh in Moab, the ancestral home of Ruth, his great-grandmother. There, he left his parents in the care of the king. In his own case, David was advised by the prophet Gad (who is called "David's seer" [1 Chron. 21:9]), to leave his Moabitish retreat and return to Judah. Apparently, the presence of David in the land was not only an expression of his personal faith in God, but it served to boost the morale of the people and increase their appreciation of their king-elect. Thus David returned to Judah, but stopping short of his former refuge at Adullam, he remained instead in the forest of Hareth. Unfortunately, this move incited the neuroses of King Saul, and it marked the beginning of Saul's militant effort to destroy David and David's supporters. The fact that even at this time Saul held court under a tree (v. 6), is evidence of the informality of the era.

The beginnings of Saul's active campaign against David led very tragically to the destruction of Ahimelech and the priests of Nob. In all, 85 priests were slain. Saul committed this senseless destruction in response to the report of Doeg the Edomite concerning the occasion when the priests had harbored the fugitive David. Some scholars have interpreted the chronologies to teach that Ahimelech was the great-grandson of Eli, and that therefore, Saul was an instrument in God's hand to bestow judgment upon the house of Eli according to prophecy. However, the kinship of Ahimelech is not clearly set forth in Scripture. It is likely that Saul's wanton destruction of men of God hurt his cause in the eyes of thinking men. Also, it led to the sole priestly survivor, Abiathar, becoming a fugitive from Saul and very predictably throwing in his lot with David. The priestly ephod that Abiathar brought with him provided David with the divinely granted insights that he needed to continue to escape the king. Psalm 52 was written at this time.

8. Further Events in Southern Judea (Ch. 23)

David left the forest of Hareth when he learned of the siege of Keilah by the Philistines. He went to liberate the city, and to subdue the Philistines according to the Lord's leading and empowering. It was apparently David's desire to make his home in Keilah, but God, through the ephod, revealed that the inhabitants of that city would betray him to Saul. Hence, David proceeded to the Wilderness of Ziph. Here, for the last time, he had opportunity to visit with Jonathan. Of this meeting Scripture says: " [Jonathan] . . . strengthened his hand in God" (v. 16). Blaikie comments:

He put David's hand as it were into God's hand, in token that they were one, in token that the Almighty was pledged to keep and

bless him, and that when he and his God were together, no weapon formed against him would ever prosper. [6]

It is held that in spite of the fact that David was kept in flight because of the treachery of those who would betray him, he nevertheless was strengthening his cause at this time. Upright men among Saul's citizens would have been increasingly disgusted at the conduct of their ruler and increasingly favorably impressed with the behavior of David. The ephod that was David's source of divinely given information was the final outer garment of the priest. It was styled something as a jumper or pinafore. It may have been that the presence of the ephod also assured the presence of the breastplate with its stones outside and Urim and Thummim within. The revelation that the men of Keilah would deliver David if he stayed (v. 12) is most unusual in Scripture; it is a case of God revealing not the actual future, but the possible future.

David's journeys continued, and according to 23:13, his followers increased from 400 to 600. Such a growth amounted to further evidence of the incompetence of rule and oppression under King Saul. However, insofar as at this time the citizens of Ziph offered their services to Saul to guide him to David, the king-elect had no alternative but to take his flight to the wilderness of Maon. Possibly, fear of Saul's retaliation led the people of Ziph to their treachery, and their reward seems to have been an empty pronouncement of benediction from the lips of Saul (v.21). David was almost captured by Saul in Maon, but a fortuitous invasion by the Philistines demanded the armies of Saul elsewhere, and thus David was able to escape. His new home was Engedi. Saul pledged to pursue David throughout "the thousands of Judah" (v. 23), probably because this tribe was the largest with perhaps up to 300,000 members. In calling the site at which Saul's armies gave up pursuit "Selahammahlekoth," he was recognizing it as a "rock of division." Psalm 54 was written at the time that the Ziphites threatened to betray David.

9. David Spares Saul the First Time (Ch. 24)

The fact that the mountains of Engedi preserved the Dead Sea Scrolls undiscovered for nearly nineteen centuries is evidence of their rugged inaccessibility. Nevertheless, as soon as Philistia was taken care of, Saul with 3,000 soldiers came to the region in pursuit of David. In the course of the chase, it chanced that Saul chose to seek seclusion, and probably to rest, in the very cave in which David and his men were concealed. Thus, Saul placed himself in

_____

[6]Blaikie, op. cit. p. 360.

David's hands, and David's men urged their leader to proceed to destroy his persecutor. However, David restricted himself to removing a portion of Saul's robe, and even this deed later brought him severe regrets. David was restrained by his clear cut and firm conviction concerning the abiding sanctity of the divine anointing upon Saul. At great personal risk, David revealed himself to Saul when the king had left the cave, and his arguments and actions at this time forced the king to confess "thou art more righteous than I." Saul went his way temporarily reconciled to David, but as each seemed to realize, the change was only temporary.

The proverb of the ancients (or Easterners) quoted by David (v. 13) is similar in thought to that of Jesus: "a corrupt tree bringeth forth evil fruit" (Mt. 7:17). The vivid imagery of the language of the day is reflected in David's description of himself as a "dead dog" or a "flea" (v. 14). In his response, Saul explicitly recognized that one day David would be king. He asked only that at such a time kindness be shown to his posterity. David's promise (v. 22) was actually a confirmation of that which he had already made with Jonathan (cf. 20:15). Following this confrontation, David chose wisely not to presume upon Saul's favor, and therefore he returned to his stronghold in the mountains of Judah.

10. Samuel's Death. David's Marriage to Abigail
(Ch. 25)

The death of Samuel (v. 1) caused genuine sorrow among the people; even those who had ignored him in his lifetime mourned his death. He had risen to be Israel's most outstanding spiritual leader since Moses, and Scripture classifies him as one of God's choice men. Blaikie has written a tribute to Samuel:

Cast in the same mould with their great leader and legislator Moses, he exerted an influence on the nation only second to that which stood connected with the prophet of the Exodus. He had not been associated with such stirring events in their history as Moses . . . but he was marked by the same great spirituality, . . . [and] profound belief in the reality of the covenant between Israel and God . . . . No man except Moses had ever done more to rivet this truth on the minds and hearts of the people. [7]

Samuel was buried at Ramah, the place of his birth and lifelong residence. The prophetic office that he vacated was not filled until Nathan was raised up a decade or more later (2 Sam. 7:2)

_____

[7] ibid. p. 378.

Following the death of Samuel, David proceeded to the wilderness of Paran, and it was there that he contacted selfish churlish Nabal. This man, whose very name means "fool," failed to live up to his honorable background, for he was a descendant of Caleb and of the tribe of Judah. Nabal not only refused food to David's messengers, but also made insulting insinuations against David. In something of a contradiction from his previous patience with Saul, David reacted in hasty impetuousness and gathering a small army of 400 men, he set forth to slay Nabal and his household.

David and his army were prevented from fulfilling their intended purpose by the intervention of the gracious Abigail, the wife of Nabal. This lady, by the presentation of a generous gift, and a most tactful and forthright defence, was able to pacify the would-be avengers. Abigail was guided to one of Nabal's own workers who had reported that the forces of David had been their protectors: "They were a wall unto us both by night and day" (v. 16). Thus, Abigail saw David as he who "fighteth the battles of the Lord" (25:28). David was so impressed by Abigail that when she was widowed a few days later, he took her as his wife. Nabal's death appears to have been a stroke of divine judgment mediated through the greediness of Nabal's spirit. For her part, Abigail no doubt recognized David's royal destiny in spite of his present low estate. She later bore David a son who was named Chileab (2 Sam.3:3).

On this occasion, Scripture reports that David also married Ahinoam of Jezreel in Judah, and that his first wife, Michal, had been given by Saul to Phalti (or Paltiel). Michal was later returned to David (2 Sam. 3:14). It is generally agreed that David's polygamy robbed him of the full compensations of family living, and in fact, rivalries in his family were the cause of bitter troubles in his later life. Abigail's interesting expression "bundle of life" (25:29) is used to designate the nature of the union between the believer who is totally dedicated, and the will and life of a sovereign God. Such unquestioning dedication identifies the will of God and the will of the believer as one and the same.

11. David Spares Saul's Life the Second Time
(Ch. 26)

The pattern of events in this chapter is very similar to that of chapter twenty-four. However, it is by no means the case that this is only another version of the previous one, for it is quite understandable that over the period of years, and the spread of territory involved, there could be an approximate repetition of events. Once again Saul pursued David in the wilderness of Ziph, and once again David refused the opportunity to slay Saul. On this occasion, David penetrated the inner sanctuary of the camp which is described as "within the trench," or in some translations "within the wagons." While the king lay sleeping, David removed his water cruse or personal drinking vessel, and also his spear. It would have been an easy matter for David to have driven the spear into Saul's body at that moment, but he was restrained by the principle: "Who can stretch forth his hand against the Lord's anointed and be guiltless?" (26:9).

When David later revealed his presence to Saul and his army, he scolded Abner, Saul's captain, for inefficiency and carelessness towards his master. Perhaps David's strategy in this incident was to promote a sense of criticism and division in the ranks of Saul. David proceeded to propose the offering of a sacrifice to God in order to appease Him if He were the cause of the spirit of enmity. If the cause was the work of wicked men, David invoked divine wrath upon them. In his reply, Saul addressed David as his son, and he confessed: "Behold, I have played the fool, and have erred exceedingly" (v. 21). It is clear that Saul's insane fury against David was really Satanic in origin, and it appears to many that it was the enemy's scheme to destroy the promised line. This meeting between David and Saul came to a close with Saul's pronouncement of a benediction, and there is no record that they ever met again.

12. David Journeys to Philistia (Ch. 27;
1 Chron. 12:1-7)

Despairing of safety in Saul's realm, David proceeded to take refuge in Gath, the Philistine capital. This move was in spite of the fact that God had commanded David to remain in Judah (22:5). It is assumed that David's family made his itinerant existence impractical, and that Achish, the king of Gath who received him, was the successor of David's former captor (21:10). Typically, the same name was given succeeding kings in Philistia. Achish took David for an ally since king Saul was his enemy, and perhaps for military reasons he proceeded to settle David in the frontier city of Ziklag. David remained in this place until the death of Saul, one year and four months later.

While David was at Ziklag his military strength steadily increased. Among his recruits was a group of Benjamites who were skillful in the use of the bow and sling, and remarkably ambidextrous. David used his armed forces to pillage the neighboring Philistine cities and towns, and by a process of utter annihilation, he managed to conceal his treachery from his Philistine sponsors. David no doubt felt justified in his acts of deception during

this period, but he would stand condemned by Christian standards. It might be argued that had he maintained his trust toward God and continued in the land, God would have taken care of him.

13. Saul and the Witch of Endor (Ch. 28)

While David was in Philistine territory, the Philistine army under Achish, and the Israelite army under Saul prepared for decisive battle. The opposing armies encamped in the great Plain of Esdraelon, a site that someday will resound to the Battle of Armageddon. The battle prospects deeply disturbed the apostate Saul, and he vainly sought a supernatural revelation of the future. When the Lord failed to answer, he surrendered his self-respect and proceeded to consult the witch of Endor. No doubt Saul's sense of being forsaken by God was responsible for his unreasonable fear, both of the Philistines and of the future. Saul went to the woman in disguise, not only to avoid the chance of capture by his enemies, but also to avoid intimidating the woman in her illegal profession. Up to this time, Saul had enforced the law which prohibited witches in Israel (cf. Lev. 19:31, 20:27; Deut. 18:10).

At Saul's request, the witch sought to bring up Samuel from the dead. The practice of consulting the dead, known as necromancy, was an official application of the religious dogma of ancient Babylon, and it was widely followed in ancient times. Even today it is practised in some circles. The apparition that appeared in response to the woman's incantations severely startled her, and clearly was not according to her expectations. The Scriptural narrative is generally considered to leave the impression that the vision was truly a revived Samuel, and that the Lord had intervened in a direct miracle. However, the outcome of these events, remarkable though they were, was simply a message to Saul, renewing his condemnation. He was told that David should succeed him, and that he should suffer destruction. Samuel declared: "Moreover the Lord will also deliver Israel with thee into the hand of the Philistines: and to morrow shalt thou and thy sons be with me" (28:19).

In spite of the woman's illegal profession, she evidently was a loyal subject of her sovereign, and she was concerned that he would look upon her with favor. She thus proceeded to serve a hearty meal to Saul, and in the strength of it he eventually recovered himself and went his way. It might be argued that even at this late date Saul could have repented and have been forgiven by God. Instead, he seems to have accepted his fate blindly, and thus he went forth to his destruction in stoic determination. Perhaps Saul is an example of one given over by God to judicial hardness.

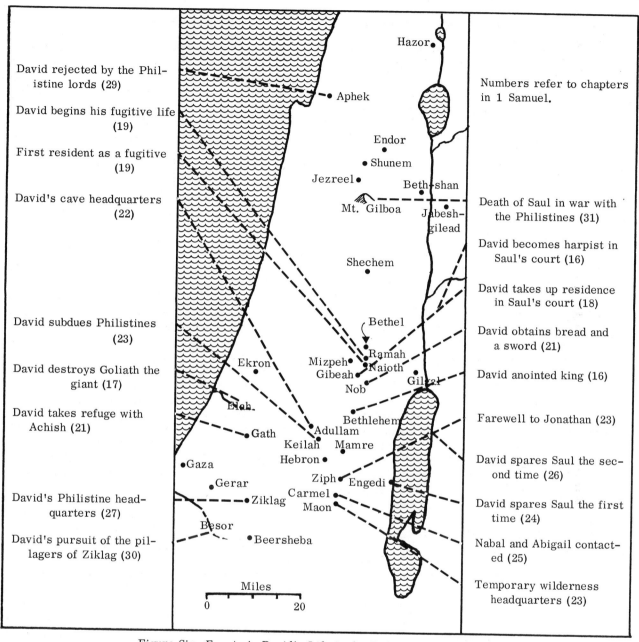

Left column labels (map):

David rejected by the Philistine lords (29)

David begins his fugitive life (19)

First resident as a fugitive (19)

David's cave headquarters (22)

David subdues Philistines (23)

David destroys Goliath the giant (17)

David takes refuge with Achish (21)

David's Philistine headquarters (27)

David's pursuit of the pillagers of Ziklag (30)

Right column labels (map):

Numbers refer to chapters in 1 Samuel.

Death of Saul in war with the Philistines (31)

David becomes harpist in Saul's court (16)

David takes up residence in Saul's court (18)

David obtains bread and a sword (21)

David anointed king (16)

Farewell to Jonathan (23)

David spares Saul the second time (26)

David spares Saul the first time (24)

Nabal and Abigail contacted (25)

Temporary wilderness headquarters (23)

Map location labels: Hazor, Aphek, Endor, Shunem, Jezreel, Beth-shan, Mt. Gilboa, Jabesh-gilead, Shechem, Bethel, Ramah, Mizpeh, Naioth, Gibeah, Nob, Gilgal, Ekron, Elah, Gath, Bethlehem, Adullam, Keilah, Mamre, Hebron, Gaza, Gerar, Ziph, Engedi, Carmel, Ziklag, Maon, Besor, Beersheba

Miles 0 20

Figure Six: Events in David's Life in the First Book of Samuel

14. David's Rejection by the Philistines (Ch. 29)

In the face of the forthcoming war between Philistia and Israel, David was confronted with an agonizing decision. He could either fight Saul and his own people, or he could openly proclaim himself a traitor to Achish, his benefactor. At the outset, David went along with Achish, and thus went through the motions of indicating that he was preparing to battle his own people. However, he was fortuitously spared the necessity of actually revealing his intentions by the voiced protests of the Philistine lords. Writes Blaikie of David's predicament:

Before him was God, closing his path in front; behind him was man, closing it in the rear, . . . it pleased God, in great mercy, to extricate him from his difficulty by using the jealousy of the lords of the Philistines as the means of his dismissal from the active service of King Achish.[8]

In his overall behavior on this occasion, David played his part well. His protests and affirmations

[8] Blaikie, op. cit., p. 401.

to Achish were ambiguous enough that Achish could be reassured, and yet there was no real commitment on the part of David. Also, he saw to it that his army departed from the Philistine camp promptly on schedule.

15. David Avenges the Destruction of Ziklag (Ch. 30)

Arriving back at Ziklag, David and his men found only rubble and destruction in place of homes and families. Marauding Amalekites had taken advantage of the absence of the fighting men to attack and pillage the city and carry off wives and families. The immediate reaction of David's men was anger -- at the outset they were ready to stone their leader. David, however, "encouraged himself in the Lord his God." There is some hint that David recognized this event as divine chastisement for his past wrongs, and that he emerged from this test with a greater measure of godliness. It is a matter of irony to remember that it had been Saul's vain kindness towards the Amalekites that had been a basic cause of his rejection; clearly God knew what was best, and now David paid the price.

The pursuit of the Amalekites was long and gruelling, but the finding of a castoff servant provided David with an informed guide. David's forces found the Amalekites engaged in a tumultuous celebration that probably, in accord with prevailing paganism, was partly religious in nature. The attack, beginning at twilight, extended for at least a full day, and resulted in all but 400 Amalekites being destroyed. In the victory, David recovered not only that which had been taken from Ziklag, but a great deal of other spoils of war as well. David proceeded to make judicious use of these goods by presenting portions as gifts to the elders of Israel. Perhaps in part, he considered he was repaying these cities for having given him refuge during his long flight from Saul. The message in verse 24 has a missionary application: "As his part is that goeth down to the battle, so shall his part be that tarrieth by the stuff: they shall part alike." This decision concerning equal rewards remained a precedent in Israel.

16. The Death of Saul (Ch. 31; 1 Chron. 10:1-14)

Saul's death in the battle against the Philistines fulfilled the prophecy that had been made at En-

dor. His three sons also died on that fateful day, and thus the king and his house were cut off. Israel's army took its stand on Mt. Gilboa overlooking the valley of Megiddo, but since it lacked chariots, the mountain site was an advantage. However, this position proved most unfavorable for retreat, and when the tide of battle turned against Israel, her forces were ruthlessly slaughtered. Israel also suffered the loss of territory, including some cities, but apparently the Philistines were satisfied with this measure of conquest. Hence, following this defeat, Israel remained free from invasions for some time.

Saul's wound evidently did not incapacitate him to the point of making him unable to commit suicide. The Septuagint indicates that the arrow had struck him in the abdomen. Suicide may have been his choice in the light of his knowledge of the customs of the day, for torture and mutilation were the common fate of a defeated warrior. According to tradition, Saul's armorbearer at this time was Doeg the Edomite, and some have suggested that the very sword by which Saul was slain was the one Doeg had used to destroy the 85 priests of Nob. The Philistines displayed Saul's body as a trophy of war upon the city wall--a process known as "gibbeting." Today's remains of the city of Beth-shan reveal the temple of Dagon and the temple of Ashtaroth side-by-side with only a narrow corridor between them, just as indicated in this account. The inhabitants of Jabesh-gilead, by rescuing the bodies of Saul and his sons, at least contributed to provide honorable last rites to their departed ruler.

The critical lack in King Saul was the absence of godliness of heart. He is portrayed as one who had no real sense of the life that enters into the highest destiny by pleasing God. Instead, his life vividly illustrates the course of the apostate who progressively departs from the worthy course. In his later life, and in his death, Saul is a pathetic example of the fruits of carnal wilfulness. As self increasingly displaced God in his life, even his original gifts and skills forsook him. Although warfare had been his special aptitude, his death resulted through an ignominious military defeat. Scripture notes that Saul's death was a stroke of divine judgment: "So Saul died for his transgression which he committed against the Lord . . . and also for asking counsel of one that had a familiar spirit, to enquire of it" (1 Chron. 10:13).

5. THE BOOK OF 2 SAMUEL

In the original Hebrew, First and Second Samuel were one book. The familiar division was first arranged as a matter of mechanical convenience at the time that the Septuagint translation was prepared. It was further perpetuated, and introduced into the Hebrew manuscript, by Daniel Bomberg, a Venetian printer, in 1516. Nevertheless, the division is thought to be justified because there is a change in style between the two books. Second Samuel is less historical, and more biographical than First Samuel. The reality of the spiritual walk, and a sense of personal fellowship with God is especially emphasized in the later book.

The Nature and Theme of Second Samuel

This book is sometimes called "The Book of the King" since it is almost entirely concerned with King David. The word "king" is found in these chapters some 278 times. King David discovered that regardless of man's status in life, he must maintain continually a close walk with God. He learned that for all men, whether they be kings or commoners, the consequences of failure are exceedingly far reaching. The Scriptural account makes evident the fact that from the time of David's great sin until his death, unhappiness and difficulty dogged his footsteps.

The Authorship of the Book

It is supposed by many that the statement in 1 Chronicles 29:29: "the book of Nathan the prophet, and . . . the book of Gad the seer" is a reference to all of Samuel after 1 Samuel 25:1 (the account of Samuel's death). The A.S.V. in 1 Chronicles 29:29 speaks of "the history of Nathan . . . and . . . the history of Gad." Thus, according to this view, the authors of the second book of Samuel would be Nathan and Gad.

The Occasion of Writing and the Scope

It is believed that Second Samuel was compiled shortly after the death of David. In 5:5 there is a reference concerning the total duration of David's reign, and it is presumed that this would only be written after his death. On the other hand, the nature and conduct of religious worship would indicate that Solomon's temple had not yet been erected. Thus, it is believed that Second Samuel describes the forty years of David's reign, and includes his rule over Judah and over all Israel.

The Key Phrase and Key Verse

The key phrase of the book is "before the Lord." The key verse is found in 5:12 "And David perceived that the Lord had established him king over Israel, and that he had exalted his kingdom for his people Israel's sake."

The Value of the Book

This book is expecially worthwhile in the moral lessons that it sets forth. Two truths are particularly outstanding:
1. No one sins at so great a cost as a believer.
2. Though sin be pardoned, it may also be punished. There is a notable Messianic implication in Second Samuel, for David is a central figure in Messianic prophecy. The ancestry of David is frequently referred to in references to Christ.

Analysis and Exposition

I. The Rise of David (Chs. 1-10)

1. The Account of Saul's Death (Ch. 1)

The news of the death of Saul and his sons was brought to David by the Amalekite messenger just two days after the event. The Scriptural account conveys the impression that David judged the messenger to be insincere and concerned only for his personal gain. In general, scholars conclude that the messenger's account was false, and that the record found in the preceding chapter is the actual report of events. No doubt the Amalekite hoped that by bringing the crown and bracelet of Saul, he might receive a generous reward. Apparently his appearance and his actions were all carefully staged and intended to impress David. The Amalekite, however, overlooked David's sense of loyalty and his shrewdness in judging human character. Thus, he fell beneath David's stroke of judgment. The episode established David's commitment to the exalted status of God's anointed, and it also cleared him of any responsibility for the death of the king, and of any possibility of being charged with rebellion.

David composed a poetic elegy, or dirge, in honor of the departed Saul and his sons. Pfeiffer describes this composition as "one of the most moving poems in all scripture." It is usually thought that the statement in verse 18 is intended to say that the name of the poem was "The Bow." The reference to a bow was in order in a poem concerned with warfare, since the bow was the principal weapon of that day. The Book of Jasher was apparently a historical account of that era, and one of the sources of data for the Bible records. This poem is in two parts, the first lamenting the fall of Saul and Jonathan, and the second commemorating the friendship of David and Jonathan. In his poetic statement, David mildly eulogized Saul, and he passed over his own sufferings at the hand of the king. One of David's main concerns was to lament the fate of King Saul and the fate of Prince Jonathan. In spite of many unpleasant experiences at Saul's hand, David loved and honored each of these men.

2. David Becomes King of Judah (Ch. 2)

At the express command of the Lord, David left the ruined city of Ziklag and journeyed to Hebron. This city of Judah, whose name means "strong fortified city," was centrally located and the strongest city of the tribe. Shortly after David, with all his associates and followers, settled in Hebron, he was anointed king by the tribe of Judah. This occasion was David's second anointing. For seven and one-half years he remained in Hebron, and from there he ruled the southern kingdom. He was thirty years of age when this period began.

Because of the opposition of Abner, the son of Saul's uncle and the captain of Saul's armies, David was not at this time accepted for the rulership of the northern tribes. Abner proceeded to select and name as king, Ish-bosheth (Esh-baal in 1 Chron. 8:33), the fourth son of Saul, and oldest who had survived the Philistine massacre. Ish-bosheth was nominally considered the ruler of all of the nation except Judah, but in reality his rule was weak, and Abner was the dominant authority. The national capital during this era was Mahanaim in Gilead. Israel continued to retain the memory of David's association with the Philistines, and thus they were slow to accept his leadership on a national basis.

It was probably about five years after David began his rule that his armed forces confronted those of Ish-bosheth about the Pool of Gibeon. As excavat-

ed in modern times, the pool has been found to be about thirty-six feet in diameter, and to have been cut out of solid rock. Since the Pool of Gibeon was in Abner's territory, it is evident that Joab, David's general, was the aggressor. The coutcome of the confrontation around the pool was a battle between twelve men from each army. The competition seems to have been intended either as a sort of sports competition, or as a battle of champions. However, the chosen twenty-four fought with such courage and ferocity that none survived. This turn of events led to such strong feelings that before long a general melee ensued, and finally Abner and his forces took flight.

As Abner fled, the brash young Asahel doggedly pursued him, threatening to attack him. Asahel was the nephew of David and brother of Joab. The harrassed Abner, after pleading to be left alone, was eventually provoked into destroying Asahel, and thus precipitating even stronger feelings between the two tribal groups. Civil war was prevented on that day by Abner's appeal to Joab, and thus the armies departed without further battle. However, the death of Asahel resulted in Joab's abiding hatred and jealousy against Abner, and his intention to destroy the rival general when he could. In this conflict David suffered the loss of twenty men, while Abner lost three hundred and sixty.

3. The Death of Abner (Ch. 3)

As the years passed, the house of David became stronger while the house of Saul continued to weaken. In a petty squabble, Ish-bosheth lost the support of Abner, and the commander proceeded to throw in his lot with David. The condition that David imposed in accepting Abner was the return of his wife, Michal, whom Saul had given to Phaltiel during the years of David's wandering. The brief Scriptural record reports that David, in asking the return of Michal, sent messengers to Ish-bosheth rather than to Abner. Apparently, David's action was all part of the total ingrigue, and this was the method chosen to determine the sincerity of Abner's approach. For David to be reunited with Michal the daughter of Saul would be to strengthen the bonds between the two kingdoms.

David's test condition that had been imposed upon Abner was wholly satisfied when Michal was returned. Thus, David was convinced of Abner's sincerity and his strategic position, and he proceeded to celebrate the reconciliation with a feast for Abner and his bodyguard. Since much of the strength of the opposition against David inhered in Abner, the reconciled captain set forth among the tribes to win them over to David. Abner was not only a military man of some competence, but as already noted, his family ties made him a cousin of King Saul. (cf. 1 Sam. 14:50, 51). Unfortunately, the narrative concerning Abner depicts him more particularly as one motivated by his own ambitions, rather than as one who understood the reality of the divine hand upon David's life.

Joab's reaction upon discovering that Abner had become an ally and supporter of David was to scheme how to destroy him with all possible dispatch. It is surprising that Abner was not more suspecting, but he naively trusted himself to Joab, and promptly lost his life. The site of the murder of Abner was at the well of Sirah, which is thought to have been a little north of Hebron. The death of Abner left Ish-bosheth without adequate support, and it was therefore, one more step in David's assumption of the full kingdom. However, the action was cold-blooded murder, completely without justification.

Once again the response of King David was to manifest genuine sorrow at the loss of a former enemy, and once again he cleared himself in the public eye of any responsibility for the murder. In a gesture of honest justice and unfeigned righteousness, David uttered an imprecation upon the house of Joab, praying that its members might suffer divine judgment. The king expressed his high regard for the departed in the words "Know ye not that there is a prince and a great man fallen this day in Israel?" (3:38). With regret, David noted that Abner had not even died as an honorable warrior. However, comparing himself to such a military man, David saw himself as weak. The Scripture reports: "And all the people took notice of it, and it pleased them" (3:36).

4. The Death of Ish-bosheth (Ch. 4)

With the desertion and death of Abner, Ish-bosheth was left with neither military support nor protection, and he seems to have lacked even a personal bodyguard. Thus, two of his own captains, Baanah and Rechab, using only the simplest of ruses, succeeded in murdering him. Their motives probably included: general contempt for a defunct ruler, the hope of reward from David, and the desire to avert civil war. It is noted also that their home city, Beeroth, had been part of the tribal grant to Benjamin, and that Saul had attempted mass destruction in this area (cf. 2 Sam. 21:1-11). It is possible that the Beerothites thus sought retaliation by slaying the son of Saul. The mention of Mephibosheth in this section (v. 4) is of interest in view of the impending death of Ish-bosheth, for with the latter's passing, Mephibosheth was the sole survivor in the line of Saul.

David was grieved by the deed of Baanah and Rechab, and he promptly had both of these men slain

and their bodies exposed. It has been well said of David "One whom God was advancing needed no crimes to promote his cause." Such stern treatment of the assassins no doubt served for a warning to all other potential anarchists in the kingdom. Ish-bosheth's head was appropriately buried in Abner's tomb, for he was Abner's cousin. David emerged from this episode with new strength and influence, and with the throne of all Israel within his reach.

5. David Becomes King of All Israel (Ch. 5;
                1 Chron. chs. 11, 12, 14)

As the outcome of Ish-bosheth's death, the northern tribes proceeded to make David their king. Although this occasion marked David's third anointing with oil, it was his first by the people of Israel. This event meant that 331,300 warriors were committing their allegiance to David. Scripture specifically reports the duration of David's rulerships (vv. 4, 5), and notes that after seven and one-half years in ruling only Judah, he was to rule the united kingdom for thirty-three years. It would appear that the reign of Ish-bosheth extended only two years (2 Sam. 2:10), and if this is so, it must have been that either he did not assume the rulership until five years after David began ruling in Hebron, or he had been dead for a like period before David became king of united Israel.

Before David could reign in Jerusalem (or Jebus), he had to gain possession of it. Though the tribe of Judah had previously had holdings in Jerusalem (Jud. 1:18), a consolidation conquest was now necessary. David laid siege to the city, and because the Jebusites were overconfident, he gained a total victory. Josephus says that the defenders actually manned the walls with cripples, and Scripture indicates that at least their attitude could have motivated such a presumptuous defense (v. 6). David's conquest of Jerusalem (also called Zion), meant that the city was to become the world's greatest religious center, sacred to Christian, Jew, and Moslem, and the emblem and type of the anticipated heaven of the believer.

Traditionally, it has been an often suggested theory that David's forces entered Jerusalem by means of a secret passage from the spring of Gihon to the interior of the city fortress. Josephus is among those who so report, and it is a possible interpretation of the reference to the "gutter" (v. 6). Certainly, from among the records of other cities and their water supplies, there is ample precedent for such a passage and such military strategy. However, archaeological remains in Jerusalem do not provide specific information concerning the time of David, because the city has been so thoroughly and completely transformed in the intervening years.

Not only man-made structures have been removed, but the contours of the land itself have been changed. Thus, any specific theory of the method of David's conquest cannot be actually substantiated. The names "Zion" and "Millo" refer to modest heights within the city, which in a day of hand weapons constituted particularly advantageous sites for military strongholds. The particular characteristic of Zion was the steepness of its slopes on three sides, and a single ridge of rock giving access to it on the fourth. It was thus most excellently situated for purposes of defense.

Scriptures notes the rapid growth of national prosperity under David, and the contributions of Hiram, king of Tyre, in providing materials and artisans. The people of Tyre were concerned for the welfare of Jerusalem because they were dependent upon Palestine for a portion of their food supply. The attacks by the Philistines during this era were an attempt to halt the growing unity of the nation under the rule of David. In two successive battles, David thoroughly defeated these enemies and permanently crushed their power. In each instance, God fought for David, and it was on this occasion that the divine empowering presence was made known by "the sound of a going in the tops of the mulberry trees." This divine signal cue may also have served to conceal the sounds of David's troops as they prepared their surprise attack. David drove the Philistines as far back as Gazer (a variant of Gezer), but apparently he did not choose to risk heavy losses of his men in attempting to capture this well-fortified city.

In later chapters in this book there are other reference to battles against Philistia. Commentators suggest that these events belong at this time. Hence, David's near destruction in personal combat with the giant Ishbi-benob (21:16), and the incident of water from the well of Bethlehem (23:16) are thought to have occurred during this era.

6. The Ark Brought to Jerusalem (Ch. 6; 1 Chron. chs. 13, 15, 16)

With his enemies at least temporarily subdued, David now set himself to the task of restoring worship. For the past 60 years the ark had been abandoned at Kirjath-jearim (Baale) in Judah, and had been stored at the house of Abinadab (1 Sam. 7:1, 2; 1 Chron. 13:6). David now felt that it ought to be brought to Jerusalem. In order to give the undertaking national attention, David employed 30,000 of his warriors, plus a group of priests. When Uzzah, for profaning the ark, was struck dead, David abandoned his project. For three months the ark was left in the household of Obed-edom who was apparently a Philistine proselyte. At the end of this

period, David once more sought to achieve his goal, and this time he succeeded in bringing the ark into Jerusalem.

In bringing up the ark, David very carefully followed the divinely prescribed procedure, and he also performed frequent sacrifices as a further mark of humility and obedience. The ark was properly carried by the Levites, and only duly consecrated priests officiated at the sacrifices. In welcoming the ark into the city, David had provided a choir, special songs and hymns, and a program of sacred dancing. The many sacrifices provided meat for the people, and David also added bread and wine for all citizens. David's own enthusiastic demonstrations on this occasion appeared to his wife, Michal, to be so grossly lacking in kingly dignity that she was moved to scornful criticism. Her attitude led to the judgment of barrenness upon her. It appears that Michal either was guilty of exaggerated falsehood in claiming that David had totally uncovered himself, or that she revealed spiritual disinterest in serious measure by her words of criticism. For a Jewish wife to bear no children was as much a reproach in David's day as it had been in an earlier era.

In order to accommodate the ark in Jerusalem, David pitched a tent, no doubt near to his own palace. He appointed a permanent choir and courses (i.e. shifts) of priests and Levites, and thus reconstituted tabernacle worship in Jerusalem. Abiathar was duly recognized as the high priest. David, in this era, adopted various musical instruments to be used in worship, including cymbals, harps, and trumpets. While it was perhaps the case that as soon as possible David brought the other articles of furniture of the tabernacle to the tent in Jerusalem, Scripture has no record of this action. It is known, however, they had been in Nob (1 Sam. 21:1) and that in Solomon's time they were found in Gibeon (1 Ki. 3, 4). Thus it appears that Zadok the priest ministered at Gibeon simultaneously with the tabernacle worship in Jerusalem, and in fact it was at Gibeon that the majority of the sacrifices were offered.

7. The Davidic Covenant (Ch. 7; 1 Chron. 17)

David's offer to build a permanent temple to God was the outcome of his sense of conviction as he contrasted the luxury in which he dwelt with the simplicity of the accommodations for the ark of God. David was restrained from actually launching the project by the intervention of God through the prophet Nathan. God specified that though David was not to build a house of worship, He would build David a house--that house being a dynasty. In a touching accommodation to the personal feelings of David, God carefully and fully rehearsed the many special blessings and privileges that David had enjoyed in his lifetime of serving God. Thus he was to know that God counted him a favorite child, and that the prohibition concerning the building of the temple was by no means an evidence of divine displeasure.

God's promise to David on this occasion is known as the Davidic Covenant, and it specified that the line of David should be enduring and that it should rule the nation perpetually. There was one condition: disobedience would result in chastisement, but not in the voiding of the covenant. It has been noted that this Bible chapter, in which the Davidic Covenant is set forth, seven times contains the word "forever," and that it thus pointedly sets forth the divine immutability regardless of characteristic human frailty. David gladly resigned himself to the will of God, and surrendering his own ambitions, prayed that the name of God should be magnified forever (v. 26).

As long as the Jewish kingdom remained, there was a descendent of David who ruled in Jerusalem. Since the time of the captivities, only one king of the Davidic line has been crowned in Jerusalem, and He was crowned with thorns. Although He is today unrecognized, and His abode is in the heavenlies, Jesus Christ remains in a very real sense the King of the Jews. The book of Revelation makes clear that this thorn-crowned One is yet to occupy His literal earthly throne, and to continue to fulfil the covenant of David. The covenant is eternal in scope because through Jesus Christ the spiritual kingship will continue throughout all the eternal ages to come.

8. David's Wars of Consolidation (Ch. 8; 1 Chron. 18)

When the safety of his frontiers was threatened, David once more turned to war. It has been suggested that the conquest of "Methegammah" (v. 1) is actually a reference to the taking of the city of Gath from the Philistines, and that Methegammah is not meant to be a name, but rather ought to be translated "bridle of the mother city" and seen as a poetic illusion to Gath. David's motivation in his conquests was not only to build an empire for its own sake, but also to assure his own kingdom against contamination from idolatry. David's conquests in these wars included the Philistines on the west, the Moabites on the east, the Syrians on the north, and the Edomites on the south. His rule came to extend as far northeast as the Euphrates River, and as far south as Ezion-geber on the Red Sea, a trading center that was to be of great importance to Solomon. Thus in David's reign the primary promises to Abraham were fulfilled. At least part of the leadership in these conquests was provided by Abishai (cf. 1 Chron. 18:12), although Joab continued as David's military commander.

In destroying two-thirds of the citizens of Moab, David evidenced unusual severity. It is possible that his parents whom he had left there had been mistreated (1 Sam. 22:3, 4), and that David now retaliated. This destruction was in fulfillment of Balaam's prophecy (Num. 24:17). For a century and a half Moab continued to pay tribute to Israel. In the providence of God, the time of David's rule was one of general weakness in neighboring nations. Egypt, for instance, was politically at low ebb with a ruling dynasty dominated by priests, and a general national weakness resulting from inefficient and corrupt officials. Although Syria lacked the strength to stand against David militarily, its spoils provided chariots, gold, silver, and brass. The metals were dedicated by David to the Lord.

9. David's Kindness to Mephibosheth (Ch. 9)

The account of David's kindness to Mephibosheth is in appealing contrast to the resorts of David's many wars. Mephibosheth, a son of Jonathan, had been injured in an accident in childhood, and hence was lame on both feet. (cf. 2 Sam. 4:4). Since his father's death, Mephibosheth had lived in the house of Machir in Lo-debar beyond Jordan. David's kindness and generosity to the young man was motivated by memories of his friendship with Jonathan. Mephibosheth was made a part of the royal household, and granted his own retinue of servants consisting of the same family of servants that had been employed in Saul's household. Insofar as Mephibosheth had no inherent merit, but was chosen and greatly favored, he aptly illustrates the grace and beneficence of the Lord. The name Mephibosheth means "one who disregards shame."

10. Victory Over the Ammonites and Syrians (Ch. 10; 1 Chron. 19)

When Hanun became king of the Ammonites, David graciously dispatched a delegation of good will to acclaim the new monarch. Hanun, either deliberately or by mistake, entirely misinterpreted David's intentions, and taking his messengers for spies, flippantly insulted them and sent them home in disgrace. Probably Hanun wished to provoke a military contest, for his own armies had been strengthened by the addition of 32,000 Syrian mercenary soldiers. Not having previously suffered defeat at David's hand, the young king was brashly confident that he could overthrow the great empire builder.

In the battle that followed, the clever strategy of Joab and Abishai proved more than a match for these new foes. The Syrians were defeated first, and upon their flight from the field of battle, the Ammonites failed in courage and also fled. The Ammonite leaders and defenders took refuge in the city of Rabbath-Ammon, and David did not see fit to lay siege to the city at that time. In a later engagement against the Syrians David's armies destroyed Shoback, the Syrian captain, along with 700 chariots (or charioteers), and 40,000 horsemen. Thus, Syria came under the total domination of Israel. Such decisive victories provided a long period of peace, and meant that the nation's boundaries and sphere of influence were extended throughout the ancient world. It is to be noted that David was provoked into most of his conquests as a matter of self-defense, and that he was not particularly territorially ambitious.

II. David's Years of Trouble (Chs. 11-20)

1. David's Great Sin (Ch. 11)

The fact that the Bible records the failures and iniquities of great men of God as well as their triumphs, is an outstanding proof that the book is divinely given. David's acts in committing adultery, and contriving the virtual murder of Uriah, are reported in all frankness. The setting for these events was the implementation of the previously postponed siege of Rabbath-Ammon (cf. 10:14). Scripture portrays Uriah as a devoted loyal warrior, and though critics question whether he and Bathsheba enjoyed a normal marriage, his conduct and attitudes were most exemplary. In arranging for the death of Uriah, David necessarily made Joab his accomplice, and in so doing, the king put himself in Joab's power.

With the death of Uriah, David took Bathsheba to wife, but Scripture notes: "the thing that David had done displeased the Lord." Under the Law, adulterers were subject to death by stoning. Bathsheba's attitude, and the measure of her complicity are not completely set forth in Scripture, but it is clear that she was by no means guiltless. One critic has remarked "Bathsheba's character is neither black nor white; it is just a shade of gray." David and Bathsheba were married seven days after the death of Uriah, and she became one of David's seven named wives and sixteen concubines. Bathsheba was the granddaughter of Ahithophel, David's wise counselor, and she was destined to become the mother of Solomon. In a later genealogy, she is called "Bath-shua" (1 Chron. 3:5).

2. David's Self Judgment and Repentance (Ch. 12)

It was not until the birth of the child of David and Bathsheba that Nathan appeared before the king. During the intervening months, David had evidently remained stubbornly impenitent. Nathan related a simple parable about a man and his little ewe lamb. In rightly judging the character depicted in the parable, David inadvertently judged himself.

Thus, for the first time, he saw himself for what he truly was. With contrite heart he heard Nathan review God's blessings upon him, and heard his conduct described as equivalent to having despised the commandment of the Lord. In effect, to have given place to his own wilful desires was to treat God's commandments as despised. Nathan prophesied that God's judgment would include: continuing warfare, family discord, marital discord, and the death of the child.

David genuinely repented, and thus showed commendable spiritual grace. Someone has commented: "Sin plus repentance does not equal innocence, but it nevertheless constitutes a moral miracle." David's fastings and prayers on behalf of his child were fervent but fruitless, and once the child was dead, David seems unquestionably to have resigned himself to the will of God. The Penitential Psalms (32, 51), are connected with this period in David's life. Thus, when sometime later Solomon was born, it was to a very different father, so far as his spiritual attitudes were concerned. The Scripture notes of the infant Solomon "and the Lord loved him" (v. 24), and this phrase is the meaning of the name "Jedidiah" which became Solomon's alternate name.

The final siege and conquest of Rabbath-Ammon is here recorded. The Ammonites who had begun by insulting David's messengers, and who had maintained an armed fortress destroying many of David's warriors, including Uriah, at last suffered their fate. In the final stages of the conquest of the city, Joab requested the personal presence of David in order that the king might receive credit for the conquest. The crown of the king that was taken as spoil would have weighed the equivalent of more than eighty pounds, and apparently served to be displayed rather than worn. In appropriating the crown of the Ammonites, David figuratively and literally assumed the rule of the people, and thus he commissioned them to menial tasks that they might contribute both wealth and laborers to the nation of Israel.

3. The Banishment of Absalom (Ch. 13)

Further domestic troubles fell upon David through the misdemeanor of his son Amnon by his wife, Ahinoam. Amnon was David's firstborn, and he might have been thought of as the heir apparent to the throne. This young man yielded to inordinate lust, and thereby brought shame and sorrow to his half-sister, Tamar, who together with Absalom had been born to David and Maacah. The behavior of Amnon was repulsive and irrational as can be expected in the life dominated by lust. On the other hand, even in the tragedy of the situation, Tamar's behavior stands forth as an example of prudence and common sense. Perhaps Amnon knew that he had no hope to be granted Tamar in legitimate marriage because the Law forbade marriage to one's half-sister (Lev. 18:11).

Absalom was outraged by the conduct of Amnon, but he remained silent and entreated Tamar to do likewise. He was willing to await an appropriate opportunity to administer revenge. Thus, it was two full years later that he contrived to invite Amnon, along with all the king's sons, to the traditional feast of his shepherds at sheep shearing time. Although David was somewhat suspicious and reluctant, he eventually permitted Amnon to go. With Amnon thus in his power, Absalom simply waited until the time was ripe to signal his servants to proceed to slay him. The murder led to the flight of the surviving sons, each of them upon his own mule. While at first the report to David declared that all the king's sons had been slain, later tidings reported the matter correctly.

Although incestuous rape, such as had been committed by Amnon, was a capital crime in Israel, it was not Absalom's prerogative to administer justice. On the other hand, king David lacked the moral strength to take action because his own personal shortcomings forced him to remain silent. David's punishment upon Absalom, the murderer, was similarly lacking in sound principles of justice, for official banishment was scarcely a valid penalty for murder. Absalom took refuge at the home of his maternal grandfather in Geshur of Syria. David maintained a deep affection for Absalom, and constantly pined to be reunited to him.

The mound of Beth-shan as it appears today. It was on the walls of the city on this site that the bodies of Saul and his sons were displayed. The mound is located in the eastern corner of the valley of Jezreel, and is about four miles west of the Jordan.

4. Absalom Restored to David (Ch. 14)

After three years had passed, Joab apparently became convinced that David was ready to reinstate Absalom to the court. In acting in the case, Joab's technique was to contrive an interview between David and a supposed widow. David listened to the woman's problems with impartiality, and in prescribing for her case on behalf of her fictitious son, clearly committed himself concerning the fair response on behalf of Absalom. He took the position of admitting that there was a higher law than that of blood revenge, and therefore there was really no basis for his son's banishment. Upon discerning Joab's hand in the incident, David had no course but to confront his general and instruct him: "Go therefore, bring the young man Absalom again."

Although Absalom was brought from Geshur to Jerusalem, David refused to restore him to his presence or allow him to return to the royal court. David may have been motivated by his sense of true justice, for after all Absalom was a murderer, or it may simply have been the pride of a stubborn man. Two more years elapsed before David finally allowed the reconciliation, and this event came to pass only because Absalom pressured Joab's intercession by setting fire to the General's barley field. It is clear that Absalom knew no penitence for his past misdeeds, and that he actually was a ruthlessly ambitious man who unscrupulously formulated his policies quite apart from moral values. Absalom embodied not only exceptional craftiness and cunning, but also unusual physical attractiveness, and Scripture declares that his hair was of such quality and weight that it weighed no less than fifty ounces. A daughter born to Absalom during his exile was named Tamar—a name of very special family significance. The reunion of David and Absalom at the close of the five year exile involved neither penitence nor valid justice, and critics have described David's role as mere "doting affection."

5. The Outbreak of Absalom's Revolt (Ch. 15)

It is evident that even though Absalom had sought to be reconciled to David, his father, he continued to nurture hostility in his heart. Thus, following his restoration, Absalom began a deliberate campaign to impress the people and to win their hearts away from David. His entire program was formulated on the basis of public relations value, including fifty heralds, his technique of telling people what they wanted to hear, and his refusal to accept servile obeisance. He contrived particularly to capitalize upon his father's problem of too many responsibilities, and too many details demanding personal attention. No doubt, Absalom was guided in part in his treacherous campaign by his aware-

ness of the declining popularity of King David. At this time, the new generation would have known their king only as an elderly man, while the pious older generation continued to be scandalized by David's affair with Bathsheba.

At that time in which Absalom thought that his following was large enough, he proceeded to initiate his revolt by assembling his forces at Hebron. In his choice of stories to provide a dishonest justification for his trip to Hebron, Absalom particularly revealed his total lack of moral discrimination. The forty years of verse seven would seem plausibly to refer to the age of Absalom, or else to be more correctly rendered "four years." The presence of Ahithophel, the wise counsellor, in Absalom's company was one of his greatest assets, and it may be explained either because Ahithophel felt there was promise for the success of the Prince, or because the counsellor, who was the grandfather of Bathsheba, was seeking to bring revenge upon David for having brought shame upon the family.

At the first news of the insurrection, David determined that he was militarily unprepared to defend his city, and thus he hastily fled. Crossing the Kidron, and partly ascending the Mount of Olives, he took up his post at what later became the site of the Garden of Gethsemane. David's supporters included Ittai, the Gittite, and his people who were actually Philistine tribes, and who perhaps may be thought of as mercenary soldiers. Although Zadok, the priest, and his assisting Levites were willing to remain with David, upon entreaty they agreed to remain in the city. Also, David arranged for Hushai and the two young priests, Ahimaaz and Jonathan, to remain in the city and serve his cause as spies. The occasion of the flight was marked by gloom and depression in David's ranks, and his sincere prayer that the counsel of Ahithophel would be turned into foolishness. It is believed that Psalm 55 set forth David's feelings at this time.

6. Absalom's Entrance Into Jerusalem (Ch. 16)

There is no corroborating evidence to confirm that Ziba's testimony concerning Mephibosheth's treachery was true. However, David may have felt that Mephibosheth was the type of person who would hope that David and Absalom would destroy one another that the way might be cleared for him to assume the throne of his father. David accepted the word of Ziba, and proceeded to award all the possessions of Mephibosheth to this servant. Apparently at a later time, David doubted Ziba's truthfulness, and he thus divided the possessions between him and Mephibosheth, his master. David chose to accept Shimei's curses as God's instruments to teach him humility, and thus he restrained his men from destroying this offensive demonstrator. To throw dust (v. 13) was a characteristic oriental mode for expressing contempt. In actual fact, David had no grounds for a sense of guilt in the matter of his treatment of the house of Saul, and Shimei's demonstration was quite unwarranted.

While David remained in his ignominious exile, Absalom proceeded to enter Jerusalem and to take full possession of the vacated throne and the royal household. Such bold action was the outcome of the counsel of Ahithophel. In particular, the act of possessing his father's harem constituted Absalom's public proclamation that the throne was transferred to a new incumbent. It dramatically announced to all the nation that Absalom intended no restraint in his taking over the throne. Ahithophel had shrewdly determined that this action would effectively establish a decisive and permanent gulf between Absalom and David.

7. Absalom's Rejection of Ahithophel (Ch. 17)

In order to determine his next actions, Absalom consulted with his counsellors, Ahithophel and Hushai. Ahithophel counselled an immediate attack in order to defeat David with one quick bold stroke. He reasoned that if David's followers could be scattered and David destroyed, the people would readily rally around Absalom. Hushai, being in reality loyal to David, counselled the exact opposite of Ahithophel, and recommended a delayed attack with a massed army. In advocating a complete military defeat, Hushai appealed to Absalom's vanity, and he further enhanced his position by exaggerating the scope of the possible victory. When Absalom accepted Hushai's advice, the disappointed Ahithophel proceeded to hang himself. It is possible that Ahithophel, in his wisdom, so acted because he saw in the future a traitor's death for himself.

While the preparations for a massed military campaign were under way, the vain Absalom had time to enjoy the pleasures of Jerusalem, but on the other hand, David had time to rally his forces and prepare his defense. Hushai took advantage of the interval to dispatch messengers to convey word of the planned strategy to David. The messengers, Ahimaaz and Jonathan, successfully delivered their message, but they were almost captured by Absalom's men. The first hiding place of the messengers in Enrogel is identified as a year-round unfailing source of water near Jerusalem. In later times, Enrogel was deepened to become a well 125 feet deep. In acting upon the information the messengers brought, David gathered his followers and proceeded to a place of safety. He and his people took refuge in Mahanaim, a well fortified city in the highlands of Gilead, east of Jordan. David's forces at this point began to gain in strength, and his loyal supporters generously made available an abundant supply of equipment and provisions of food.

8. The Battle Between the Forces of David and Absalom (Ch. 18)

While the two armies prepared for battle, some two or three months elapsed. In this period David's forces increased greatly, and he found it necessary to divide his army into thirds and place each portion under a general. Among his supporters were Joab, Abishai, and Ittai, the three generals, plus Shobi who represented the city of Mahanaim, and Machi and Barzillai who were responsible for freely provisioning David's armies. Although David's fighting men may have been outnumbered, he had vastly superior military and tactical leadership, and in fact, almost all of the important men of the kingdom remained on his side. Only Ahithophel had supported Absalom, and now he was dead. It is believed that Psalms 3, 4, 61, and 63 were written during this period.

When the battle actually took place, the site was selected by David's forces in what was then a wooded area east of the Jordan. David himself was dissuaded from personally taking to the field. It soon became evident that Absalom's forces, in spite of their probable numerical superiority, were poorly disciplined. As the battle proceeded, confusion and heavy losses characterized the performance of the armies of Absalom. The prince made no effort to rally his forces, and by the close of the day there were 20,000 fatalities, and Absalom was apparently in flight. It was in this humiliating action that he suffered the accident of having his hair caught in a tree, and being left suspended when his mule ran from beneath him. When Joab learned of Absalom's predicament, he hastened to the spot, and with the help of ten armor bearers, attacked and slew him.

No doubt Joab desired the death of Absalom, for had the treacherous prince succeeded, Joab probably would have been among those executed. Absalom's body was covered with stones as a mark of contempt, and Scripture notes that the only memorial to his life was the pillar that he had himself erected. Josephus reports that the king's dale was a site near to Jerusalem. The death of Absalom and the accompanying defeat of his armies meant the end of the war and the reestablishment of the authority of David. Although the news of Absalom's death was reported to David as tactfully as possible, the king was nevertheless smitten with extreme sorrow and grief. It has been suggested that Ahimaaz actually knew the truth, but out of concern for David's feelings, and possible concern for the fate of the messenger who brought such tragic tidings, Ahimaaz preferred not to tell it. Part of the reason for David's extreme grief may have been his own self-reproach and sense of failure as a father.

9. David's Return to Jerusalem (Ch. 19)

In having so indulged Absalom in life, and in so extravagantly mourning him in death, David quite clearly was in error. Joab's disobedience in destroying Absalom, and his impudence in rebuking the king were also obvious errors. David's attitudes were based solely upon his own wishes and he was quite oblivious to the will and justice of God in these matters. As Joab pointed out, David's gloom turned the victory of his loyal soldiers into defeat. Joab's arrogance on this occasion was a preview of his later conspicuous efforts to dominate the king.

Although the ten tribes promptly invited the return of David to the nation's throne, Judah was delayed in acting. David thus solicited an official invitation, on the strength of which he might return to Jerusalem and assume the leadership of the people. As one of his reforms in returning to office, David pledged that he would appoint Amasa as his general in place of Joab. This move may have had political value, but it certainly lacked plausibility, for Amasa had just suffered a defeat as leader of the rebels against David, while Joab had just won a great victory for his king. It is not surprising that Joab bitterly resented his demotion, and that at first opportunity he would take action to dispose of his rival. David showed his magnanimity by forgiving Shimei who had cursed him, and in this act the king won a thousand Benjamites to his side. As previously noted, he partly restored Mephibosheth, but he did not deprive Ziba of all of his reward. At this time also, David bestowed a blessing upon Barzillai who had helped to support his troops.

Although the ten tribes had been the first to acknowledge the continuing kingship of David, when the late coming tribe of Judah did arrive, they dominated the homecoming ceremony. This argument over formalities and prestige was of course a manifestation in miniature of the same kind of tensions that had led to the recent civil war. Although the differences in this instance were peaceably settled, the fact that there could be such a dispute indicated the presence of the seeds of future national differences. Just a generation later, at the time of the death of Solomon, the schismatic spirit once more asserted itself, and the outcome was the permanently divided kingdom.

10. Revolt By Sheba (Ch. 20)

David had no sooner returned to Jerusalem than a new rebellion threatened. Sheba, the son of Bichri, a Benjamite, announced himself the leader of the tribes, and he proclaimed a new campaign of independence. Although Scripture depicts Sheba as a worthless radical, the fact that he was a Benjamite, and thus of the same tribe as Saul, gave him favor in the eyes of the people of the ten tribes. Followers rapidly gathered about Sheba, and it appeared that a new civil war was imminent. David charged newly appointed Amasa with the task of organizing his forces, but after a three-day delay, Amasa was still not ready for battle. At this point, Joab entered the picture, proceeded treacherously to murder Amasa, and then once more assuming the leadership of David's army, set forth to deal with Sheba.

In a very short time Sheba was no longer able to offer active resistance, and he was forced to take refuge in the city of Abel. Joab's forces laid siege to the city, and began the process of beating down its walls. The attack was halted upon the entreaty of a wise woman who promised the head of Sheba if Joab would refrain from the destruction of the city. A short time later, Sheba's head was tossed over the wall and all fighting ceased. The conclusion of these events meant that David was once more secure in office as king of all the nation, and Joab was again the unchallenged general of the armies of David.

III. David's Later Years (Chs. 21-24)

1. The Penalty for the Broken Covenant (Ch. 21)

After the third year of a severe famine that befell the land, the Lord revealed to David that the cause was Saul's violation of the covenant with Gibeon. Joshua had promised to protect and spare this nation (Josh. 9:16), but on some unknown occasion, Saul had violated the promise. There is no record of the occasion, nor how many Gibeonites had been slain. Since Saul had committed the offence while he had ruled as king, all of the nation was required to suffer the consequences. David brought an end to the famine when he delivered seven of Saul's grandsons to be publicly hanged in the city of Gibeah, the original home of Saul. In this act of judgment, David chose to spare Mephibosheth. Scripture records the pathetic concern of Rizpah, the mother of two of the victims. In a most exemplary display of mother love, Rizpah watched over the exposed bodies of her sons for what was probably a six-month period.

The account of the hand-to-hand combats against the Philistine champions is considered to belong historically prior to David's conquest of Jerusalem (cf. Ch. 5). Since Israel now held Jerusalem, it is not likely that the Philistines would be causing uprisings in these regions. This record of personal victories sets forth the military prowess of David's

Only nondescript rocks now mark the site of Nob, the religious center of Israel during Saul's rule. It was here that David first proceeded when he began his exile, and here Ahimelech provided David with the shewbread and Goliath's sword. The site is located about two miles north of the modern city of Jerusalem.

mighty men and the fact of Israel's persistent victories. Apparently, David was almost overcome by Ishbi-benob, who was "of the sons of the giant" (v. 16). David escaped only because Abishai intervened, but the incident led to a pledge that David must not again engage in combat in the battlefield. Scholars have suggested that the Philistine identified as "the brother of Goliath" (v. 19) should more properly be described as "the son of Goliath."

2. David's Song (Ch. 22)

The composition recorded in this chapter could be entitled "A Song of Victory." Its theme: God's deliverance illustrates His vindication of the innocent and His sovereign government. As recorded in this chapter, the song is substantially identical with Psalm 18, and it is concluded that slight revisions were probably for convenience in singing it. Commentators disagree concerning the time of the writing of this song, and it has been sug-

gested that David wrote it in his earlier years, and simply kept it at hand until this time. It is concluded that David's affirmation of his righteousness (v. 25) was meant either to describe his state prior to his sin with Bathsheba, or it is meant to testify of his awareness of God's forgiveness. David's song, as recorded here, is traditionally used by the Jews in their conduct of liturgical worship.

3. David's Last Words (Ch. 23, 1 Chron. 11:15-25)

The "last words" of David constitute more specifically the last of his inspired writings. In this passage an acceptable definition of "inspiration" is set forth (v. 2), and also a stirring Messianic prophecy (v. 4). David's mighty men are here enumerated, and it is noted that including Uriah, the husband of Bathsheba, they numbered thirty-seven. Twice elsewhere in Scripture (1 Chron. 11, 1 Chron. 27), David's mighty men are listed, but either because the personnel of the group changed over the years, or because certain individuals had more than one name, the three lists only partly agree. The incident of the well of Bethlehem, that is here reported, is believed to have taken place either while David was fleeing Saul (1 Sam. 21:1), or in the period when David was assuming the monarchy (2 Sam. 5:18-24).

4. David's Sin in Numbering the People (Ch. 24, 1 Chron. 21)

The project of numbering the people seems to be presented as a temptation to which David succumbed. It is usually concluded that the wrong was not likely in the census itself, but in the use to which David intended to put it. A detailed census would have served to exhibit the military and national might of Israel, and thus become the ground for a far departure from David's original humble trust upon God. Even Joab saw that the program was dangerous, and sought to dissuade the king from his plan. After nine months and twenty days the project was completed, and the count reported 800,000 in Israel and 500,000 in Judah. Only males age 20 and older were counted. It has been concluded that the approximately 300,000 who were royal body guards, and the 30,000 who were frontier guards, were not made part of the totals. The report in Chronicles adds these, and thus the apparent discrepancy.

Because David had committed a wrong, God prescribed punishment and He presented the king with three choices. David, preferring to fall into the hands of God, chose the three days of pestilence rather than famine or military defeat. The outcome was the death of 70,000 newly enumerated citizens. David was moved to genuine penitence, and by his devout prayer that God would punish him rather than the people, he joined the company of the great intercessors of the Bible. Evidently David's heart had been particularly moved because God had granted him a vision of the angel of the Lord being restrained in his work of destruction. God's spokesman in His dealings with David throughout this episode was the prophet Gad.

Upon the prophet's instruction, David undertook to make offerings to God upon an altar which he erected on Araunah's threshing floor. Since Araunah (or Ornan) was a Jebusite chieftian and not an Israelite, it was necessary that David purchase the land for his use. After considerable oriental ceremony, David proceeded to pay fifty shekels for the title to the land. The particular significance of this incident is that this altar was the last of some six that had been erected in various parts of the land. It was on this site that Solomon built his temple, and that each of the subsequent temples of Israel was built.

6. THE BOOK OF
1 KINGS

The fact that 1 Kings begins with the conjunction "now" or "and" indicates that the author meant to maintain a complete continuity with the preceding books of Samuel. However, because the style of writing and the point of view of the writer are so distinctive in Kings, it is generally agreed that this work is by a different author. It is usually concluded that the books of Kings are by a later generation of prophet-scribes than the books of Samuel.

General Characteristics of the Books of Kings

In the Hebrew canon, first and second Kings were one book, and they were classified among the Earlier Prophets. The books were divided in the Septuagint translation because the more extended Greek version would have made a single roll too long and heavy. Taken together, the two books of Kings tell the entire story of the flowering of Israel's kingdom, and then its steady decline and final destruction at the hand of the invader. The books were evidently drawn from contemporary records, and a number of source materials are documented. These include:
1. The Book of the Chronicles of the Kings of Israel (used 17 times).
2. The Book of the Chronicles of the Kings of Judah (used 15 times).
3. The Book of the Acts of Solomon (used once in 1 Ki. 11:41).
In spite of the single reference to the Book of the Acts of Solomon, one plausible theory holds that virtually all of the first eleven chapters of 1 Kings are derived from this source. In the case of Bible portions from other sources, it is held that the inspiration of the Holy Spirit guaranteed the divine choice of material and assured that what purported to be true actually was true.

As a general rule, there is reference to source material in the case of all kings except those who died a sudden or violent death. It might be assumed that in these cases either the king did not survive long enough to prepare court annals, or else those who destroyed him also destroyed the records of his reign. There is a specific pattern in reporting the parallel northern and southern kingdoms so as to avoid confusion. Manley reports this as follows:

The writer [of 1 and 2 Kings] solves skillfully the problem of writing the parallel history of the northern and southern kingdoms. He begins with the first king of Israel and continues to the end of his reign, then begins the history of Judah and continues to the end of the reign of the last king who overlapped the reign of the first king of Israel. So he turns from one to another, giving all the time careful time-notes indicating in what year of the reign of each northern king the next king in the south began his reign and vice versa. [1]

Critical scholars sometimes place a good deal of emphasis upon real or imagined discrepancies in the books of Kings. Just as with all Bible materials, so here, it is often true that a more thorough understanding of the situation completely removes the discrepancy. However, it is recognized these books are subject to occasional textual errors that may lead to a certain type of discrepancy. Angus points out:

It is well known that the text of Samuel, Kings, and Chronicles is in worse condition than that of any other of the inspired writings; nor must we ascribe to the author what may be due to the errors of the copyists. [2]

The Nature and Theme of First Kings

The first book of Kings is a historical account of the kingdom of Israel from the time of the death of David through the reigns of Ahab and Jehoshaphat. Keil reports the nature of this book as: "the development of the kingdom of God under the kings." Included in this portion is the report of the division

---

[1] G. T. Manley, The New Bible Handbook (Chicago: The Inter-Varsity Christian Fellowship, 1948), p. 174.

[2] Joseph Angus, The Bible Handbook (Grand Rapids: Zondervan Publishing House, 1952), p. 248.

of the kingdom, and the parallel reigns of the northern and southern kings. The basic purpose of the first and second book of Kings is not to set forth history, but rather from history to establish the fact of the providential hand of God in the lives of His people. The reader is meant to discern the presence of Jehovah as the invisible, but nevertheless real, King of the nation. In view of the basic purposes of the books, the spiritual ministries of the prophets are given significant space along with the histories of the kings, and the two are interwoven into a composite historical account. Though the books of Kings indeed present history, it is history written with a religious and practical aim.

The Authorship of the Book

There is clear evidence that there is a difference in authorship between the books of Samuel and the books of Kings. Distinctive characteristics of these books setting them apart from Samuel include: the characteristic formulas by which the reigns of kings are introduced and concluded, the formulas describing the death and burial of the kings, and the language describing the personal virtues of the kings. In these books, these matters are uniformly reported in a manner to establish a single unique author. Further, the chronological references in the books would intimate that he lived into and during the time of the Babylonian captivity, but not up to the time of the return of the remnant. Thus, scholars seeking to identify the author of Kings look for someone not linked with the earlier books of Samuel, but who was exposed to the Babylonian captivity, and who probably suffered captivity himself.

A prominent individual who would qualify under the foregoing, and one long endorsed as the author by tradition, including the Talmud, is Jeremiah. The following are arguments supporting the claim of his authorship: 1) The books of Kings and Jeremiah include parallel passages that are almost identical (e.g. The story of the fall of Jerusalem, 2 Ki. 24:18 - 25:30 and Jer. 52:1-34), 2) There are unique Hebrew words that are found only in these two books (e.g. "cruse" 1 Ki. 14:3 and Jer. 19:1,10; or the special word for "hide" [Heb. chabah] in 1 Ki. 22:25 and Jer. 49:10), 3) A distinctive special interest in the Pentateuch is common to both. Facts that do not confirm Jeremiah's authorship are as follows: 1) There is reason to believe that Jeremiah died in Egypt and therefore he probably was not carried into bondage in Babylonia, 2) It is quite doubtful that Jeremiah lived to the period of mid-captivity and the liberation of Jehoiachin which is described in 2 Kings. Had Jeremiah still been alive he could not have been younger than 86, and it is very doubtful if at that age he could still produce a creative literary work.

Although it may not seem warranted to ascribe authorship directly to Jeremiah, it is generally agreed that his hand is discernible in these books. Specifically, it is said: "The author, if not Jeremiah was a man like minded with Jeremiah, and almost certainly a contemporary who lived and wrote under the same influences." A student of Jeremiah's has been suggested, and thereby similarities of vocabulary and style would be accounted for. It is possible that this student used notes prepared by Jeremiah, and therefore portions would actually be the personal composition of the master.

The Scope of the Book

The first book of Kings records the history of Israel and Judah for approximately 125 years.

The Key Phrase

The key phrase is: "as David his father." These words, or their equivalent, occur at least 25 times in 1 Kings.

The Value of the Book

The first book of Kings, in careful detail, traces the history of the nation and the fate of the throne of David which was vitally linked to the divine covenant. The story of the division of the kingdom following the death of Solomon is, of course, a fundamental event to be taken into account for all the remainder of the history of the nation. The narratives of this book give a background for the ministry of the prophets, and thus give them relevance and application in the times in which they occurred. The fortunes of the kingdom of Israel rose to their greatest height within the scope of this book, for never again has the nation achieved such wealth and greatness. The Lord Jesus used the first book of Kings, and in His ministry quoted from it twice (1 Ki. 10:1, 17:9).

Analysis and Exposition

I. The Establishment of Solomon's Kingdom
(Chs. 1, 2)

1. The Plot of Adonijah. Solomon Proclaimed King
(Ch. 1)

As the book begins, King David is introduced as having become feeble and decrepit and requiring the care of Abishag as a wife and nurse. Evidently David had aged prematurely, for he was likely not more than 70 at this time. Upon learning of this state of affairs, David's son Adonijah, determined that they were grounds for the immediate transfer of the throne. It is assumed that Adonijah was the oldest surviving son of David, although actually he had been born fourth in line and was next to Absalom. Since Adonijah would be about 35 at this time, he was probably at the peak of his productive life, and his assets would have included a display of previous achievements together with a gratifying potential for the future. Even Joab the general, and Abiathar the priest forsook David to cast in their lot with this promising pretender to the throne.

When news of Adonijah's campaign reached Nathan and Bathsheba, they immediately appealed to David on behalf of Solomon. Although there were ten or more sons in the line of succession between Adonijah and Solomon, it was a fact that David had promised Bathsheba that her son should succeed to the throne. No doubt Bathsheba also had personal interests in the matter, for had Adonijah become king, Bathsheba and Solomon would certainly have lost status, and they possibly could have lost their lives. David agreed to maintain his pledge on behalf of Solomon, and he enlisted Zadok the priest, Nathan the prophet, and Benaiah the captain of the guard on behalf of his cause. These leaders met with the young Solomon outside the city, and there they anointed him and proceeded to parade him into Jerusalem with a great deal of ceremony. The Cherethites and Pelethites who directed the procession (1:38), were foreign mercenaries who served as David's personal bodyguard. This anointing of Solomon appears to have marked the official beginning of the record of his reign, even though for a time he served with David, his father, as co-regent.

The rousing cry of Solomon's supporters reached the place of Adonijah's feast, and before long a messenger brought an explanation. The guests, finding themselves supporters of the losing candidate, promptly melted away. The pretender himself, realizing that his bold self-proclamation actually amounted to an act of treason, took refuge at the altar of sacrifice. For the time being, Solomon laid no charges, and Adonijah was permitted to go free. The altar to which Adonijah clung would either be that of the tabernacle at Gibeon, or it would be David's special altar that had been erected on Araunah's threshing floor.

2. David's Death. The Accession of Solomon
(Ch. 2; 1 Chron. 28, 29)

Chronicles tells the story of an official gathering in Jerusalem arranged by David at this time in order to present Solomon to the tribal leaders. In his address, David exhorted faithfulness to God's commandments, and he commissioned Solomon and the people to proceed with the building of the temple. In the report in Kings, David is depicted upon his death bed delivering his final charges to Solomon. He exhorted: "Be thou strong therefore, and show thyself a man" (v. 2). He charged Solomon to administer justice to Joab, to avenge Shimei who had so vehemently cursed David, and to return kindness to the generous sons of Barzillai. David died at age 70 after having ruled for a period of 40 years. In the historical books, Scripture records the biography of David, while in the Psalms it records his inner

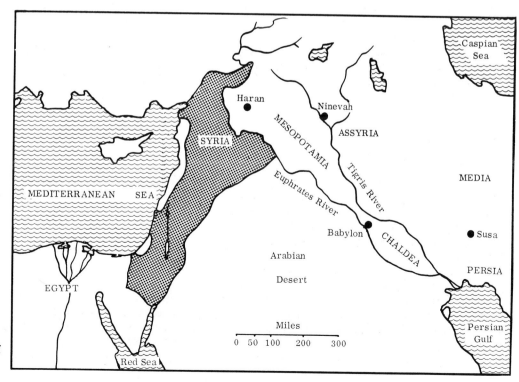

Figure Seven: David's Empire (shaded area) at the time of his death.

feelings and emotions. The New Testament reports God's testimony of David: "I have found David the son of Jesse, a man after mine own heart" (Acts 13:22).

The rule of David was one of the high points in the history of the nation of Israel. He united the people, gave them a well-organized central government and law; he fostered a national consciousness, and he achieved for the nation an individual identity including their own capital city. Solomon inherited a kingdom extending from the Mediterranean to the Euphrates, and from the mountains of Lebanon to the Red Sea. His subjects have been estimated to have been not fewer than 5,000,000. Evidently, one of David's greatest projects was assembling the materials for the building of the temple. It is inferred from 1 Chronicles 28 and 29 that David acquainted Solomon with his plans and enough of his detailed building specifications that Solomon was able to proceed in the first year of his reign. Scripture honors King David, among other ways, by naming him 1,087 times in the Old Testament and 47 times in the New Testament.

With David's death, Solomon assumed the full rulership. The duration of the co-regency is not given, and estimates vary from a few months to as much as seven years. Solomon appears to have gained the crown in stages, and Chronicles notes that he was: "made . . . king the second time" (1 Chron. 29:22). However, once he did become entrenched on the throne, Solomon proceeded to rule with firm efficiency. When Adonijah requested the hand of Abishag in marriage, Solomon interpreted the move as an attempt upon the throne, and he promptly had the petitioner put to death. Even Bathsheba had seen no harm in Adonijah's request, although it was widely accepted that the one who possessed the former king's harem was to be counted his successor politically as well. In quite a different vein, Farrar hints that Solomon's horror at Adonijah's request was because he was in love with Abishag the Shunamite himself, and that she was the Shulamite of the Song of Solomon.

In further settling past wrongs, Solomon deposed Abiathar the priest, but out of respect for his sacred office, the king spared his life. Abiathar was banished to his own land at Anathoth. Solomon determined that justice upon Joab should involve maximum severity, and therefore he ordered that Joab be slain. At least twice Joab had committed virtual murder, and Solomon felt it to be his duty to bestow punishment. Joab died at the hand of Benaiah and at the express personal command of the king. For the time being, Shimei's punishment was the restriction of travel, but later, Solomon had him slain because he violated his probation. Shimei had

agreed in a solemn oath to remain within the city of Jerusalem, and his careless journey to Gath was a flagrant violation that justified his fate. Solomon filled the vacancies that these judgments created by confirming Benaiah as captain of the army, and Zadok the chief priest.

II. Solomon's Reign (Chs. 3-11)

1. Divine Gifts to Solomon (Ch. 3, 2 Chron. 1)

Solomon proved himself to be a very wise young man even before he received supernatural wisdom from the Lord. Scripture reports: "And Solomon loved the Lord, walking in the statutes of David his father" (v. 3). Solomon demonstrated his shrewdness and wisdom in making covenants with the neighboring nations, and by this means he greatly strengthened his empire. In keeping with eastern custom, he sealed several of his political alliances with marriages, and the most important of these was his marriage to Pharaoh's daughter. It is assumed that Pharaoh would have given his daughter to Solomon as a diplomatic gesture in the face of the rising strength of Israel. It is noted that Solomon did not discontinue the high places (v.3), and God apparently permitted this practice because Solomon's faith transcended the legal and organizational significance of his action.

At the time that Solomon received the divine gift of wisdom, he had gone to Gibeon to sacrifice, for the great brazen altar of the tabernacle was evidently still located there. Although the Lord appeared to Solomon in a dream, the transactions and relationships established at that time had all the validity of an ordinary event of waking experience. In a noble and unselfish prayer, Solomon chose the gift of wisdom from among all that God offered. He determined that what he most needed was true practical insight, and an appreciation of genuine righteousness. God announced that because Solomon chose wisdom rather than riches, the life of his enemies, or long life, He would bestow these gifts also. However, long life was to be conditional, and was to depend upon obedience to God. Solomon's settlement of the case of the two disputing mothers was an impressive demonstration of the operation of his gift of wisdom.

2. The Possessions of Solomon (Ch. 4)

Solomon encouraged the growth of titled families in Israel, and he governed through a circle of high officers who held the rank of princes. Scripture reports also: a series of premiers who in succession held office for one month, priests, scribes, the court recorder, the army captain, superintendents, the high steward, and the chief tax collector.

There is evidence that David had previously organized Judah on this basis, and that Solomon now extended the organization to all of Israel. It is noted that some officers had very large territories, for Geber was the only officer in the entire Eastern tableland. Zadok, the chief or high priest, recognized by Solomon, was of the line of Eleazar in contrast with Abiathar who had been of the line of Ithamar.

In its earlier years, Solomon's reign represented happiness, peace, and prosperity. The entire court and governmental staff shared Solomon's table, and estimates of this body range as high as 14,000 persons. Each day's rations included: flour, meal, some 30 cattle, 100 sheep, and other foods. Solomon maintained extensive horse stables reported in Kings as numbering 40,000, but in Chronicles as 4,000 (2 Chron. 9:25). Solomon's wisdom and his writings were widely admired and respected, and he included in his studies the complete science of growing things from the cedar to the hyssop. Of Solomon's 3,000 proverbs, some 375 are preserved in the Old Testament; of the 1,005 songs, only two songs (Psa. 75 and 117) and the Song of Solomon have been preserved. It is inferred that his "dromedaries" were either race horses or racing camels. In general, Scripture notes that Solomon's wisdom exceeded that of the Egyptians and the "sons of the east" (i.e. the Arabians and Chaldeans).

3. Solomon Prepares to Build the Temple (Ch. 5; 2 Chron. 2)

In negotiating a treaty with Hiram (or Huram) the king of Tyre, Solomon simply capitalized upon the goodwill that already existed between the two nations. By this means, Israel obtained a supply of cedar and fir lumber in exchange for wheat and oil. Solomon paid Hiram for the lumber, and he also paid the workmen (2 Chron. 2:10). It was apparently a coincidence that in each case the amount of wheat paid was the same--20,000 measures. The number of supervisors appears to have totalled 3,850, and under them there was a great army of workers from among Solomon's subjects who were actually little more than slave laborers. It has been suggested that the majority of these workers would be Canaanites rather than Israelites. Hiram's workers are here called Sidonians, which is simply a variant name for Phoenicians. It is noted that the workers also prepared building stones for use in the project, and it is suggested that the word "stonesquarers" (v. 18) is actually the name "Giblites." These were the inhabitants of Gebal (or Byblos) and they had the reputation of being skilful workers and artisans.

4. The Construction of the Temple (Ch. 6; 2 Chron. 3)

The beginning verse of this chapter is very important in Bible chronology, even though its interpretation remains in dispute. The beginning of the building of the house of the Lord is identified as "the four hundred and eightieth year after the children of Israel were come out of the land of Egypt, in the fourth year of Solomon's reign over Israel" (v. 1). The exact dating of this verse is disputed because there is a question concerning the beginning of Solomon's reign. Many hold that he was twice anointed king. (cf. "And they made Solomon the son of David king the second time" 1 Chron. 29:22). The fourth year of Solomon's reign may have been dated from this second anointing. Further, it has been suggested that the reign of Solomon began prematurely due to Adonijah's intrigues, and that possibly for the first seven years of Solomon's forty year reign, he was co-regent with David. It is clear that while this chronological anchor point greatly helps in relating events and eras in Old Testament times, it gives no certain bases for unsupported dogmatism in Biblical chronologies.

Solomon's temple was built upon the general plan of the tabernacle with three areas: the holy of holies, the holy place, and the courtyard. The overall proportions of the two worship centers were identical, but all the tabernacle dimensions were doubled for the temple. The basic structure of the temple was comprised of immense stones that have been estimated to have been as much as nine feet thick at the base, but to have become thinner as the structure rose in height. Panels of cedar covered the inside walls, and timbers of fir covered the floor. The one curtain that was retained from the tabernacle plan was that between the holy place and the holy of holies. It apparently formed a second covering in addition to the doorways between the two compartments.

The furniture and vessels of the temple correspond only loosely with those of the tabernacle. In the temple there was a great deal of emphasis upon the laver, and ten additional lavers were constructed. The large central laver was a cast piece that held upwards of 18,000 gallons of water. It is inferred that the temple provided ten tables of shewbread (2 Chron. 4:8), and ten candlesticks. The ark itself was not rebuilt, but was simply installed in the new structure when all else was finished. However, Solomon constructed two impressive cherubim to overshadow the ark in the holy of holies. These were made of olive wood, and overlaid with gold and so placed that when the ark was in position it rested beneath their wings.

All of the materials of the temple were prepared to size and shape at their source, so that in the actual erection of the building there was no sound of axe or tool of iron. Concern for these matters confirmed the sanctity of the temple and set it apart from ordinary residence or business houses. While the temple was being constructed, the word of the Lord came and confirmed to Solomon the need for divine enthronement within the human heart as well as in the temple. As it were, the physical temple was God's pledge that He would maintain His presence with His people. He promised: "I will dwell among the children of Israel, and will not forsake my people Israel" (v. 13).

It is often held that in view of the Phoenician assistance that Solomon received, his temple was probably styled somewhat by Phoenician standards. If so, it would have been very massive and heavy in construction, and the two columns, Jachin and Boaz, that are described so thoroughly in the next chapter, would have been free-standing pillars that flanked the entrance. Apparently, the building was lighted by windows just beneath the ceiling, in what is known as clerestory construction. Not only was the interior stonework covered by wood, but the wood in turn was covered with carvings of flowers and overlaid with gold. All other appointments of the temple were likewise appropriately finished. In all, the building of the temple required seven and one-half years, even though a good portion of the preliminary preparation had already been completed in David's time.

5. Solomon's Palaces. The Temple Furnishings (Ch. 7; 2 Chron. 4)

In addition to the temple, Solomon built a royal residence and military headquarters known as "the house of the forest of Lebanon" (vvs. 2-5); the pillar hall with the porch (v. 6); the throne hall and judgment hall (v. 7); his personal residence and a house for Pharoah's daughter (v. 8). Only meager details concerning these various buildings are given, and in fact, Josephus reports that they were not separate buildings, but simply sections or wings of one royal palace. Scripture indicates that in architectural style and basic building materials, Solomon's secular structures were very similar to the temple. At this point, the two temple pillars or monuments which were to mark the temple entrance are described. The name of the right pillar "Jachin" means literally "establishment," and carries the inference: "let this temple stand forever"; while "Boaz" simply means "strength."

To insure the best craftsmanship in temple equipment and furnishings, Solomon imported from Tyre an expert metal worker named Hiram who was,

however, a different individual from the king. It has been suggested that the divine prohibition upon the making of images had discouraged the development of this type of craftsmanship in Israel. Not only did Hiram cast the two entrance pillars, but also the great brazen laver (or sea), and the ten smaller lavers. All of these castings were in enduring bronze. Archaeologists have determined that there was indeed a well-advanced smelting and refining industry based at Ezion-geber on the gulf of Aqabah that made possible such elaborate projects. It is estimated that the great bronze laver would have weighed between 25 and 30 tons, although there is some uncertainty as to its exact form because of the discrepancy between the diameter (10 cubits) and the circumference (30 cubits). Apparently it was not a perfect circle, or else the measurements are only approximate.

The altar is minimized in the description of the temple construction, but it is mentioned and briefly described in 2 Chronicles 4:1. Evidently it had the form of a very large square box made from bronze. The inner furnishings of the temple were made of gold and were elaborate and decorative. The equipment of the temple included: 10 candlesticks, snuffers, basins or deep dishes, knives, 100 bowls or vessels for wine libations, and flat vessels for incense. Estimates of the value of the temple materials and cost of construction range upwards of five billion dollars in modern currency. It has been noted that the labor force employed in its construction included 30,000 Jews, and no less than 153,000 Canaanites.

6. The Dedication of the Temple (Ch. 8; 2 Chron. 5:1-7:10)

The temple was completed in the eighth month of the seventh year of construction (6:38). The dedication was in the seventh month of a later year, and apparently coincided with the Feast of Tabernacles. The interval between the completion and dedication would have been at least 11 months, and it could have added additional years as well. Multitudes assembled for the dedication, and the highlight was the installation of the ark within the newly completed temple. In confirming His pleasure, God bestowed blessing and glory so manifest that the priests were unable to stand to minister. Many have seen this incident as a preview of the Kingdom glory. Solomon used the occasion to deliver a brief address, to pray a public prayer of dedication, and to pronounce a blessing upon the nation. The assembly was an Old Testament counterpart of a modern church service.

Solomon's prayer at the dedication of the temple has been described as: "one of the grandest devotional utterances to be found in pre-Christian devotional literature." The prayer includes two statements of doctrinal significance: "But will God indeed dwell on the earth? behold the heaven and heaven of heavens cannot contain thee; how much less this house that I have builded" (v. 27), and "If they sin against thee, (for there is no man that sinneth not)" (v. 46). The first Scripture indicates the immensity and infinity of God, and the second is a clear statement of the universal depravity of mankind.

Since Exodus forbade that the carrying staves were never to be drawn from the rings which attached them to the ark (Ex. 25:15), it is taken that verse 8 is not a description of a violation of this command, but rather the Scriptural way of explaining that it was being kept. The staves were so adjusted as to be readily visible in order that all would know that God's command had been obeyed. The sacrifices at this time were most numerous, and in one day 22,000 oxen and 120,000 sheep were offered. There would have been 2,000 or more officiating priests, and it is noted that Solomon provided additional temporary altar facilities in the middle of the court. Much of the flesh of the offerings would be returned to the people for food during the days that they were in attendance at these festivities. It is assumed that by combining seven days of dedication activities with seven days of observing the Feast of Tabernacles, the complete series of events totalled fourteen days (v. 65). It is noted in Chronicles that the people were sent home on the twenty-third day of the month (2 Chron. 7:10).

7. The Covenant to Solomon. His Building Activities (Ch. 9; 2 Chron. 7:11-8:18)

Shortly after the temple dedication services, Solomon was again honored by the appearance of the Lord, just as at Gibeon. On this occasion, the Lord reaffirmed the Davidic covenant and repeated the warning that disobedience would bring chastisement. To a large measure, the warning on this occasion is a repetition of that spoken by Moses during his farewell sermons (cf. Deut. 28:37, 45, 63; 29:23-26). The Lord declared that if they should turn from following Him "Israel shall be a proverb and a byword among all people" (v. 7). During much of Israel's history this unfortunate state of affairs has prevailed, for characteristically the Jewish

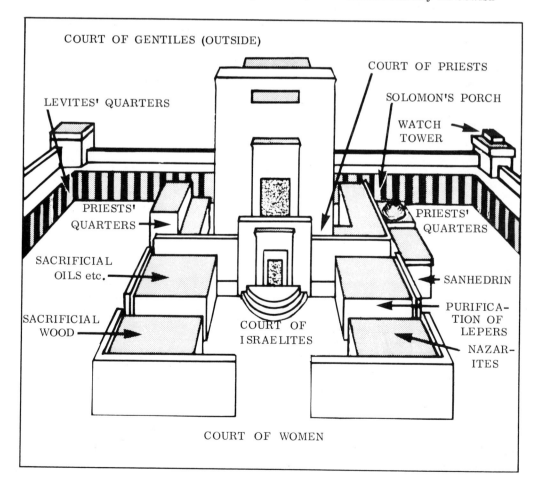

Figure Eight: Solomon's Temple as seen through Shushan Gate. (From the model by J. Jehuda)

people have been the targets of criticism and ridicule.

A portion of Solomon's payment to Hiram of Tyre for the supplies of building materials is reported to have been twenty cities. Hiram's inspection of the cities left him disappointed and somewhat contemptuous. One suggestion is that "the land of Cabul" means "the pawned land" and in a veiled way such a name would be hinting that the land was of no value. Hiram evidently returned the cities to Solomon, and the debt was instead paid in gold. A proposed improved rendering of verse 14 would read, "Hiram had sent the king 120 talents of gold." This amount seems to have represented the indebtedness to Hiram that Solomon accrued through his massive building program.

Solomon's exploits, his fame, his influence, and his alliances continued to increase. Scripture notes (9:16) that Gezer, a Canaanite city that had resisted Israel from Joshua's time, had been captured by Pharaoh and given as a gift to Pharaoh's daughter, Solomon's wife. It is suggested that the city may have been her wedding gift. Solomon rebuilt Megiddo (9:15), and apparently made it one of his chariot cities. Archaeologists report the remains of extensive stables on the site of the city. In general, Solomon subdued his enemies both within and outside of his state, and he transformed the economy of Israel from an agricultural to a mercantile basis. Part of Solomon's technique was to use conquered people as forced laborers in his projects (v. 21). Solomon, with the help of Hiram of Tyre, established a successful merchant navy and developed trade with Syria, Arabia, Egypt, and India. It is concluded that the Bible name "Ophir," refers either to India or Arabia.

Solomon's development at Ezion-geber (v. 26) was two-fold in its purpose: both a seaport and also a mining center. In modern times, archaeologist Nelson Glueck simply followed the literal account of Scripture and thus rediscovered king Solomon's mines. Because modern operations are more efficient, Israel today is able to exploit copper lodes that were passed over in Solomon's time as too lean. Thus far, no particular remains of Solomon's seaport have been identified as such by the archaeologists. The climatic conditions in the region of Ezion-geber are so undesirable to humans that it is assumed that workers there were actually slaves, and that they were prevented from escaping by a very high wall around their smelter. All of this would accord with what is otherwise known about Solomon's administration.

8. The Visit of the Queen of Sheba (Ch. 10; 2 Chron. 9)

Sheba (or Saba) is believed to be a state in southwest Arabia and it may have been the home of the Sabeans. In the New Testament (Mt. 12:42), this queen is referred to as "the queen of the south." In Arabic legends her traditional name is Balkis. This illustrious woman ruler arrived for her visit with Solomon with an impressive retinue of attendants and a multitude of questions. She brought with her a gift of gold equivalent to five million dollars, plus a great store of spices and precious stones. It is proposed that one reason for the queen's visit was that she might establish an agreement with Solomon concerning competition between her land caravans and Solomon's merchant navy. The queen summed up her impressions of Solomon's reign: "Behold, the half was not told me." Theologians have long debated whether the queen became a proselyte to Judaism, but no information is given.

Two rather interesting traditions concerning Solomon's demonstrations of wisdom before the queen of Sheba are reported. When Solomon was asked to distinguish between identically dressed boys and girls, he simply ordered them to wash their hands. The groups were easily identified when the boys failed to roll up their sleeves before plunging their hands into the water. In another test, Solomon distinguished between real flowers and artificial by ordering the window opened and then observing which flowers attracted wild bees.

The almug trees (vv. 11, 12) are believed to be a species of red sandalwood native to India. It is proposed that the text infers that Solomon used this material to build stairways in the temple. The "targets" (v. 16) of gold would be ornamental shields used on state occasions. The "navy of Tharshish" appears to be a general expression identifying a fleet of merchant vessels. The name "Tharshish" or "Tarshish" itself is thought to be a form of "Tartessus" in Spain, a Greek colony there exporting gold, silver, iron, and lead. Solomon's ships returned from the Orient with such exotic cargoes as: gold, silver, ivory, apes, and "peacocks" (modern translators suggest that the reference is to another kind of monkey). Even the Mohammedan Koran devotes six chapters to the exploits and wisdom of Solomon, and he stands as unquestionably the wisest and most wealthy man who has ever lived.

9. Solomon's Wives and Adversaries. His Death. (Ch. 11)

In his later years, even the great Solomon failed God. Scripture pointedly notes that his falling

The site of Gibeon where Solomon received the gift of divine wisdom. At the farthest side of the mound is the modern village of El-jib. This view looks northward.

away was not the outcome of wealth, power or honor, but specifically his incredible exercise of plural marriage. With no less than 700 wives and 300 concubines, Solomon stands with the all-time record of history. (Second place goes to Darius Codomanus with 1 wife and 329 concubines.) The totals no doubt include all who were received into Solomon's harem in his lifetime, and the entire group would not have been present in his court at any one time. Nevertheless, it is clear that such a harem provided Solomon with neither a home nor love, and instead, was responsible for leading him into idolatry. Although some of the international relationships established by marriage may have been to Israel's advantage, the accompanying idolatry meant a far more devastating loss to Israel's national heritage.

God appeared to Solomon and censured him for his declension and pronounced the future disruption of the kingdom. In addition, the Lord established adversaries against Solomon to cause him

distress from that time onward. In his latter days, Solomon found himself actively opposed by: Hadad the Edomite, Rezon of Syria, and Jeroboam the son of Nebat. Actually, Hadad and Rezon had already emerged, but their activities only began to be a threat in the era of Solomon's idolatry. As an Edomite, Hadad had come under Joab's fierce attacks and therefore he lived in exile in Egypt. Rezon was an outlaw who had gathered sufficient strength to assume the rule of the city of Damascus. While these men, with Jeroboam, engaged in hostile agitations, Solomon appears to have become increasingly detached from the hearts of his people. Even more pathetically, Solomon continued to depart from God and to become unhappy, restless, and lonesome.

Although Hadad and Rezon conducted nuisance raids, Solomon's chief threat was Jeroboam, son of Nebat. This man, while yet a youth had distinguished himself as "a mighty man of valour" and one who was "industrious." (v. 28) Apparently, in perform-

65

ing the usual forced labor under Solomon, he happened to be assigned to the fortifications of Jerusalem. Solomon was so impressed that he placed him in charge of the labors of the tribe of Joseph. However, it does not appear the Jeroboam's virtues were the reason for his divine choice to rule the ten tribes; Abijah the prophet made clear that Solomon's failures were responsible. With the divine acknowledgement of Jeroboam's forthcoming role, the measure of his threat to Solomon was evident, and the king sought to destroy him. However, Jeroboam took refuge in Egypt, and he remained in exile in Solomon's later years as a constant center of harassment and threatening.

Solomon died after reigning forty years. He was about sixty years old at the time of his death, having lost the gift of long life because of his failure to meet the divine provisions. Solomon's spiritual state at the time of his death is a matter of conjecture, but many commentators have felt that a man so possessed of insights and values such as revealed in Proverbs would surely have returned to the Lord in his last days. Solomon's personal and national indulgences largely bankrupted the country, and to a large measure the world that he knew vanished at his death. The book of Chronicles entirely passes over Solomon's fall, and it makes no mention of his many wives nor his approval of idolatry.

III. The Disruption and Decline of the Kingdom
(Chs. 12-22)

1. Rehoboam's Stubbornness and the Secession of
   the Ten Tribes (Ch. 12), 2 Chron. 10, 11)

At Solomon's death, it was assumed that his son Rehoboam, "the liberator of the people," should succeed him, and Rehoboam's coronation at Shechem was planned. No reason for the choice of Rehoboam is given, but somewhat remarkably, in spite of all the wives and offspring of Solomon, Rehoboam is the only son that the Bible mentions. His mother was Naamah, the Ammonitess. The coronation of Rehoboam was hindered by a protest movement which began in the tribe of Ephraim but before long included all of the ten tribes. The bargainers came basically with two requests: 1) that taxes be reduced, 2) that forced labor be abolished. Rehoboam was granted three days to consider the matter, and it was in this interval that he sought out the young counselors (lit. "the boys"). Rehoboam was 41 years of age at this time.

After a three-day interval, Rehoboam's answer in keeping with the advice of the young men, was rash and violent. He threatened: "my little finger shall be thicker than my father's loins . . . my father chastised you with whips, but I will chastise you with

scorpions" (1 Ki. 12:10, 11). Clearly, Rehoboam identified with those aspects of his father's reign that had been painful to the people. The great luxury and wealth of Solomon's court had been at the cost of demanding human labor and the appropriation of the people's resources, and even that magnificent rule amounted to a chastisement with whips. The cry "to your tents, O Israel" was the signal to disperse in the face of the breakdown of negotiations. The ten tribes not only withdrew from all part in the coronation ceremonies, but they later proceeded to stone the tax collector whom Rehoboam sent to them. Rehoboam's stubbornness cost him upwards of three million subjects.

Rehoboam's kingdom comprised basically only the tribe of Judah. Later, his subjects were augmented by the Benjamites and Levites, and at least some representatives from the ten tribes who did not approve of Jeroboam's rule. Although Rehoboam nominally served Jehovah, and was somewhat responsive to Him, at the same time he appears to have been partly contaminated by idolatry. It may be assumed that his Ammonitish mother inclined him toward idolatry, and that he would have considered Jehovah simply as one among many tribal gods. When the tribes proceeded to elect Jeroboam as their king, Rehoboam accepted God's direction to refrain from warfare against the secessionists. Through the ministry of the prophet Shemaiah, God at this time confirmed that the division was according to His sovereign plan. One significant advantage enjoyed by Rehoboam was that the men of Judah and Benjamin were the outstanding warriors of the nation.

It is evident that Jeroboam had very quickly returned from his Egyptian exile upon news of the death of Solomon, and he thus was available as a spokesman and leader of the ten tribes. As king, one of his first acts was to deepen the rift between the two kingdoms by establishing worship centers at Bethel and Dan within his own kingdom. In these centers, Jeroboam erected golden calves which seem to have been intended either as objects of worship themselves, or as beasts of burden to convey Jehovah to His people. This latter was a common practice among pagan nations, and it may have been that Jeroboam's theory was that these were mere platforms for the invisible God. In either case, of course, he was guilty of idolatry, and he was simply conforming to the pagan Egyptian worship of the bovine form.

In his actions in general, Jeroboam appears to have been motivated far more by political and tactual considerations than religious. It is clearly evident that he really cared little for religion or for the welfare of the people in matters of morals and truth. In order to fortify his frontiers, and possibly to emphasize further his break with the past, Jeroboam developed the city of Penuel east of Jordan and an important and strategic point in the kingdom. He considered Shechem to be the capital, although he located his own palace at Tirzah which was presumably a nearby residential community. Apparently, each move by Jeroboam was determined according to political expediency.

When Jeroboam found that many priests from his kingdom were migrating south to join Rehoboam's kingdom, he simply recruited priests indiscriminately from among his own subjects. It appears that all who were able to offer the required sacrifice (1 bullock, 7 rams, cf. 2 Chron. 13:9), were considered eligible for the priesthood. In providing for these new priests, he likely withheld tithes from the legitimate Levites, and he would therefore naturally promote their exodus. Jeroboam proceeded to change the date of the feast of Tabernacles, the national feast day, from the seventh to the eighth month. He stands in Scripture as a destructive religious innovator, probably not wicked or evil in himself, but nevertheless motivated by human ambition and the appeal to expediency. Throughout Scripture, Jeroboam is identified by the repeated epithet, that it was he who "caused Israel to sin."

2. The Broken Altar and the Unfortunate Prophet (Ch. 13)

The first of two object lessons taught in this chapter was to Jeroboam. God forcefully demonstrated to the king that his altar and religion were objects of divine displeasure. Jeroboam's altar was smitten by God and left shattered and useless. Likewise Jeroboam's arm, in a foretaste of divine judgment, was made withered and helpless. Not only was Jeroboam's altar destroyed, but inasmuch as the ashes were poured out, God made clear that that the very sacrificial service performed upon that altar would be desecrated. Although Jeroboam was brought to the place of humbly entreating the prayers of the prophet of God on his behalf, he appears neither to have profited by nor to have learned from the incident, for at a later time he continued his rebellious course without improvement.

The second object lesson involved the man of God who had been commissioned with the task of declaring God's displeasure at Jeroboam's false altar. This guileless prophet permitted himself to be enticed into disobeying God's command, and the result was that he was slain by a lion as he journeyed homeward. Presumably the prophet was held so strictly accountable to obey God's command because he was especially privileged in knowing God's will. Although this prophet lost his life, and the elderly prophet of Bethel did not, this latter suffered disgrace and sorrow of heart at such a turn of events.

3. Jeroboam's Wife and Ahijah the Prophet. Nadab Succeeds Jeroboam (Ch. 14; 2 Chron. 12)

The sickness of Abijah, the son of Jeroboam, appears to have been a divinely imposed judgment. In his extremity, Jeroboam sent his wife to Ahijah, the prophet at Shiloh, that the mind of God might be known. Jeroboam's wife disguised herself and took only a simple gift to the prophet so that she would not be recognized as the queen. Neverthless, the message of Ahijah was one of condemnation, and it included the announcement of the certain death of the child, and the termination of the line of Jeroboam. Just as predicted, the child Abijah died when his mother returned to Tirzah, but even in the face of such events, Jeroboam remained impenitent. Thus, his line was to end as prophesied with the death of his son. Jeroboam ruled Israel for 22 years, and upon his death was succeeded by his son, Nadab.

In the meantime, Rehoboam of Judah was by no means conducting himself as he ought. He too sponsored idolatry and allowed immorality, and thus likewise provoked the anger of the Lord. Within five years after Solomon's death, Rehoboam's apostasy was so complete that God permitted the invasion of the Egyptians under Shishak. Rehoboam had hoped to repel the attackers by fortifying 15 cities of his kingdom and equipping them for military garrisons, but these efforts were in vain. Shishak was a new pharoah in Egypt and he had overthrown the father-in-law of Solomon. He came against Judah with 12,000 chariots and 60,000 horsemen. Primarily, the invasion may be explained on religious grounds, for Shishak was simply God's instrument of chastening upon His disobedient people.

Chronicles tells the story of national repentance in the face of this attack: "Whereupon the princes of Israel and the king humbled themselves; and they said, The Lord is righteous" (2 Chron. 12:6). In response to this repentance, God agreed to spare the city of Jerusalem and the lives of the people. Thus Rehoboam escaped Shishak's conquest by paying an impressive ransom, and although the land was pillaged and impoverished, life was permitted to continue. Shishak did not press his advantage and maintain his conquests in Palestine, although he proclaimed his conquest to all posterity by engraving it upon a temple pylon at Karnak near Luxor in Egypt. There, he reported the conquest of some 156 towns and cities in Judah and Israel, and his carving includes an illustration of long rows of captives tied neck to neck. The shield of each captive is inscribed with the name of the city that he represented. In 1938 a mummy that was identified as Shishak was found in a burial chamber at Tanis in Egypt.

Scripture reports that Rehoboam had 18 wives and 60 concubines, and that he was the father of 28 sons and 60 daughters. His favorite wife was Maachah, the granddaughter of Absalom. She became the mother of Abijah, his successor, and outlived both her husband and her son. In general, Rehoboam is thought of as an unworthy ruler who fostered idolatry and apostasy in the kingdom of Judah, and who lacked both political and military skill. One of his few wise acts was his arrangement of provision for his 88 children with whom he "dealt wisely," and his distribution of governmental posts among his sons (2 Chron. 11:23). When Rehoboam died at age 58 after 17 years of reign, he was succeeded by his son Abijam (called Abijah in Chronicles).

4. Abijam's Rule, Jeroboam's Death, Asa's Reformation (Ch. 15; 2 Chron. 13-16)

The Bible account declares that Abijah: "walked in all the sins of his father . . . and his heart was not perfect with the Lord his God" (v. 3). Abijam's (or Abijah's) war against Jeroboam of Israel is recorded at some length in the book of Chronicles, and it is the main feature of his life recorded there. Abijam first attempted a form of psychological warfare by an appeal to the Israelites to refrain from hostilities against Judah. He exhorted: "God himself is with us for our captain . . . O children of Israel, fight yet not against the Lord God of your fathers" (2 Chron. 13:12). Such persuasion was to no avail, however, and Jeroboam persisted in pressing hostilities. The battle proved to be an overwhelming victory for Abijam. "God smote Jeroboam" and even though Abijam had been outnumbered two to one, his forces inflicted no less than 500,000 casualties upon Jeroboam's 800,000 man army. Scripture reports: "Neither did Jeroboam recover strength again in the days of Abijah" (2 Chron. 13:20). Abijam died after only a three year reign, and he was succeeded by his son Asa. A further detail concerning Abijam reported in Scripture is that he had 14 wives and that he begat 22 sons and 16 daughters.

In refreshing contrast, Asa the son of Abijam, and the third king of Judah, was a reforming king. He proceeded to rid the kingdom of the glaring manifestations of idolatry, including destroying the idols he found in the land, removing the sodomites (probably male prostitutes who served in the temple of Ashtoreth), and above all, deposing Maachah, the queen mother and widow of Rehoboam. Maachah had been the leader of the idolaters and had given them support from within the royal household itself. Scripture commends Asa: "Nevertheless Asa's heart was perfect with the Lord all his days." In addition to religious reform, Asa, in the early years of his reign, also strengthened Judah politically and improved the defences of the key cities of the land. However, Scripture notes that Asa was able effectively to implement all of the reforms that he intended, and in spite of his good intentions the high places were not removed.

Chronicles reports Asa's victories over the armies of Zerah, who commanded a coalition of Egypt and Ethiopia. Zerah's host is the largest army mentioned in the Old Testament, for it boasted upwards of one million men against Asa's half million. No doubt Asa prayed with feeling: "help us, O Lord our God; for we rest on thee, and in thy name we go against this multitude" (2 Chron. 14:11). The defeat of Zerah was the greatest victory of Israel's entire history, and for at least three centuries following, the kingdoms of North Africa made no further attempt to conquer the lands of Asia. When Asa returned in victory, he was met by the prophet Azariah who exhorted to faithfulness to God. The prophet declared the basic principle: "the Lord go with you, while ye be with him; and if ye seek him, he will be found of you; but if ye forsake him, he will forsake you" (2 Chron. 15:2). It is noted that both because of military victories and because of basic piety, that appealed to many during Asa's reign, there was a significant tide of immigration from the northern kingdom and many from all tribes chose to throw in their lot with Judah.

In spite of his many virtues, Asa in his later years departed from a dedicated walk with God. When provoked by Baasha of Israel, he chose to take the remaining store of temple treasure and employ it as a bribe to hire the Syrian mercenary soldiers of Benhadad of Damascus. These tensions between the two kingdoms resulted because Baasha attempted to construct a border fortress at Ramah, just five miles from Jerusalem, to restrain his own people from their immigrations to Asa's kingdom. When the prophet Hanani rebuked Asa for his lack of faith in these matters, the king countered by casting the prophet into prison. Although Asa's forces defeated Baasha, the victory probably cost him more than its value. Asa died of "diseased feet" (probably senile gangrene) and he is remembered as one who "sought not to the Lord but to the physicians" (2 Chron. 16:11). These latter were probably heathen sorcerers. The life of Asa serves to illustrate one who fails God, not because of sin, but because he lives beneath his privileges in God. Jehoshaphat, his son, succeeded him to the throne.

In Israel, in the meantime, Nadab had proved to be a sinful ruler. After two years he was murdered by Baasha of the tribe of Issachar. Upon succeeding to the throne, Baasha proceeded ruthlessly to destroy all survivors of the house of Jeroboam, just as

Ahijah had prophesied (1 Ki. 15:29). Officially, Baasha had no claim to the throne except that of having murdered his predecessor, but to a people who preferred a strong ruler to a weak one, apparently this was claim enough. Baasha's defeat in battle in the conflict with Asa of Judah has already been noted. Among the cities that were destroyed in this war were: Abel-beth-maachah, Ijon, Dan, and as well, a portion of the territory of Naphtali was lost to the southern kingdom. Baasha ruled for twenty-four years, and he is remembered as one of Israel's wicked kings.

5. From Baasha to Ahab (Ch. 16)

This chapter commences with a prophecy by Jehu, son of Hanani, against Baasha of Israel. Although God had honored and favored this man in raising him from total obscurity to a place of status,

Baasha in no measure responded. He had fulfilled his role in exterminating the house of Jeroboam, apparently motivated by personal ambition and apart from any more worthy objectives. There were virtually no redeeming aspects in Baasha's twenty-four year reign, and at his death, his son Elah succeeded him. Elah proved to be a wicked king, and after reigning not quite two years, he was slain by Zimri while he was in a drunken stupor. Thus ended the dynasty of Baasha just as Jehu had prophesied (v. 3). Scripture consistently compares the reign and dynasty of Baasha to those of Jeroboam, and from a spiritual standpoint, both were a total loss.

Zimri had been a commander of one-half of Elah's war-chariots, and he was clearly committed to militarism. Thus, without hesitation, Zimri proceeded to execute all the males of the family of Baasha. This act, however, and the rule of Zimri

The general view of Tirzah as it appears today. For the first half century of the kingdom of Israel, Tirzah was the site of the royal residences. The particular site of Jeroboam's palace is visible at the right, just behind the buildings in the center background.

generally, was markedly distasteful to Israel, and they promptly rebelled. Their new leader was Omri, who also was a military man, and who is described as "the captain of the host." Omri's army had been besieging the Philistine city of Gibbethon, but upon the news of the usurping rule of Zimri, the army promptly diverted its siege energies to Tirzah where Zimri was entrenched. The city soon fell, and Zimri, realizing that he lacked popular support, chose to commit suicide by setting fire to the royal palace and remaining within to be cremated. Zimri had ruled Israel for only one week.

After a struggle with Tibni that extended for 14 years, Omri finally emerged as the undisputed ruler of Israel. His rule proved to be impressively strong, and even though he was comparatively evil he is remembered for having founded one of the most powerful dynasties of Israel's existence. The Moabite Stone[3] acknowledges his conquest of Moab, and from his time onward in Assyrian monuments the nation of Israel is known as the house of Omri (i.e. Beth-Omri). It appears that so far as the world scene is concerned, Omri was one of the most important of the kings of Israel. Scripture limits him to just seven verses, evidently because his spiritual influence was of no great consequence. Omri died after ruling for 12 years, and he was succeeded by his son Ahab.

A noteworthy achievement by Omri resulted from his abandonment of Tirzah in the sixth year of his reign and his purchase of the hill of Samaria as a site for the new capital city of Israel. The name "Samaria" means "watch-tower." The new site had important military advantages, and it gave Omri adequate lines of communication with Tyre so that he might enjoy a military alliance with the Phoenicians against the Syrians. Samaria was a more or less symmetrical hill, and the fortifications provided for a series of walls at various terraced levels on the slope of the hill. Archaeologists report that the masonry at Samaria is the finest that is found in Israel. One feature was the provision of

_____

[3]This stone, found in 1868, is now in the Louvre Museum in Paris. It is written in Phoenician, dated in the ninth century B.C., and names at least 14 places that are named in the Bible. The Moabite Stone appears to have been prepared in the time of Omri's grandson in order to recognize Moab's rebellion against their vassal state established at this time. The stone begins: "I am Mesha, son of Chemosh . . . king of Moab, . . . Omri, king of Israel . . . oppressed Moab many days." The rebellion that it describes took place during the reign of Joram almost a century later.

many large cisterns intended to provide water in times of siege. One characteristic of archaeological finds at Samaria is an abundance of fragments of carved ivory that evidently was used generously for decorative purposes.

With the ascension to the throne of Ahab and Jezebel, Israel descended into oppressive spiritual darkness. Jezebel was the daughter of the king of Sidon, and she was determined to develop Baal worship as the basic religion of Israel. The golden calves of Jeroboam became the basis of out-and-out idolatry, and the official worship in the land became that of Baal and Ashtoreth. Not only was idolatry sponsored and promoted, but the surviving worshippers of Jehovah were viciously persecuted. It is said that in every instance in which Jezebel is mentioned in Scripture (at least 22 times) her name is linked with evil.

At this point Scripture records the rebuilding of Jericho (v. 34) in defiance of God's ancient curse (Josh. 6:26). As noted elsewhere, heathen practices directed that such an event required a living child to be sealed within the foundations of the city.

6. Elijah and the Barrel of Meal (Ch. 17)

It was at this juncture that the prophet Elijah appeared upon the scene of Bible history. In response to "Israel's worst ruler," God raised up His "greatest and most powerful prophet." Elijah came from the town of Tishbi in Gilead, and it has been suggested that the rugged, stern, majestic region of Gilead was reflected in the remarkable character of Elijah. He was not meant to be an ordinary man, for he was God's especially chosen prophet who was to be an answer to Baal. Newell describes him as: "The truest earthly friend Israel had in the awful years of rainless desolation." Even though Elijah promptly incurred the wrath of Ahab by his announcement of God's displeasure and a consequent forthcoming drought, his presence assured the continued existence of the nation. Likewise, it proclaimed the fact of God's persistent mercy. Even the appearance of Elijah was striking, for he dressed in a cloak of sheepskin or coarse camel hair, and he permitted his own hair to remain uncut (2 Ki. 1:8).

In response to Ahab's violent resentment, and at the express command of the Lord, Elijah took refuge at the Brook Cherith. God may have desired Elijah's isolation in order that the prophet should not be available for premature entreaties for the halting of the drought. At Cherith, the Lord provided Elijah with bread and meat until, in accordance with Elijah's prophecy, even that brook dried up. In divine fashion, when one channel of divine care ceased, another became available. Thus, from the Brook

Cherith, Elijah proceeded to Zarephath and there he met the widow gathering twigs for firewood. While on the one hand Elijah requested that she use the last of her flour to prepare bread for him, at the same time he extended to her the promise of the unfailing provision of God. This promise of God was validated in the continual multiplication of the oil supply of the widow. Further, when in the passage of time her son fell violently ill and died, Elijah restored the child to life by means of divine miracle-working power.

7. Elijah and the Prophets of Baal (Ch. 18)

At the close of the three years, Elijah emerged from his retreat and once more appeared before Ahab. The latter, seemingly caring more for his royal mules than his human subject, happened to be out hunting for grazing land. Ahab's response upon meeting Elijah was immediately to accuse the prophet of causing the unhappy plight of the nation. Elijah pointed out, however, that it was Ahab's own idolatry that was responsible for their national troubles. To prove his point, Elijah suggested that a contest be arranged. By mutual agreement, the details were quickly arranged so that the encounter took place on Mount Carmel. It resulted in the defeat and death of 450 prophets of Baal (and probably the 400 prophets of the groves of Ashtoreth) and an overwhelmingly great victory on behalf of Jehovah.

The classic challenge of Elijah on this occasion: "How long halt ye between two opinions?" (v. 21) may be correctly rendered: "Why do you limp along?" The spiritual destructiveness of the lack of true commitment and the withholding of dedication is thus emphasized. Elijah's procedures in achieving his victory included the rebuilding of the broken altar of the Lord. There was both actual and symbolic significance in such an act. The prophets of Baal achieved no more success by praying "in blood" than by any other means because, of course, their cause was utterly invalid.

Immediately after the contest was concluded, Elijah advised Ahab to partake of food, and he reported that the promised rain would soon come. By faith, Elijah detected the sound of abundance of rain and he saw the end of the drought. Elijah continued in prayer only until his servant reported a tiny cloud and then the prophet immediately prepared for the homeward journey. This cross country dash was made in what became a torrential rain, and although Ahab rode his chariot, Elijah ran on ahead. The distance was about ten miles. It is noted that in pagan terms, Jehovah not only vindicated His promises at Carmel, but He proved Himself the God of fertility and harvest by faithfully sending the rain.

8. Elijah and the Juniper Tree (Ch. 19)

Elijah's greeting at Jezreel was a threat of death from Jezebel the queen. Wearied and distressed, he could only flee. Although it is proposed that the expression "went for his life" (v. 3) more correctly could be rendered "went for the sake of his soul" this rendering would suggest that he desired to be in a wilderness place so that he could commune with God without disturbance. Nevertheless, the wilderness was to him a place of discouragement. After a day's journey from Beersheba, he was found beneath the juniper tree in a state of abject despondency. There, he requested that he might die. God rejected this request, but instead sent him nourishing food at the hand of an angel. That food, consisting of a cake baked on coals, and a cruse of water, was sufficient to sustain him throughout a forty-day pilgrimmage.

It was while he sought refuge in the cave of Horeb as a somewhat despondent runaway, that Elijah heard God's voice: "What doest thou here, Elijah?" (v. 9). God patiently heard Elijah's sad rehearsal, and then He led him forth upon the mountain. In an impressive threefold manifestation, the Divine presented Himself to Elijah as: the wind, the earthquake, and the fire. Thus, at the cave entrance, high upon the mount, Elijah communed with the still small voice. By this means, God assured Elijah that there were still 7,000 faithful worshippers, and that God's work for the prophet included: 1) to anoint Hazael king of Syria, 2) to anoint Jehu king of Israel, 3) to ordain Elisha his successor in the prophetic ministry.

In proceeding to fulfill his duties, Elijah first ordained Elisha to be his successor. This he did by casting his mantle upon the young man while he plowed in the field at Abel-meholah in the Jordan valley. Elisha promptly left all, and thenceforth he followed Elijah as his ministerial assistant. Elijah's words: "what have I done to thee?" (v. 20) are taken to imply that the call to the prophetic ministry was not a necessary reason for Elisha to lose all personal freedom. Although called and commissioned, he served because he chose to do so, and not out of necessity. Since Elisha had been plowing with twelve yoke of oxen, he evidently came from a prosperous family, but his dedication was such that he was willing for even the most menial tasks in serving God and in his associations with Elijah.

9. Ahab and Ben-hadad of Syria (Ch. 20)

Ben-hadad, the king of Syria, had been increasing in power during this era, and at this time he asserted himself by demanding tribute and submission of Israel. His unreasonable demands eventually goaded Ahab into armed resistance, even though Ahab's forces were greatly outnumbered. God intervened in the battle, and Israel won a decisive victory and Ben-hadad himself was slain. Humanly speaking, the fact that Ben-hadad was an inveterate drunkard no doubt confounded his military strategy, and he placed his men at a great disadvantage requiring them to take the Israelites alive.

A year later, the Syrians had largely recovered their strength, and once again they attacked Israel. Their doctrine that Israel's God fought only in the hills and not on the plain gave them fresh courage. Inasmuch as such an outlook simply invited God to vindicate Himself, the outcome was another crushing defeat for the Syrians as God aided Israel. In the one day of battle 100,000 Syrians fell. On this occasion, Ahab unwisely spared the aggressive king (called Ben-hadad just as his predecessor) in a pattern similar to Saul's sparing of Agag the Amalekite. It is possible that the prophet (v. 13), and the man of God (v. 28) would have been either Elijah himself or his disciple. The fact that a representative of Jehovah had access to Ahab's court is evidence that Elijah's ministry had attained an important measure of success.

Though Ahab may have been motivated by diplomatic reasons in sparing Ben-hadad, his actions were clearly in error. It has been suggested that Ahab preferred not to crush Syria totally, for he visioned Syria as a buffer state to protect him from the rising power of the great Assyria. The procedure of the prophet to attract Ahab's attention and to convey the divine message was indeed unique. The prophet's message was severe, for it actually constituted the pronouncement of the death penalty. In permitting personal injury to himself in order to dramatize the message that he wished to convey, the prophet performed a "mimic" action. Other prophets used similar techniques and they conveyed their message by the clothing that they wore, the names that they gave their children, or by various physical actions.

10. The Tragedy of Naboth's Vineyard (Ch. 21)

Near to the royal residence in Jezreel was a vineyard that was owned by Naboth. Ahab chanced to develop a desire to possess this property, and he requested Naboth to sell it to him. Naboth, however, refused on what actually constituted religious grounds. In his commitment to the religious tranditions of the nation, Naboth saw family inheritances as part of his divine legacy. In his view, property was not a saleable commodity. Thus, Ahab and Jezebel in their attitudes in this matter manifest impious contempt for the prevailing religious traditions. In his personal reactions on this occasion, Ahab became so

emotionally disturbed that he proceeded to pout over the matter in the manner of a spoiled child.

Queen Jezebel, with the consent of her husband, proceeded to take steps to achieve his desires. It would appear that she proclaimed the citizens of Jezreel to be guilty of treason or blasphemy and thus subject to public trial. Since Naboth was a leading citizen of the city, he was required to bear the brunt of the charges. Apparently it was alleged that since the king was the representative of God, that to blaspheme the king was as wicked as to blaspheme God. False witnesses to testify against Naboth were readily arranged, and thereby, even though justice was mocked, the form of just procedures and legality was maintained. As an outcome Naboth was dragged forth and slain by stoning. Jensen comments: "the ease with which the judicial murder was arranged with the leading citizens is an index of how little regard was then being paid to covenant law."[4]

Ahab soon made his way to Jezreel to possess the vineyard, but on the way he found himself confronted by a hostile Elijah. The prophet announced that for this act Ahab would suffer a violent death and his ruling house would be cut off. Jezebel too, would die an ignominious death. Ahab appears to have repented quite genuinely in response to this message, but unfortunately, the repentance was too late to do more than postpone the punishment. The literal fulfillment of Elijah's pronouncement occurred when the body of Joram, Ahab's son, was cast into Naboth's field. However, the threat concerning Jezebel was fulfilled directly upon her.

11. Micaiah and Ahab. Jehoshaphat's Reign
(Ch. 22; 2 Chron. 17-20)

Once more Syria and Israel prepared for war. Because Ahab sought to regain control of the frontier city of Ramoth-gilead, he became the aggressor. In planning the attack, Ahab enlisted the aid of Jehoshaphat of Judah. Since Jehoram, the son of Jehoshaphat, was married to Athaliah, the daughter of Ahab, the two monarchs were united by a family tie. Jehoshaphat promptly agreed to help, and then almost as an afterthought, sought the divine will in the matter. God's spokesman was Micaiah the prophet. Micaiah first made clear that he would declare God's message regardless of the consequences, and then he frankly declared to Ahab and Jehoshaphat that their armies would be defeated and Ahab would be slain. The vain Ahab denounced the prophecy, consigned Micaiah to prison, and marched to war. Jehoshaphat foolishly followed.

---

[4]Joseph Jensen, God's Word to Israel. (Boston: Allyn and Bacon, 1968), p.175.

The outcome of the battle was just as Micaiah had predicted. Although Ahab disguised himself, he was struck by a chance arrow, and that day he died. His leaderless armies dispersed with no further will to resist. Scripture notes that Ahab's blood was washed from his chariot "by the pool of Samaria" (v. 38). A large pool excavated in Samaria is tentatively identified as this very site. With the death of Ahab, his son, Ahaziah, succeeded him to the throne. Jehoshaphat managed to escape from the battle site without physical injury, but in such an association and outcome he lost both his dignity and his exemplary walk with God.

Figure Nine: Sites of events in First and Second Kings

An important event in the lifetime of Ahab was the Battle of Karkar (or Qarqar), although it is not mentioned in Scripture. This battle resulted when a coalition of western nations in a military thrust attempted to halt the growing power of Shalmaneser III of Assyria. Interestingly, Israel joined Syria, her usual avowed enemy, on this occasion. Shalmaneser's inscription (a monolith now in the British Museum) mentions Ahab the Israelite and reports that he provided 2,000 chariots, while Hadadezar (Ben-hadad) provided 1,200. The inscription claims a victory for Shalmaneser against the coalition, but the fact that the supposed victor did not press his advantages makes the victory questionable. Thiele dates the Battle of Karkar at 853 B.C., and notes that it constitutes the earliest definite historically parallel date identifying events both in Assyria and Israel--such dates are called "synchronisms." On the basis of subsequent events in Israel, Thiele concludes that this date also marks the year of the death of Ahab.

The ascension of Jehoshaphat to the throne of Judah is noted in 1 Kings 15:24, and brief reports concerning him continue in the books of Kings until 2 Kings 8:16. More detailed and systematic reports of Jehoshaphat are found in 2 Chronicles. Scripture notes that he reigned 25 years, and in general: "he walked in all the ways of Asa his father; he turned not aside from it, doing that which was right in the eyes of the Lord" (v. 43). However, he did suffer occasional spiritual lapses when he allied with the ungodly. His disastrous league with Ahab is reported in this chapter. His ill-fated coalition of two decades later with Jehoram, Ahab's son, is reported in 2 Kings 3. This latter involved the valley of ditches.

Both Kings and Chronicles mention Jehoshaphat's merchant navy (1 Ki. 22:48, 49; 2 Chron. 20:35-37). He apparently planned to trade with his immediate Eastern neighbors, as well as with those in the Far East. A disaster destroyed the ships in port in Ezion-geber--"the giant's backbone." Kings declares that Jehoshaphat refused to unite with Israel's king Ahaziah in these ventures; but Chronicles says he did form such a partnership. It is assumed that two separate occasions are described, and it is usually concluded that in spite of losses and disputes of partnerships, Jehoshaphat did on occasion operate a merchant navy. Such international trade would explain his general prosperity: "Now Jehoshaphat had riches and honour in abundance" (2 Chron. 18:1).

Jehoshaphat's noteworthy achievements included providing teams of travelling educators to teach the book of the Law to the people (2 Chron. 17:7-9), and the implementation of regional courts in each city with a central court of appeals in Jerusalem (2 Chron. 19:5-11). His miraculous victory over the Southern Coalition (2 Chron. 20:1-30) is not recorded in Kings, but might be associated with the early ministry of Elisha. It was on this occasion that a choir singing praises to Jehovah preceded the army to the field of battle. In the resulting divine intervention, the opposing armies proceeded to destroy one another, perhaps motived in part by internal jealousies, while Judah watched. For three days Jehoshaphat's armies gathered spoil. Jehoshaphat was succeeded on Judah's throne by Joram (or Jehoram), and it is usually concluded that the latter began his rule two years before Jehoshaphat's death (cf. 2 Ki. 8:16).

7. THE BOOK OF
2 KINGS

In the Hebrew canon, First and Second Kings are one book. Today's customary division is the outcome of the Septuagint translation. This division was probably necessary because the Greek version was more lengthy than the original Hebrew, and it was no longer practical to contain the entire portion in a single scroll. On this account, the two books may be expected to conform in: style, type of content, and general theme.

The Nature and Theme of the Book

Second Kings takes up the historical narrative with the account of the reign of Ahaziah of Israel (Ahab's successor), and the continuation of the story of Jehoshaphat of Judah. However, it has already been noted that Jehoshaphat's death had been reported, even though his further exploits are included in the Second Book of Kings. This book proceeds to record history up to the account of the conquest and deportation of Judah, and it ends with an account of the final state of Judah's captive king.

The spiritual significance of the deeds of the kings is especially emphasized throughout the books of First and Second Kings. Thus, there are lengthy portions in this book dealing with the life of the prophet Elisha. As well, the thread of history concerning the Davidic line is carefully set down and preserved. God is depicted as being long-suffering and gracious, but confirmed in His resolve to effect His eternal purpose.

The Authorship of the Book

Evangelical scholars usually agree that both books of Kings have a single author. Thus, if it is established that Jeremiah wrote the first book, it is agreed that he wrote the second. As already noted, however, it is usually concluded that the author was not Jeremiah but someone of similar attitudes and circumstances. Above all, he shared with Jeremiah a burden and concern for the national apostasy.

The Scope of the Book

The Second Book of Kings covers something more than two and one-half centuries of historical time when its personalities are related to accepted secular datings, although datings derived from the addition of lengths of reigns extend the scope by as much as fifty years. Current chronologies tend to reject the previous theory of gaps between rulers, called interregnums, and to see overlappings or co-regencies involving certain kings.

The Key Phrase and Key Verse

The key phrase: "according to the word of the Lord" reveals the divine interest and concern in all the events of the nation. In a similar manner, the expression, "man of God" is used some thirty-six times in the Book. A suggested key verse is found in 10:10 "Know now that there shall fall unto the earth nothing of the word of the Lord, which the Lord spake."

The Value of the Book

Second Kings records the lives of twenty-seven of the kings of Israel and Judah, and in most cases reports the degree and effect of the divine dealings with them. Nearly a dozen of the prophetic books were produced during the scope of this Book, and hence the period it represents is sometimes known as: "the Elizabethan era of Jewish literature." Second Kings constitutes the conclusion of the systematic Biblical account of Jewish national history, and thereafter, until the time of the New Testament, all that is known of this era must be gleaned from references in the prophets and in secular history.

Analysis and Exposition

I. The Close of Elijah's Ministry (Chs. 1:1 - 2:11)

1. The Death of Ahaziah (Ch. 1)

King Ahaziah of Israel, with whose accession the First Book of Kings concludes, is revealed to have been confronted with two serious problems. On the one hand he was faced with the rebellion of the supposed subject nation of Moab, and on the other, he suffered a severe physical injury because of a fall through a palace skylight. Evidently, the Moabites had seen the opportunity to be free from domination by Israel in view of the latter's defeat by Syria and the death of Ahab. In his extremity at this time, Ahaziah sent messengers to secure help from Baalzebub, a Philistine god of medicine.

Under divine direction, Elijah proceeded to intercept Ahaziah's messengers. In the fashion of that day, knowledge of the future was considered the key to its control, and therefore God chose this means in order adequately to impress Ahaziah. Elijah instructed the messengers to return to their master and to report to him that he would not recover from his accident. God chose thus to administer His disciplinary wrath upon Ahaziah because this king had consistently maintained both the calf worship of Jeroboam and the Baal worship of his parents. Although the messengers did not recognize Elijah, from the description that they brought, Ahaziah immediately knew who had spoken.

The king, in apparent hostility and retribution, dispatched three successive military squads in order to capture Elijah. Scripture depicts the prophet's residence at this time as being upon a mountain. In their summons, the first two captains evidenced indifference or contempt for the prophetic office in the person of Elijah, and thus they were destroyed by fire from heaven. When the third captain came in respect and humility, Elijah agreed to go with him into the presence of the king. There, he simply repeated his message, and with Ahaziah's ensuing death, saw it fulfilled. Ahaziah was succeeded by Jehoram (Joram), who was his brother and thus also, a son of Ahab and Jezebel. The total reign of Ahaziah was not more than two years.

2. Elijah and the Chariots of Fire (Ch. 2:1-11)

The man of God prepared for his departure by paying a farewell visit to his disciples, the sons of the prophets, who had been divinely advised of events to come. As the last hour approached, Elijah, accompanied only by Elisha, miraculously divided the Jordan and crossed to the other side. He paused to discuss Elisha's request for a spiritual inheritance, then at the final solemn moment, a fiery chariot descended, and he was swept to heaven in a whirlwind. Elijah had succeeded in restoring the kingdom of God to Israel, and now his eternal reward awaited. Elisha sought the double portion no doubt in the sense of the firstborn (Deut. 21:17), for he saw this as his need if he were to perpetuate Elijah's work. Such a gift was a "hard thing" because it involved the power of God rather than mere human power. As Keil notes: "A dying man cannot leave to his heir more than he has himself."

II. The Ministry of Elisha (Ch. 2:12 - 13:21)

1. The First Miracles of Elisha's Ministry
(2:12-25; 2 Chron. 20:1-30)

Even as Elisha witnessed the translation of his master, he uttered a cry which has been paraphrased: "My father--so much better than all chariots and horses; in thy absence the chariot of Israel and the horsemen thereof are useless." Upon retrieving Elijah's mantle, Elisha proceeded to duplicate the feat of his master in dividing the Jordan. This initial ministry confirmed Elijah's prediction of the transmitted spiritual blessing, and as well, accredited him in the presence of the sons of the prophets. The confident faith of Elisha sharply contrasts with the unbelief of the other disciples of Elijah who insisted upon forming a search party to look for their master in the wilderness. Elisha's second miracle was the purifying of the water supply at what is taken to be Jericho. Elisha's technique of casting in the cruse of salt is considered to have been of symbolic merit only, for the waters were actually purified by divine power.

As Elisha next made his way to Bethel, a group of "little children" mockingly taunted him. On the basis of the trends and culture of that day, it is concluded that Elisha's tormentors were more properly "young men," and that almost surely they were youths who were committed to idolatry. The prophet responded by pronouncing divine wrath upon them, and God vindicated His servant by producing two vicious she-bears that attacked forty-two of the mockers and seriously mauled and injured them. This event is considered a judicial miracle. The youths deserved their fate inasmuch as their actions were in effect an insult against God. Following this incident, Elisha journeyed first to Carmel, and later to his home in Samaria.

2. Joram and the Valley Full of Ditches (Ch. 3)

Upon Joram's (or Jehoram's) ascension to Israel's throne, Mesha of Moab had chosen to repudiate his tribute-paying status that had prevailed under Ahab. Thus, Joram undertook to establish his sovereignty over Moab by force of arms. Joram enlisted the aid of both Judah and Edom, and Jehoshaphat's promise of support was given in the identical words that he had used to pledge himself to Ahab (cf. 1 Kings 22:4; 2 Kings 3:7). For strategic reasons the armies marched in a very difficult round about route, and when expected water supplies were lacking, they were on the point of perishing from thirst. It was in this hour of extremity that they gladly turned to the prophet Elisha for counsel.

Though the prophet scorned the spiritually

unworthy Joram, who had continued calf worship and had tolerated Baal worship, yet for the sake of Jehoshaphat, Elisha instructed the kings to dig ditches throughout the valley. The following morning, God miraculously filled these ditches with water, and in a double stroke, both provided refreshment for the weary armies and their livestock, and at the same time, confused and bewildered the Moabites so that they were easily destroyed. Only by the gruesome strategy of Mesha, Moab's king, wherein he publicly offered his son as a burnt offering, did the Moabites manage on this occasion to maintain their independence. Mesha's act was so revoltingly horrible, that it put a cessation to the warfare.

The events pertaining to the valley full of ditches marked the last recorded exploit of Jehoshaphat. It has already been noted that he died at sixty years of age after twenty-five years of reign (cf. 2 Kings 8:16). During at least part of the reign of Jehoshaphat, he was a co-regent. Thiele suggests that for the first four years of his reign he shared the throne with his father, Asa, and during the last six years he shared with his son, Joram.

3. The Increase of the Widow's Oil (Ch. 4)

According to Josephus, the impoverished woman was the widow of the prophet Obadiah. Her debt had occurred when Obadiah took 100 prophets into his care to preserve them during the persecution under Ahab. If this is true, Elisha's concern for her and her sons is clearly understandable. The "pot of oil" possessed by the woman would be actually a small flask used to contain oil for the anointing of the body. The conditions of the miracle that was accomplished were simply that there must be willingness to receive. As in most instances involving the Lord's provision, the more that was shared, the more there was. This Old Testament incident has much in common with the New Testament story of the multiplying of the loaves and fishes. By this divine work, the widow's needs were met and her sons were spared from slavery.

Elisha's travels next led him to Shunem, and there he was the guest of a prosperous and remarkably hospitable woman. This hostess, by having an annex built on her house, even provided a special room for the prophet. Elisha rewarded her by performing a healing of her barrenness that she might bear a son. In later years, when the child of promise was a growing boy, Elisha ministered to restore him to life after he suffered a sunstroke and died. It is noted that no miracle was wrought by Elisha's staff, but only by the faith and personal intervention of the man of God. God's choice of channels for the exercise of divine power is always people and not physical objects.

Elisha's next recorded miracles were at Gilgal where he first made edible a large pot of poisoned pottage or vegetable stew. It is concluded that the poisoned fruit in the stew would be either cucumbers or colocynths. The meal that he added would not have cured the poison, but would have been simply a symbol of divine intervention. Scripture does not so much stress that Elisha accomplished a miracle in feeding one hundred men with twenty barley loaves and some ears of corn, but rather that he simply predicted that God would make these provisions adequate. It is noted that the bread and corn were brought as an offering of the firstfruits. In the absence of the regular priesthood in the Northern Kingdom, this offering was given to the prophet that he might feed those in need.

4. Naaman the Leper of Syria (Ch. 5)

Even though Naaman was captain of the armed forces of Syria, he was also a victim of leprosy. Apparently he was able to continue in his post only because the Syrians did not quarantine lepers as in Israel. Upon news of the miracle-working ministry of Elisha in Israel, Naaman quickly journeyed southward with generous gifts and a letter from the king of Syria to the king of Israel. The letter, not surprisingly, caused Joram of Israel great consternation, for he took it to be a subtle, but deliberate, military provocation. Undoubtedly, Joram was greatly relieved when Elisha volunteered to concern himself with Naaman's problem. It may be concluded that at this time Israel's capital was at Samaria and Elisha's residence at Gilgal.

The seemingly harsh and indifferent treatment that Elisha bestowed upon Naaman was necessitated by Naaman's state of mind. God's healing touch depended upon humility of heart and obedience of will. It was thus necessary for Naaman to accept his casual treatment at Elisha's hand, and to dip seven times in the insignificant Jordan because the attitudes of heart and mind thus manifested were exactly those that God sought. Naaman's triumph stands in stark contrast with the spiritual and practical failure of Gehazi. Because he obeyed God, Naaman was delivered from leprosy; because he disobeyed God, Gehazi became its victim. Gehazi not only was guilty of greed, but also he misused the prophet's name and misrepresented his word. The healing of Naaman has many parallels in the conversion of the unbeliever. Naaman almost stumbled over the very simplicity of his message of deliverance, and his problem was not in learning more, but in being willing to put aside that which he felt he already knew.

5. The Siege of Samaria (Ch. 6)

The recovery of the lost axe is one of the

most interesting miracles of Scripture. On behalf of the concerned young man, Elisha was able to cause the iron to float and thus it could be recovered and the task of building continued. It may be assumed that the particular campus being enlarged at this time was located at Jericho. The poverty of the student worker is evident in the fact that he was unable to buy his own axe. It is possible that "borrowed" could be rendered "begged" or more appealingly "donated by request." This miracle of the floating iron appears to show that God is willing and able to relieve earthly needs even by miraculous power.

Elisha's next exploit was his encounter with the Syrians. These invaders were seeking to subdue Israel by means of surprise attacks, but Elisha's prophetic powers enabled him constantly to inform King Joram of their strategy. When the Syrians sought to capture Elisha at Dothan, the prophet caused the army to be blinded, and he then led them peaceably to Israel's stronghold of Samaria, a city some four hours distant. It was on this occasion that Elisha's servant became greatly alarmed at the sight of the attackers, but when granted spiritual insight he saw a great company of chariots and horses of fire round about. Elisha's sword was the Word of God, his armament was the Most High, and therefore he had nothing to fear from the armies of men.

The events of the latter part of the chapter represent a lapse of time from those of the earlier section. Once again Syria attacked Israel, and this time laid siege to Samaria. A severe famine within the city resulted, and the people took to eating vile and unclean food and even began cannibalism. Whether or not "dove's dung" (v. 25) is to be taken literally, or to be counted a figurative expression signifying the most miserable kind of food, remains a disputed matter. Joram appeared in a mourning garment, but his heart was impenitent and critical, and he became unreasonably hostile toward Elisha and threatened to destroy the prophet. Elisha remained somewhat calm in the situation because he was aware that divine Providence would care for him.

6. The Retreat of the Syrians (Ch. 7)

At the very height of the famine, Elisha insisted that relief would come, and he predicted that by the next day flour would sell for the equivalent of five dollars a hundredweight, and barley for half that. Though the king's advisor scoffed at Elisha, the prophet saw his prediction wholly fulfilled, including the death of the scornful advisor. This dramatic change in Samaria's lot was the outcome of a miracle accomplished by God through an aural delusion. The Syrians had evidently imagined that they heard the tramp of an approaching army of Egyptians or Hittites, and they thus fled in confusion.

Even their horses and asses had been left behind. The discovery of the flight of the Syrians was by four leper-outcasts, and their conclusion: "This day is a day of good tidings and we hold our peace" (v. 9) is often used as a text with a gospel application. Joram's scouts investigated warily, and upon their report the starving Samaritans swarmed upon the spoil.

7. Elisha Visits Damascus. Jehoram of Judah dies. (Ch. 8; 2 Chron. 21:1-22:6)

Scripture reports the difficulties of the Shunammite woman as she sought to recover her land after a seven-year sojourn in Philistia during a time of famine. She had gone to Philistia at the direction of Elisha, and now it was his servant in the court of Joram of Israel who assured her that her land would be restored. Not only was she to be given title to her land once more, but also all of the harvests that it had produced during her absence were to be returned to her. Following this incident, Elisha was directed by God to Damascus that there he might fulfill Elijah's commission that had been given by the still small voice at Horeb (1 Kings 19:15). When confronted there by Hazael, the messenger of ailing king Ben-hadad, Elisha was moved to weep in prophetic insight at all of the atrocities that this man was yet to do in Israel. Elisha also prophesied that king Ben-hadad would soon die, and that Hazael would succeed him. The prophecy was expedited when Hazael, shortly after his return to the palace, murdered king Ben-hadad and proceeded to assume the throne of Syria.

In Judah, in the meantime, king Jehoram (Joram) died, after reigning a total of eight years. Jehoram's relatively brief reign in Judah was full of sins and calamities, and he is remembered as a king who sanctioned Baal worship and virtually discredited and discontinued the worship of Jehovah. Jehoram was largely led by his wife, Athaliah, a daughter of Ahab of Israel. Among Judah's misfortunes during Jehoram's rule were: 1) the rebellion of the Edomites, 2) the rebellion of Libnah, 3) the invasion of Jerusalem by the Philistines and Arabians and the consequent kidnapping of members of the royal family. A possible understanding of events involving Edom (vv. 20-22) is that Jehoram's forces at Zair were surrounded, but by night they broke through the enemy lines and returned home thus escaping utter destruction. One of the lesser crimes of Jehoram was the murder of six younger brothers and the execution without due cause of a number of princes and nobles (2 Chron. 21:4).

Ahaziah, the son of Jehoram and Athaliah, began to reign at age twenty-two, and he reigned not more than two years. He too is remembered as a

This mound, identified as the remains of Dothan, is located sixty miles north of Jerusalem. It was to this place that God sent horses and chariots of fire to protect Elisha against the armies of Syria. The name means "two wells."

wicked ruler, and Scripture reports that his mother, Athaliah: "was his counsellor to do wickedly" 2 Chron. 22:3). One of the few noteworthy acts of Ahaziah was his association with Joram of Israel in a war against Syria. Except that Israel managed to recover the city of Ramoth-gilead, the war was otherwise fruitless. Ahaziah's enthusiasm for idolatry led him to remove valuables from the temple of Jehovah and install them in the temple of Baal. This chapter prepares for events to come by concluding with an account of a visit of Ahaziah of Judah to Joram of Israel. This latter ruler had been injured in battle, and he was residing in the royal palace at Jezreel while he convalesced.

8. Jehu Slays Joram, Ahaziah, and Jezebel
(Ch. 9; 2 Chron. 22:6-9)

At the command of Elisha, one of the young prophets proceeded to Ramoth-gilead and there

anointed Jehu to be king of Israel. Jehu at first made light of his anointing, but when he reported it to his fellow army officers, their pent-up hostility against King Joram asserted itself. They proceeded to acclaim Jehu king by hastily carpeting the steps with their clothes as a touch of royal luxury and then sounding the royal trumpet. For his fellow army officers to proclaim Jehu king amounted to treasonable rebellion. Thus, Jehu sealed the city gates and proceeded as speedily as possible to Jezreel, some thirty-five miles away. He drove furiously because it was crucially essential that he arrive at the city before any other word of the rebellion. Only by this means could he be assured that Joram would not have taken counter measures.

At Jezreel, Jehu promptly gave vicious battle to the invalided Joram and readily slew him. Jehu threw Joram's body on the site of Naboth's vineyard, at the very place where fifteen years before, Jehu had witnessed Ahab arranging the murder of Naboth (vs. 25). Jehu next proceeded to inflict a fatal wound upon Ahaziah of Judah, the visiting guest. Ahaziah fled by way of Megiddo, and there he died. When Jezebel, the dowager queen, sought by her cosmetics and regal display to overawe and subdue the conquering invader, she too fell victim to his stroke of judgment. The death of Joram and his family marked the end of the fourth dynasty of Israel. Joram had reigned twelve years.

9. The Reign of Jehu (Ch. 10)

Jehu swept into power as a reformer, and he promptly set about to exterminate completely the house of Ahab. After craftily requiring the local authorities to profess their loyalty to him rather than to the sons of Ahab, he required these leaders to destroy seventy of the young princes of the line of Ahab. Jehu also slew forty-two, apparently innocent, princes of the royal house of Judah who merely happened to be passing by. These men were apparently unaware of the rebellion that had taken place in Israel, and they made the mistake of being friends of Jehu's late enemies. Other victims of Jehu's reforms were Samaritan members of the family of Ahab, and these Jehu slew in the presence of Jehonadab the Rechabite, a man of piety whom Jehu particularly desired to impress.

Jehu's next strategy led him publicly to declare himself favorable to the worship of Baal. By edict, he provided for the gathering of all Baal worshippers in their temple, and for a time he officiated at their worship. However, at the chosen moment, he withdrew and eighty fierce soldiers at his command fell upon the worshippers and destroyed them utterly. Jehu proceeded to pillage and destroy the temple of Baal so as to make it thenceforth a refuse ground for the city. Inasmuch as the supporters of Ahab were worshippers of Baal, there was a political motive in Jehu's reforms, but regardless of motive, they served so completely to rid Israel of Baal worship that never again was it a notable force.

In the year 1845, the Black Obelisk of Shalmaneser III was found at Nimrud (Calah) on the Tigris River. The Obelisk has been dated at approximately 842 B.C. Its inscription includes a report of the subjection of Israel by Assyria, and it mentions that Israel was required to pay tribute. The Obelisk pictures Jehu kneeling before Shalmaneser, and it records Shalmaneser's report: "silver, gold, a golden bowl, a golden vase, golden goblets, pitchers of gold, lead, staves for the hand of the king, javelins, I received from him." The Obelisk is of particular interest because it presents the earliest pictures of Israelitish people known to history.

God had His commendation for Jehu, and declared that he had "done well" (v. 30) in purging Israel of the dynasty of Ahab and the accompanying Baal worship. Hence, He promised that Jehu's children of the fourth generation would sit upon the throne of Israel. Nevertheless, God noted that Jehu "departed not from the sins of Jeroboam, which made Israel to sin." God, therefore, permitted chastisement to come upon Jehu in the form of plundering raids by Hazael of Syria. When Jehu died, after twenty-eight years of rule, he was succeeded by his son, Jehoahaz. Jehu's dynasty was the most powerful and longest-lived of all of Israel's dynasties, and extending more than a century, it included five individual monarchs.

10. The Rule of Athaliah, Joash the Boy King (Ch. 11; 2 Chron. 22:10-23:21)

The untimely death of king Ahaziah of Judah while still in his twenties, meant that he left only small children as his successors to the throne. It was obvious that in this situation some sort of regency would be necessary. Thus, recognizing this fact, and choosing to take advantage of it, Athaliah, the queen mother, proceeded to usurp the throne. To secure her position, she committed the reprehensible act of murdering all the known royal princes. She thereby became the only usurping monarch in all of Judah's history. Athaliah's general conduct matched her actions on behalf of the throne, and she is remembered as one who expended her energies to encourage the worship of Baal and Ashtoroth.

Divine providence was undoubtedly involved in the successful concealment of the little prince Joash (Jehoash) from the villainous Athaliah. For six years, the child dwelt in the temple residence under the protection of the priest, Jehoiada. When the seven years of Athaliah's usurping rule was completed, Jehoiada, with the help of the officers of the army, launched a coup d'etat to place Joash on the throne and depose Athaliah. Jehoiada employed both the priests and the Levites, and also the palace guard, in a well-engineered scheme that escaped suspicion. He arranged both for a watch upon the palace and Athaliah's activities, and full protection for the little prince, Joash. Though this was a rebellion, except for the slaying of Athaliah, it was bloodless.

In the early years of young king Joash (Jehoash), Jehoiada the priest served as regent, and he proceeded to lead the people in a splendid religious revival. The reign of Joash was pledged to be upon the "testimony" (i.e. the Scriptures), and it was upon this basis that the revival was implemented and directed. The organization of the temple workers was renewed, and worship in the Levitical pattern was once more established. At this time, there was further suppression of Baal worship, and an effort was launched to erradicate this false religion totally. It is possible that the plagues of locusts described by the prophet Joel occurred during this era of Israel's history.

11. The Temple Restored (Ch. 12; 2 Chron. 24)

A commendable project in the reign of Joash was the restoration of the temple. Joram, Ahaziah, and Athaliah had all actively opposed the worship of Jehovah, and for a seventeen-year period the temple had been allowed to fall into decay. Its foundations were crumbling, its treasures and instruments plundered and lost, and its ceremonies either ignored or conducted by unclean and unworthy people. Joash's project of restoring the temple had a poor beginning, and it was only when he suspended the regular priestly expenditures and devoted all of the income to the building fund that success began to result. Jehoiada, the priest, assisted Joash by preparing a chest with a hole in the lid to receive offerings beside the altar. This plan had the desired effect, and the people were moved to give enough to repair the temple and to secure the vessels and furniture for it as well.

In the later years of Joash, after the death of Jehoiada, listlessness and indifference, and even idolatry, again arose. As an outcome, God permitted Joash to be defeated at the hand of Syria. To satisfy the victors, Joash gave over to them all of the temple treasures and valuables that he had formerly so enthusiastically collected. His acts earned for him the scorn of his people and even their open hatred. When Zechariah, the son of his great benefactor, Jehoiada, dared to reprove Joash's apostasy, the king proceeded to approve his stoning. This incident stands as one of the tragedies of the Bible, and it is explicitly mentioned in the New Testament (Matt. 23:25). Joash, while still incapacitated by wounds suffered in combat with the Syrians, was ignominiously slain by his own servants, and Amaziah his son succeeded him. He had ruled in Judah for forty years.

12. The Reigns of Jehoahaz and Joash of Israel. Elisha's Death (Ch. 13)

The scene once more shifts to the nation of Israel and reports the beginning of the rule of Jehoahaz following the death of Jehu. In the early years of his rule, Jehoahaz permitted idolatry to flourish, and thus he became the subject of God's anger. As His scourge, God used the rulers of Syria: Hazael, and later Ben-hadad III, since this nation was Israel's longtime enemy. It is to the credit of Jehoahaz

that he repented under oppression, though unfortunately, he did not succeed in leading his subjects in a similar repentance.

The changed attitude on the part of Jehoahaz resulted in divine intervention and deliverance from the Syrians. Ancient inscriptions declare that at this time, Assyria under Adad-nirai III came up against Hazael of Syria. While the Assyrians did not entirely crush the power of Syria, they sufficiently weakened the nation of Syria that its forces found it necessary to withdraw from Israel. It is to be noted, however, that in later history, Syria continued to make temporary disastrous inroads upon Israel.

When Jehoahaz died after some seventeen years of rule in Israel, he was succeeded by his son, Joash (Jehoash). It was in the reign of this ruler that the prophet Elisha suffered illness that proved fatal. During this illness, Elisha provided for Joash to strike the ground, or shoot arrows into it, in a symbolic gesture to determine the number of future victories over Syria. It is assumed that the ritual depicted the discharge of an arrow into someone else's territory and thereby achieving conquest and victory. The king was, unfortunately, without enthusiasm and demonstrated faith in the incident, and only three victories over Syria were portrayed by his actions. Commentators note that Christians are frequently as careless in appropriating Scriptural promises in prayer.

For the most part, Scripture presents a favorable picture of the material aspects of the reign of Joash of Israel. Though he did not depart from the sins of Jeroboam, he did much to make Israel once more a strong power. During his reign, he established Samaria as an independent and respected state. It is noted that in conflict with Judah, he achieved victory to the point of breaking down a portion of the walls and plundering the city of Jerusalem. Rawlinson describes Joash of Israel as a superior monarch, and Josephus, also, gives a favorable report of this ruler. There is a possibility that the destructive siege of Samaria previously described (2 Kings 6:24-7:20), actually took place in the reign of Joash rather than in that of Jehoram. At least some scholars consider that the exploits of Elisha are arranged topically rather than chronologically, and they therefore assign the siege to this period.

Elisha must have been upwards of ninety years of age at the time that he died, and for sixty years he had been Israel's leading citizen. However, there is no specific Scriptural record of the final forty-five years of his life. Even after his death, Elisha's bones were responsible for the resuscitation of a corpse which chanced to come into contact with them. This miracle was a reminder and confirmation of the promise that by divine power, Israel should three times defeat Syria. Elisha stands as a choice Old Testament servant of God, and his memory is fragrant with good works and miracles wrought for the glory of God. Twenty-four separate miracles are recognized during his lifetime, a total that exceeds the record of any other Bible character apart from Jesus Christ.

III. The Decline and Fall of Israel (13:22-17:41)

1. The Threefold Victory Over Syria (13:22-25)

When Hazael, king of Syria, died, he was succeeded by his son, Ben-hadad III. Joash of Israel took advantage of the fact of a new monarch, and he proceeded to attack the Syrian strongholds in Israel. He was thereby able to recapture Israelitish towns on the west bank of the Jordan, and there were three victories just as Elisha had prophesied.

2. Amaziah of Judah and Jeroboam II of Israel (Ch. 14; 2 Chron. 25)

Amaziah, son of Joash of Judah, began as an aggressive ruler who gave promise of restoring strength and prestige to Judah. He speedily punished the murderers of his father, Joash, and he led his nation in a memorable victory against the Edomites in a battle beside the Dead Sea. In his later years, Amaziah became excessively self-confident, and by provoking a needless war with Israel at Beth-shemesh, suffered defeat, capture, the spoiling of the temple, and the destruction of the defences of Jerusalem. Amaziah reigned twenty-nine years, and he is considered only moderately good, for he lacked the out-and-out zeal of a true reformer. He died in Lachish at the hands of conspirators, and he was succeeded by his son, Azariah (Uzziah).

Jehoash of Israel died after having humiliated Amaziah, and he was succeeded by his son, Jeroboam II. This man proved to be an able and aggressive ruler, but not a religious reformer. He retained image worship, and in the sight of God his moral life was evil. Nevertheless, Jeroboam II was a capable political leader so that he strengthened Israel's borders and led the nation to be once more a world power. Pfeiffer refers to the reign of Jeroboam II as "a kind of Indian summer in Israel's history." Archaeological findings identified with this era reveal many evidences of prosperity and even class

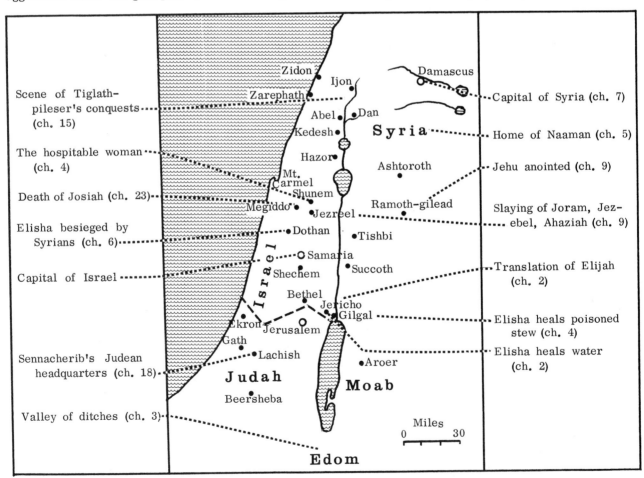

Figure Ten: Further sites and events in Second Kings

distinctions among the people, with a prosperous middle and upper class. The prophets Amos and Hosea may be assigned to the time of this rule. Jeroboam II, after a forty-one year rule, was succeeded by his son Zachariah.

It should be noted that the grievous spiritual and social problems in the time of Jeroboam were, to a large measure, the outgrowth of the growing class distinctions. The fashion of the day was an overall personal selfishness that encouraged a consciousness of class status and fostered the conspicuous social and material promotion of a few. Though the nation thrived and prospered overall, it was at the expense of the common people. The oppression and exploitation of the poor was particularly the burden of the ministry of the prophet Amos.

3. Judah's Temporary Prosperity. Jotham's Rule. Anarchy in Israel (Ch. 15; 2 Chron. 26, 27)

The unfortunate toleration of idolatry in Judah continued during the reign of Azariah. Nevertheless, because he achieved the greatest measure of material prosperity since the time of Solomon, he is remembered as one of Judah's better kings. Azariah strengthened Jerusalem, built fortresses, encouraged agriculture, and put the army on a fighting basis. The rebuilding of the port of Elath (Eziongeber) is specifically reported in the preceding chapter (14:22). He proceeded totally to suppress the land of Edom as a hostile neighbor. His irrigation projects included the digging of wells in order to provide water for agriculture, for vine growing, and for extended grazing lands for cattle.

In the latter part of his fifty-two year reign, Azariah apparently sought to copy the heathen pattern that provided that the civil ruler was also the high priest. Because he thus transgressed upon the priesthood, God afflicted him with leprosy. His illness made necessary the establishment of a regency under his son, Jotham, and this arrangement seems to have continued for perhaps as much as ten years. Interestingly, the ruins of a small palace-style structure adjacent to the government buildings and dated at the time of Azariah, have been proposed as a possible quarantine palace for the leprous king. Upon his death, Azariah the leper-king was buried in Jerusalem in the burial field of the kings, but not in the royal family tomb. His death was noted by Isaiah as the occasion when the prophet was granted a special divine vision (Isa. 6:1). Ahaziah was succeeded by his son, Jotham, and there was no marked change in the policies of government.

In the meantime, Israel was experiencing a series of six sovereigns who reigned for brief periods, and only one of which lived out his natural life.

Older chronologies set forth a more expanded period of time that called for gaps between some of the kings of this era (called interregnums), but Thiele's approach is to shorten the total period and to resolve difficulties by recognizing co-regencies. In several instances he distinguishes between the time when a ruler first began to rule and the time when he became the sole ruler. In the case of Zachariah, the son of Jeroboam II, the reign extended only six months. This ruler chose to perpetuate calf worship in Israel, and God, therefore, bestowed His stroke of judgment. His death marked the end of the dynasty that had been founded by Jehu. The murderer of Zachariah, Shallum, reigned just one month, and then he, likewise, was murdered. In his one-month rule, Shallum represented a new dynasty. His murderer was Menahem who was the only one of this series of sovereigns not violently slain.

Menahem began his ten-year rule with a ruthless attack upon the rebellious city of Tiphsah on Israel's Euphrates' frontier. However, this seems to have been his one and only victory. He soon fell under the domination of Pul (Tiglath-pileser III), one of the greatest of Assyria's conquering monarchs. Tiglath-pileser imposed a heavy tribute, and Menahem was forced to levy a property tax of fifty shekels upon all those who could pay. The annals of Tiglath-pileser tell of payment of tribute by Menahem, including: "silver, colored woolen garments, and linen garments."[1] Pekahiah, the son of Menahem, reigned after his father's death, but he was a mere puppet and he was murdered by Pekah after a reign of two years. With Pekahiah's death, the seventh dynasty was terminated.

The Assyrians were an ancient Old Testament nation, believed to be identified with Asshur in Genesis 10:11. Their land was rough and infertile, and consequently the people were hunters, herdsmen, and warriors. According to archaeological findings, they first came to grips with Israel in the time of Ahab, but apparently they did not make any serious inroads at that time. The Assyrian Empire is usually thought of as beginning about 1120 B.C., and enjoying revived power after 800. It was this latter revival that especially made itself felt upon Israel.

Although the Assyrians had apparently already stripped Palestine of her wealth, they again invaded in the time of Pekah. The target of their attacks was Gilead and the region about Galilee in the land of

---

[1]Thiele persuasively argues that the tribute payment was in 743 B.C. cf. Edwin R. Thiele, The Mysterious Numbers of the Hebrew Kings (Grand Rapids: Wm. B. Eerdmans Publishing Co., 1965), pp. 94-115.

Naphtali. Not only did they annex his territory, but they carried its people into captivity into Assyria. This event marked the beginning of Israel's Assyrian captivity. It is possible that this invasion was at the request of Judah whom Pekah had attacked (see 16:5-8).

The received text assigns twenty years to the rule of Pekah (v. 27), but an eight-year reign would more readily harmonize with the chronologies. Thiele, and others, suggest that Pekah first set up a rival dynasty in Gilead, and that for twelve years he reigned there while Menahem and Pekahiah were the recognized kings of Israel. Thus, although Pekah personally saw himself as king for twenty years, his actual rule in Israel was only eight. His rule ended when he perished by the sword, just as he had disposed of Pekahiah. Scripture notes that throughout his lifetime he had persisted in the idolatrous ways of his predecessors. Pekah's murderer, and his successor to the throne, was Hoshea the son of Elah. The annals of Tiglath-pileser tell of public hostility to the king, and the succession of Pekah by Hoshea. However, Assyria takes credit for the outcome: "they overthrew their king, Pekah, and I placed Hoshea as king over them." With Pekah's death, the eighth dynasty came to an end.

Scripture notes that Jotham was twenty-five when he began to reign over Judah, and that he reigned sixteen years. He is depicted as a good king who "did that which was right in the sight of the Lord." Nevertheless, just as his predecessors, he permitted the neighborhood high places and he thereby weakened the basic impact of Biblical Judaism. He built a temple gate (probably the north or upper gate where all sacrifices were slaughtered), a wall or tower, cities in the mountains of Judah, and other castles and towers. In a battle against the Ammonites, Jotham won a decisive victory, and he thereby became the recipient of massive payments of tribute. Scripture reports: "Jotham became mighty, because he prepared [or established] his ways before the Lord his God" (2 Chron. 27:6). Upon his death, he was succeeded in Judah by Ahaz his son.

4. Ahaz and Tiglath-pileser (Ch. 16; 2 Chron. 28)

Ahaz, son of Jotham, was a youth of twenty when he came to the throne of Judah. He largely repudiated the worship of Jehovah and chose instead the way of idolatry. Scripture reports that he: "made also molten images for Baalim . . . and burnt his children in the fire, after the abominations of the heathen" (2 Chron. 28:2, 3). Before long, Ahaz found himself engaged in a war against both Pekah of Israel and Rezin of Syria. It has been suggested that at least part of Pekah's objectives was to force Judah to ally with Israel and Syria against Assyria. In response, Ahaz sought Assyria's aid against his attackers, and he even pillaged the temple and sent its treasures as a bribe to the Assyrians. Scripture reports: "Tilgath-pilneser king of Assyria came unto him, and distressed him, but strengthened him not" (2 Chron. 28:20). Thus Ahaz' efforts really came to naught, and in his day "the Lord brought Judah low because of Ahaz king of Israel; for he made Judah naked" (2 Chron. 28:19).

In spite of the foregoing, it is to be noted that Ahaz was responsible for launching Assyria against Damascus and thereby assuring the overthrow of his Syrian foes. It was while Ahaz was in Damascus in a meeting with Tiglath-pileser that he saw an altar that he determined to copy. Under his direction, an altar of this pattern was built to replace Solomon's altar in the temple. Ahaz also removed the twelve brazen oxen from beneath the laver, and he either used them for decorative statuary elsewhere or he melted them to reclaim their metal. In all of his diverse exploits, Ahaz appears as a confused and deluded man who denied himself the divine help he might have had. Most tragically, he chose to ignore the wise counsel spoken to him by Isaiah: "If ye will not believe, surely ye shall not be established" (Isa. 7:9). After a sixteen-year reign, Ahaz died, and he was succeeded in Judah by Hezekiah his son.

5. The Downfall of Samaria (Ch. 17)

In Israel, in the meantime, Hoshea was devoting his energies to securing himself upon the throne. Once firmly established, he took advantage of a change of rulers in Assyria to withhold payment of the required tribute. Concurrently, he negotiated a treaty with king So of Egypt, in order that he might be assured a military ally. The prophet Hosea advised against such a rash rebellion (Hos. 12:1), but Hoshea paid no heed. The new Assyrian king, Shalmaneser V, responded to the challenge by launching a siege upon Samaria that eventually extended for three years.

The date of the fall of Samaria was formerly given as 721 B.C., but 722 B.C. is now considered a better authenticated date, and some scholars place it as early as 723 B.C. At this time, the Northern Kingdom of Israel, or the ten tribes, as an independent state, came to an end. Hoshea was deposed and imprisoned, and there is no further record of him. He represented the ninth dynasty of the kings of Israel. From the time of Jeroboam I to the downfall under Hoshea had been approximately two centuries. Not one of Israel's rulers throughout this period had been genuinely spiritual in outlook, and the warnings of God's prophets remained unheeded (cf. v. 13). The people of Israel were carried into captivity (v. 6),

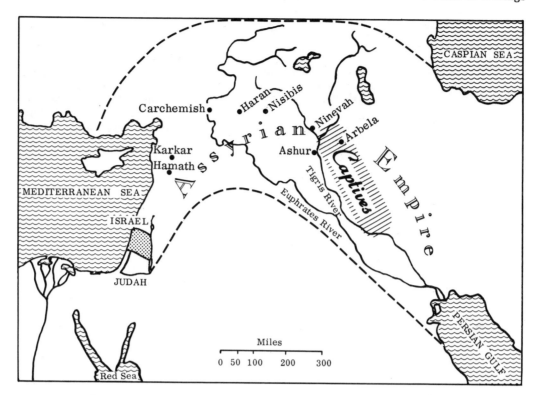

Figure Eleven:
Scene of the captivity of the ten tribes (Israel) or Samaria.

and Scripture pointedly enumerates the causes that were responsible (vv. 7-23). Primarily, Israel as a nation was guilty of idolatry and open disobedience to the commandments of Jehovah.

Contemporary evidence indicates that shortly after Shalmaneser conquered Samaria he was succeeded on the throne of Assyria by his brother, Sargon II. In later inscriptions, Sargon proceed to claim to himself the credit for having conquered Samaria. Several scholars suggest that it is possible that Sargon was a commander or other military official under Shalmaneser at the time that the city fell. Thus he felt justified in claiming the victory as his own. Scripture does not specify which king was ruling when Samaria was conquered, and therefore the only source of data is secular records. According to Sargon, 27,290 Israelites were deported, a governor was placed over the land to receive tribute, and among the spoils of war obtained by the Assyrians were fifty chariots.

To discourage sedition and prevent further resistance of the conquered people, the Assyrians deported the ten tribes into what is now Persia and Kurdistan. In turn, the land of Israel was settled by other conquered peoples. The Assyrians allowed an Israelite priest to return to Bethel to teach Judaism, but the outcome was a spiritually invalid syncretism. Thus "they feared the Lord, and served their own gods" (v. 33). The intermarriage of these immigrants with the remaining Israelites produced the nation known as the Samaritans. To this day, a remnant survives in Palestine in the towns of Nablus (Shechem) and Haik. They scrupulously observe Old Testament ceremonies, although from the time of Ezra they have been officially hostile to the Jews. There was never any systematic return of the members of the ten tribes, although representatives came back with Jeshua and Zerubbabel.

IV. The Decline and Fall of Judah (Ch. 18-25)

1. Hezekiah Reigns King of Judah. Sennacherib Invades (Ch. 18; 2 Chron. 29:1 - 32:16)

Hezekiah, son of Ahaz, assumed the throne of Judah at age twenty-five. At the very outset he implemented sweeping spiritual reforms, purging the land of heathen idols, and cleansing and rededicating the temple to the worship of Jehovah. He decreed a Great Passover festival to which he invited even the Israelites. He assigned priests in divisions, reinstituted tithes, and built and filled royal granaries and treasuries. Scripture reports Hezekiah's revival most favorably: "The priests and Levites arose . . . and their prayer came up to his holy dwelling place, even unto heaven" (2 Chron. 30:27); "So there was great joy in Jerusalem: for since the time of Solomon . . . there was not the like in Jerusalem" (2 Chron. 30:26). Two possibilities are suggested to account for the Israelites at Hezekiah's Great Passover: 1. The event took place in the closing years of Hoshea's reign and in the face of impending destruction many people defied Hoshea's restrictions to make the pilgrimage or 2. The event took place after the deportation, but involved the remnant who had been left behind.

It is proposed that Hezekiah's commendable godliness was especially to the credit of his mother, Abi, who is specifically named in Scripture. His reforms found a ready response in the people, and they resulted in a remarkable sense of unity and great joy. His concern was to relate Jehovah to the needs of his day, and when the venerated brazen serpent of Moses' day hindered in this regard, he did not hesitate to destroy it (v. 4). Scripture notes that the temple was so cluttered with debris at this time that it took a corps of priests and Levites a full week to clear it. The Valley of the Kidron was used as a dumping ground. Hezekiah gave evidence of his assurance of divine blessing and help by proceeding to repudiate his annual tribute payment to Assyria. Not surprisingly, his action was followed by an effort by Sennacherib to collect by force of arms.

Sennacherib was the son of Sargon II, and he became ruler of Assyria upon the death of his father. He attacked Judah only after having first subdued the Egyptians. The date of Sennacherib's attack is disputed by scholars because of difficulties in dating the beginning of Hezekiah's rule. Systems now used, including Thiele's, require rather drastic textual emendations. However, the chronology notwithstanding, it is clear that Sennacherib conquered and pillaged freely in Judah, and that he levied a burdensome tribute upon Hezekiah. Even though Hezekiah dutifully turned over the temple treasures to pay the imposed tribute, Sennacherib proceeded to besiege Jerusalem and generally remained overbearing and demanding. Sennacherib's commander-in-chief, Rab-shakeh (a title, not a name), sought by shouted speeches to intimidate the defenders of Jerusalem's walls. Such strategy failed because Hezekiah's soldiers were stoutly loyal.

Excavation at Lachish (v. 14) has indeed confirmed that this city at that time bore the brunt of Sennacherib's invasion. Back in Ninevah, Sennacherib prepared a stone relief showing his capture of the city and the complete conquest of its defenders. Lachish at that time was a large city, some eighteen acres in extent. The remains include evidences of a large palace with extensive royal granaries associated with it. A great burial tomb at Lachish contains the bones of at least 1,500 people, but they are a mass conglomerate suggesting that the remains of decomposed bodies were gathered and thrown into a common pit.

The incidental reference to the Syrian or Aramaic language (v. 26) is of considerable interest to scholars. It is noted that Hezekiah's ambassadors were able to speak Aramaic, but they did not consider that it would be understood by the common people. By the time of Christ, Aramaic was the everyday language, and Hebrew was reserved for special religious ceremonies. During this era, including the dark days of the Jerusalem siege, the prophet Isaiah ministered, and he served Hezekiah as spiritual advisor and counsellor. It is likely that Micah, too, was in Jerusalem in these days, and that he wrote his book during the siege of the city.

2. The Fate of Sennacherib's Army (Ch. 19; 2 Chron. 32:17-23; cf. Isa. 37)

The siege of Jerusalem by Sennacherib virtually developed into a holy war for Judah because of the Assyrians' defiance of Jehovah. When Sennacherib sent a threatening letter to Hezekiah, the king referred the situation to God by taking the letter to the temple and spreading it out before the Lord. Thereupon, Isaiah promised divine intervention and deliverance for Judah. That night, God sent a death angel throughout the camp of Assyria, and by morning 185,000 Assyrian soldiers were dead. The "angel of the Lord" is identified in exactly the same manner as the death angel upon the Egyptians in the time of the plagues. Sennacherib left Palestine in great haste, for verse 36 literally reads: "he decamped, departed and returned." Elsewhere, Scripture says of Sennacherib: "So he returned with shame of face to his own land" (2 Chron. 32:21).

Sennacherib lived for some time after his defeat in Judah, but Scripture makes plain that he attempted no more attacks upon the Jews. God's final stroke of judgment upon Sennacherib came later when his own sons murdered him. The Assyrian god, Nisroch, in whose temple Sennacherib was worshipping at the time of his murder, was the Assyrian eagle-deity that is frequently depicted on Assyrian monuments. Sennacherib's ignominious death following his disastrous defeat seems doubly to discredit the pagan deity to whom he ascribed religious homage.

An account of Sennacherib's conquests in Judah is set forth in the Prism of Sennacherib. This splendidly preserved cylinder of baked clay is written upon its six sides in cuneiform script. The cylinder reports only Sennacherib's victories, and wholly passes over his defeats. It mentions that the people whom he conquered agreed to submit to servitude and the payment of tribute. Egyptian sources make mention of Sennacherib's defeat in the conflict with Judah, but assign credit for the victory to Egypt. It is reported that the Egyptian god sent field mice into the camp of the Assyrians to eat their bowstrings and hence prevent their giving battle.

3. The Illness and Later Death of Hezekiah (Ch. 20; 2 Chron. 32:24-33; cf. Isa. 38)

Some scholars have concluded that Hezekiah's illness was not a later event, but actually an incident during Sennacherib's siege of Jerusalem. This view is based somewhat plausibly upon verse 6: "I will deliver thee and this city out of the hand of the king of Assyria." In this incident, Hezekiah's illness is depicted somewhat as God's scourge to cause the king once more to establish adequate prayer contact with God. By means of the illness, and through the ministry of the prophet Isaiah, God conveyed the necessary lesson. Through the instrumentality of Isaiah, and in a test of obedience involving a lump of figs, God effected a healing in the body of Hezekiah. As evidence of the reality of the healing, God caused the sundial to move backward ten degrees. The exact implications of this incident are debated by scholars, but the overall outcome is clear enough. Among some, the reversal of Hezekiah's sundial is linked in the earth chronology with the long day of Joshua. It is interesting to note that although Scripture does not record Hezekiah's prayer to God on this occasion, it does record God's response: "I have heard thy prayer, I have seen thy tears; behold I will heal thee" (v. 5).

Although King Hezekiah had successfully met the spiritual and military challenge of the fierce hostility of the Assyrians, his response to the warm approval of the Babylonians can only be described as a failure. Apparently, the Babylonians had been particularly impressed by the miracle of the sundial, and thus they made their journey to Judah. Scripture notes: "Howbeit in the business of the ambassadors of the princes of Babylon, who sent unto him to inquire of the wonder that was done in the land, God left him, to try him, that he might know all that was in his heart" (2 Chron. 32:31). Hezekiah unwisely showed off his treasures to these visitors, and thus, God, through Isaiah, responded with a rebuke. The king learned that in some future day God would punish such vanity by permitting the nation of the visitors to carry away the very treasures that he had so proudly displayed.

One factor in Hezekiah's failure may have related to the origin of his treasures. In the invasion by Sennacherib, Hezekiah had been forced to surrender all of the national wealth; that which he displayed to the Babylonians was newly acquired. Therefore, Hezekiah probably took personal credit for all that he displayed. In the overall, God was tolerant of this failure in Hezekiah, and Scripture testifies of this man: "He trusted in the Lord God of Israel; so that after him was none like unto him among all the kings of Judah, nor any that were before him. For he clave to the Lord, and departed not from following him" (2 Ki. 18:5, 6).

An outstanding engineering project achieved during Hezekiah's time was a conduit cut through solid rock to bring water to Jerusalem. It led from the Virgin's Fountain or Gihon Spring to the city reservoir known as the Pool of Siloam. The passage is 1,750 feet (about one-third of a mile) long, and was first explored in 1838. In 1880, the ancient script still visible on the walls was noted and analyzed, and insight gained from the study is still useful today in identifying Hebrew writing styles. The tunnel shows a good deal of engineering skill, for workers began from either end but quite accurately met in the middle. It may be assumed that the water tunnel was built by Hezekiah in preparation for the expected siege by Sennacherib.

4. The Reigns of Manasseh and Amon (Ch. 21; 2 Chron. 33)

Manasseh, son of Hezekiah, born three years after his father's great illness, proved to be a particularly wicked king throughout most of his long reign. He went to extremes in restoring the degraded system of heathen worship and in desecrating what was sacred to Jehovah. His most serious offence was the setting up of an image, presumably of Ashtoreth, in the temple of Jehovah. Scripture notes that Manasseh led the people in more wickedness than that of the Canaanites whom Jehovah had destroyed before them (cf. v. 11). Under Manasseh, the nation fast ripened to judgment, and thus the prophets were moved to tell of impending divine destruction: "I will wipe Jerusalem as a man wipeth a dish, wiping it, and turning it upside down" (v. 13).

The latter-day repentance of Manasseh is one of the ironies of Scripture. "In affliction, he besought the Lord his God, and humbled himself greatly before the God of his fathers, and prayed unto him: and he was intreated of him, and heard his supplication, and brought him again to Jerusalem . . . Then Manasseh knew that the Lord he was God" (2 Chron. 33:12, 13). Although the repentance provided that Manasseh was released from his personal captivity in Assyria, the change was too late to recover the nation. Even though he would have wished to have blotted out his past evil deeds, he could neither restore the innocent lives he had taken nor could he halt the practices of idolatry that he had launched. Second Kings chooses not even to mention Manasseh's repentance, evidently because it had no national consequences. According to tradition, one of Manasseh's victims was the prophet Isaiah who was sawn asunder with a wooden saw. That God would accept the person of Manasseh upon his repentance is a striking evidence of divine mercy and grace.

The fifty-five year reign of Manasseh (during part of which he may have been co-regent with his father) exceeded that of all other kings of Judah in duration. When he eventually died, he was succeeded by his son, Amon, who reigned for just two years. Amon was as evil as his father had been, and he was murdered by his own servants. The people of Judah proceeded to mete out justice to Amon's murderers, and then they placed his son, Josiah, upon the throne. At the time of his ascension, Josiah was a lad of eight years.

5. Josiah and the Book of the Law (Ch. 22; 2 Chron. 34:1, 2, 8-33)

Josiah was an unusually righteous king in Judah and he did all that he could to restore the true worship of Jehovah and reestablish obedience to the Law. He once again instituted a fund for the restoration of the temple, and commissioned work-

ers for the task. In the process of this work, the book of the Law was rediscovered and Shaphan the scribe read it before the king. Josiah's reaction, upon being thus informed anew of God's requirements for the people, was personal penitence together with a sincere search for the will and plan of God on behalf of the nation. Although Josiah's life had been based upon Biblical principles, it would appear that not until this discovery did he actually possess a copy of the Law. In his spiritual quest at this time he was greatly aided by Hilkiah the high priest and Huldah the prophetess. God was highly pleased by Josiah's penitence, but He nevertheless revealed that His wrath was determined upon Jerusalem and the people because of their prolonged total apostasy under Manasseh and Amon.

Ruins excavated at Megiddo. This level is associated with the time of Josiah, although the structures, which were either a temple or similar public building, may have been originally built in an earlier period. At one time this site was identified with Solomon's stables, but this identification has since been rejected.

6. Josiah Eradicates Idolatry. Jehoahaz and Jehoiakim (Ch. 23; 2 Chron. 34:3-7, 35:1-36:5)

Continuing his program of penitence and reform, Josiah called a great national assembly and there, before all the people and their leaders, he read aloud the book of the Law. He then led the people in solemn outward profession agreeing to obey what had been read. Scripture reports: "All the people stood to the covenant," but it may be inferred from the preceding chapter that their participation was external more than truly of the heart. Josiah's next campaign was that of destroying all that pertained to idolatrous worship. He recalled or deposed false priests, he destroyed groves given to idolatry, and he defiled, appropriated to the state, or ruthlessly destroyed these sites and facilities. It is inferred that part of his program of reform involved recalling to Jerusalem and the temple those wayside priests of Jehovah who were tending toward idolatrous customs in encouraging a concept of local shrines and community deities. Those who were clearly priests of Baal he slew outright (v. 20).

Josiah extended his reforms beyond his own borders, and at Bethel he destroyed Jeroboam's schismatic altar and its accompanying high place. Even the cemetery which was a memorial to the religion of Jeroboam suffered his stroke of destruction, although he spared the grave of Judah's prophet who had foretold this very destruction (1 Ki. 13:1-4). It is somewhat surprising that Josiah should assume this measure of domination in Samaria, but apparently he regarded himself as sovereign there, at least in religious matters, since the kingdom of the ten tribes was now dissolved. It is probable that he acted only with Assyrian approval. Returning to his own land, he reestablished the observance of the Passover, and he once more enforced Scriptural injunctions against necromancers and those with familiar spirits. It is assumed that the prophet Jeremiah had a part in Josiah's reforms, for this great man of God exercised his ministry at this time, but Scripture passes over Jeremiah's role in this regard.

Of all the kings of Judah, only Josiah and Hezekiah are identified as "good" without qualification. Nevertheless, at this late date in national history, even the reforms of Josiah did not avert the divine schedule for destruction upon a nation that had ripened to judgment. Josiah's rule was terminated after thirty-one years when he was slain in a battle against the Egyptians at Megiddo. The nature of events is disputed by scholars, but there seems reason to infer that Pharaoh Necho actually was travelling north to give his support to the king of Assyria against Babylonia. Thus, the amended rendering: "Pharaoh Necho king of Egypt went up to the side of the king of Assyria . . ." (2 Ki. 23:29). Apparently Josiah achieved his goal but forfeited his life, for by hindering the ally, Egypt, he assured the downfall of oppressive Assyria. At least one school of historians notes that in the Battle of Harran (Haran) in 608 B.C., the Assyrians, deprived of the full measure of help that they had expected from the Egyptians, were finally crushed by the Babylonians.

At the death of Josiah, Jehoahaz his son succeeded to the throne, but he ruled only ninety days. He was an evil king of whom Ezekiel wrote (Ezk. 19:1-9), and under the figure of a young lion described as a violent tyrant. Jehoahaz' rule ended when Pharaoh Necho of Egypt carried him into bondage in chains and put the land under tribute. Thus Necho assumed control of Palestine in spite of the interest and wishes of rising Babylonia. Necho proceeded to place Jehoiakim (formerly Eliakim) upon Judah's throne, and at the same time exacted a renewed tribute that Jehoiakim could pay only by imposing heavy taxes upon the people. Though he was only a puppet ruler under the domination of Egypt, Jehoiakim proved to be fundamentally evil and committed to cancelling the spiritual gains that had been made under Josiah. It was under Jehoiakim that the prophet Jeremiah suffered his first imprisonment.

7. The First and Second Babylonian Invasions (Ch. 24; 2 Chron. 36:8-14)

During this era of Judah's history, the domination of Palestine passed from that of the Assyrian-Egyptian alliance to that of Babylon. Jeremiah speaks of the Battle of Carchemish and declares that Pharaoh Necho of Egypt was there defeated by Nebuchadnezzar of Babylon (who apparently at this time commanded Babylon's army and was not yet king) in the fourth year of Jehoiakim's reign (Jer. 46:2). Historians date the Battle of Carchemish in 605 or 604 B.C., and consider it the occasion when Necho lost to Babylon all his colonial possessions. At the outset, the power of Babylon over its territories was restricted, and even Jehoiakim made bold to rebel after three years of submission. Although divine providence dictated events, it is proposed that in the natural the harassing attacks upon Jehoiakim by the Chaldees, Syrians, Moabites, and Ammonites were all directly or indirectly contrived by Nebuchadnezzar who used these subject peoples as his instruments against Israel. The Babylonian king withheld his personal intervention because he was too occupied attempting to secure his own throne.

Jehoiakim was responsible for much evil, and Scripture reports: "He filled Jerusalem with innocent blood; which the Lord would not pardon." (v. 4). Many of the details of his reign are recorded by Jeremiah, including God's scorn upon Jehoiakim's person whereby: "He shall be buried with the burial of an ass, drawn and cast forth beyond the gates of Jerusalem" (Jer. 22:19). An important chronological synchronism is noted: ". . . in the fourth year of Jehoiakim the son of Josiah king of Judah, that was the first year of Nebuchadnezzar king of Babylon" (Jer. 25:1). It appears that Nebuchadnezzar took possession of Palestine at that time, and in fact temporarily put Jehoiakim in chains, but later proceeded to permit his continued rule as already noted. Jeremiah reports that in Jehoiakim's fifth year "they proclaimed a fast to all the people in Jerusalem" (Jer. 36:9). It is concluded that the fast was not evidence of true penitence in Jehoiachin, but simply a technique that he invoked as a possible method of casting off the Babylonian domination. It was shortly after the fast that Jehoiakim contempuously burned the scroll of Jeremiah's prophecies. Scripture describes the spiritually hardened monarch cutting out and burning each section of the book as it was read to him.

The details of the death of Jehoiakim after eleven years of reign are not recorded, but undoubtedly Jeremiah's prophecy of his burial was fulfilled. It has been suggested that perhaps his own subjects slew him and threw his body out of the city in order to conciliate some of the marauding bands (cf. v. 2). His son, Jehoiachin (also known as Jeconiah or Coniah), a youth of 18, succeeded him. Since the royal city was by now greatly weakened by so much warfare, Nebuchad-

nezzar promptly intervened, and after only three months' rule Jehoiachin was forced to yield himself to Babylon. This event is dated in 597 B.C. He, the best of his people, and most of the remaining treasures were deported to the lands of his conquerors. More details concerning Jehoiachin's fate in captivity follow in the next chapter. The 10,000 deportees on this occasion included the nation's leaders, its strong men and those apt for war, and its craftsmen and smiths. The prophet Ezekiel also was among the captives.

The prophecy of Jeremiah sets forth God's appraisal of the nation during the reign of Jehoiachin and the reason for the second Babylonian invasion: "They have forsaken the covenant of the Lord their God, and worshipped other gods, and served them" (Jer. 22:9). God's judgment upon Jehoiachin personally is also recorded: "Thus saith the Lord, Write ye this man childless, a man that shall not prosper in his days: for no man of his seed shall prosper, sitting upon the throne of David, and ruling any more in Judah" (Jer. 22:30). God's pronouncement whereby Jehoiachin was to be counted childless constituted the break in the royal line that disqualified all future direct posterity from assuming the throne. Jesus Christ was exempt from this curse because He was the legal, but not the natural son of Joseph.

Nebuchadnezzar placed Zedekiah (or Mattaniah) upon the throne of Judah, and life in the land

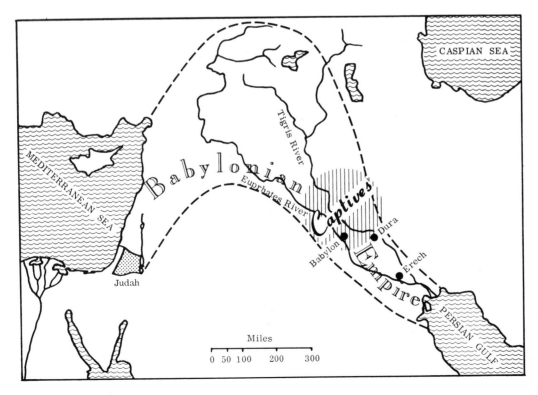

Figure Twelve: Scene of the captivity of the Southern Kingdom (Judah).

returned to some degree of normalcy. Zedekiah was a son of Josiah and was therefore the paternal uncle of Jehoiachin, although Chronicles describes him as "brother." Scripture depicts Zedekiah as one that "did that which was evil in the sight of the Lord." Jeremiah portrays him as a man weak in character and dominated by his associates in the Kingdom (cf. Jer. 38:5, 24). Zedekiah's rebellion against Nebuchadnezzar in the latter years of his reign was in the divine providence that the final judgment against the nation might come to pass. In the natural course of strategy it was a most unwarranted and foolish action.

8. The Downfall of the Kingdom of Judah (Ch. 25; 2 Chron. 36:15-23)

Although the prophet Jeremiah warned of the folly of counting upon Egyptian aid, it would appear that Zedekiah's rebellion was based upon such a hope. However, Nebuchadnezzar surprised the plotters by his speedy attack upon Palestine, and Egypt appears to have abandoned the project. For eighteen months Zedekiah endured a siege upon Jerusalem, but at this time lack of food precipitated his flight and the flight of his armies. Some of the horrors of the siege of Jerusalem are commemorated in the book of Lamentations (cf. Lam. 2:20). Zedekiah was captured, his sons were slain as he watched, his eyes were put out, and he was carried to Babylon in chains. The Babylonians proceeded in their ruthless destruction of the city of Jerusalem, including destroying the 400-year old temple, the walls of the city, the public buildings, and even private homes. All but the poorest class of the people were carried into captivity in Babylon, while some sixty men who were the principal officers of the temple and city and leaders of the population were executed. These events are dated at 586 B.C.

During the siege of the city, Jeremiah remained in Jerusalem and sought to advise the people in godliness and prudent strategy. He came into popular disfavor because he predicted the uselessness of the alliance with Egypt, and the certain victory of Babylon. When his counsel went unheeded and he became subject to opposition and actual persecution, he sought to leave the doomed city. His action was interpreted as treacherous and thus he was taken into custody and imprisoned. He remained in prison until Nebuchadnezzar captured the city and freed him. Later, Jeremiah was forcibly deported into Egypt by his own people. Tradition says that in Egypt Jeremiah was stoned because he persistently denounced the idolatry and ungodliness of the exiled Jews.

At the time of the destruction of Jerusalem, Nebuchadnezzar also destroyed other cities of Judah (cf. Jer. 34:6, 7). One method of destruction used by the Babylonians was to roast the limestone walls by building huge bonfires against them. The heat caused the stones to crumble into powdered lime, while the countryside was stripped of trees to provide fuel. Great heaps of lime have been found on sites of ruined cities. No ruins of Jerusalem are definitely assigned to the time of Nebuchadnezzar, but history notes that the destruction was so complete that two centuries were required for the city's recovery. It is interesting to note that in contrast, in Babylon, Nebuchadnezzar was a great builder and to him is credited the second wonder of the ancient world--the hanging gardens of Babylon. This artificial mountain of terraced gardens was built for the pleasure of Nebuchadnezzar's Queen Amhuia.

To provide for the administration of the Jews remaining in the land, Nebuchadnezzar appointed Gedaliah, a better class Jew, as governor. Gedaliah had been a friend of Jeremiah, and he once had saved the prophet's life (Jer. 26:24). This deputy ruled wisely for a brief two months, and then he was murdered by Ishmael, a survivor of the royal line who perhaps himself had ambition to rule. Gedaliah's loyal general, Johanan, had warned him of Ishmael's intentions, but because Gedaliah himself was above intrigue and disloyalty, he did not take Johanan's warnings seriously. Following the murder of Gedaliah, Ishmael took refuge in Ammon (Jer. 51:4-15), while Johanan, in spite of advice to the contrary by Jeremiah, led a party of migrants into Egypt.

The book of second Kings closes with the account of the latter day elevation of the blinded Jehoiachin in his Babylonian captivity. After thirty-seven years of his imprisonment, Evil-merodach came to the throne of Babylonia and at the very outset of his rule he chose to favor his Judean prisoner. As befitting a king, Jehoiachin was given appropriate garments and an income, and he was made a member of Evil-merodach's court along with other similarly deposed kings. While such a gesture may have been primarily for the purpose of increasing the status of the king of Babylonia, it no doubt was a comforting sign to the people of Judah who were still in their land of bondage. Actually, God favored Jehoiachin, and it was through him that the Messianic line was transmitted (cf. Mt. 1:11, 12). At least the pious among the people would have known that God had promised restoration at the end of seventy years, and in the interim, whatever confirmed their national identity contributed to this hope. Even as they languished in captivity they continued to add to their sacred writings, and an anonymous poet wrote: "By the rivers of Babylon, there we sat down, yea we wept, when we remembered Zion" (Psa. 137:1).

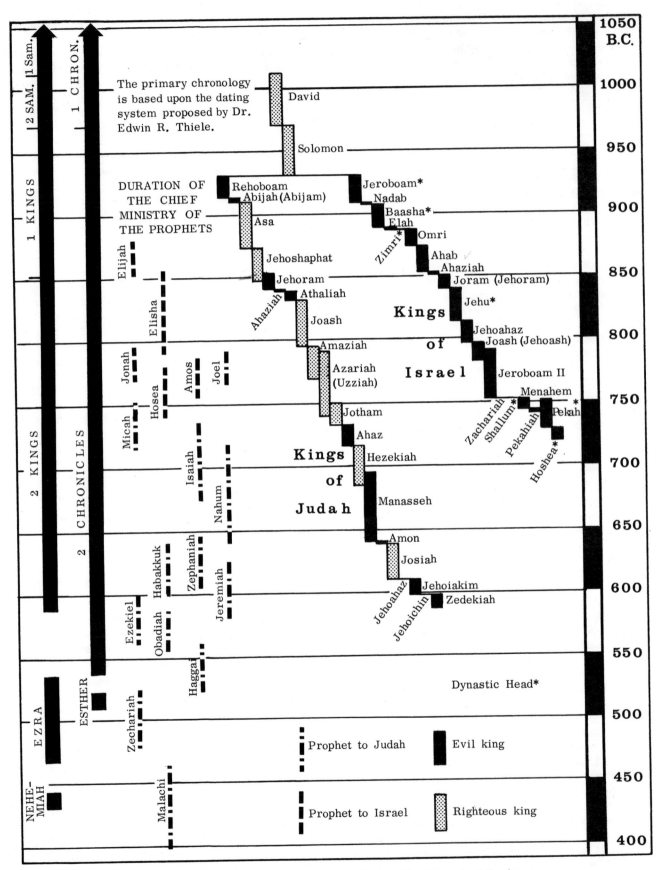

Figure Thirteen: Comparative Chronology of the Historical Books

8. THE BOOKS OF CHRONICLES

For the most part, the books of Chronicles do not contain new material. Rather, these books review, and to some degree repeat and apply, the historical data of the books of Samuel and Kings and the opening section of the book of Ezra. One authority has counted twenty-seven narratives in Chronicles not found in the other historical books, but most of these events are of limited significance. Inasmuch as the student has already considered the facts of Chronicles while he has studied the other historical books, a separate study chapter-by-chapter is not necessary.

The Background and Name of Chronicles

In the Hebrew canon the two books of Chronicles were preserved as a single book until 1517. The Hebrew title up to that time is variously rendered: "Annals of the Times" or "Events of the Times" or "The Words [Events] of the Days." The Hebrew canon associated Chronicles with Ezra-Nehemiah (one book in the canon) and Daniel. These three books stand last in the Hebrew Kethubhim or Sacred Writings. The Septuagint version proceeded to divide the books of Chronicles, and it gave them a name translated "Things Omitted" or "Things Left Untold" (Gk. Paraleipomena). Our familiar title derives from Jerome's Latin Vulgate, for his name for the books was "Chronicon."

The Authorship of the Books

As they stand in our Bibles, the books of Chronicles are anonymous. However, it is thought by many, including traditional Jewish scholars, that these books were compiled by Ezra the scribe except for those portions that concern his death. The book of Ezra directly continues the narrative of Chronicles, and the books of Ezra and Chronicles are related in the following manner: 1) Both books employ occasional Chaldaisms, 2) Both mention the Persian coin known as the dram (1 Chron. 29:7; Ezra 3:4), 3) Both books use the same formula in quoting the Law: "according to the law of Moses" (cf. 1 Chron. 23:31; Ezra 3:4), 4) The point of view of both is priestly, 5) The literary style is notably similar.

According to 2 Chronicles 36:9-23, the writer lived in Babylon which was the home of Ezra in his early years. The author obviously was scholarly, as Ezra would have been, for the frequent reference to authorities is a mark of a well-trained and careful historian. The fact that the books of Chronicles trace the descendents of David to the sixth generation after Zerrubbabel (1 Chron. 3:19), indicates their composition during the latter era of the Restoration Period, at a time contemporary with Ezra.

The Nature and Theme of the Books

The books of Chronicles are historical accounts of the course of events in the national lives of the chosen people from the death of Saul to the end of the exile under Nebuchadnezzar. The particular nature of the books of Chronicles, as distinct from Kings, may be set forth comparatively:

KINGS	CHRONICLES
Written after beginning of the captivity	Written after restoration from the captivity
Compiled by a prophet	Compiled by a priest
Emphasis: earthly	Emphasis: heavenly
Both Israel and Judah considered	Judah main theme; Israel incidental
Political and kingly	Ecclesiastical & priestly
Closes with beginning of bondage	Closes with beginning of restoration

The books of Chronicles mention a large number of source books from which their material is compiled, or in which additional information may be found. These include: the book of Nathan the prophet (1 Chron. 29:29), the book of Gad the seer (1 Chron. 29:29), the prophecy of Ahijah the Shilonite (2 Chron. 9:29), the book of Shemaiah the prophet (2 Chron. 12:15), the commentary of the prophet Iddo (2 Chron. 13:22), the commentary on the book of Kings (2 Chron. 24:27), the book of Samuel the seer (1 Chron. 29:29), and the words of Jehu the son of Hananai (2 Chron. 20:34). These original works, of course, have long ago been lost to scholars.

In their historical presentation, the books of Chronicles deal almost exclusively with the kingdom of Judah. The writer seems to assume that his readers are already familiar with the story of Israel, and he purposes to give further data in tracing the ruling house of the promised line. It is interesting to note that quotations from the books of Kings are without credit or acknowledgment, seemingly on grounds that for those who would read these books, no such credit would be necessary. The books of Chronicles are written particularly from the standpoint of the priests of Judah; they report priestly genealogies carefully and completely, and include many incidents and events especially of interest to the priests. On the other hand, the prophets Elijah and Elisha are almost unmentioned in Chronicles, for their lives were not particularly germane to the objectives of the books.

Since the books of Chronicles were completed at the time that Judah was being restored to the land, they particularly sought to report factual information necessary to the restored people. Family genealogies in general now mattered, and certainly the genealogy of the king and the background of the priestly line which was very prominent in the leadership of the people deserved accurate reporting. Land allotments were determined according to family connections, and it was critically important for each man to know the location and boundaries of his own family grant. In the spirit of tracing genealogies, it is interesting to note that the books of Chronicles begin with the person of Adam.

The Scope of the Books

Apart from the genealogical reports which extend as far back as Adam, these books cover nearly 500 years of the history of Judah.

Key Thoughts and Verses

A right understanding of Chronicles reveals that it is a history of the chosen people written from a spiritual and heavenly standpoint. The concern of the writer is to magnify God and to give Him the place He merits among His people. Key verses include: "Both riches and honor come of thee, and thou reignest over all; and in thine hand is power and might" (1 Chron. 29:12), or "Believe in the Lord your God, so shall ye be established; believe his prophets, so shall ye prosper" (2 Chron. 20:20). Hence, these verses

set forth the truth that God is sovereign, and that blessing and value in life are found through obedient service and devotion to Him.

The Value of the Books

As already noted, the books of Chronicles provide only a few historical facts not found elsewhere. Nevertheless, these books constitute a valuable unveiling of the divine words and thoughts which underlie the known historical facts. Chronicles provide a detailed listing of the courses and divisions of the priests and Levites, and the books report the procedure in the establishment of public worship in the reigns of David, Solomon, Hezekiah, and Josiah. To the returning exiles, this detailed report of natural lineage and spiritual relationships would have been a most valuable document.

In some instances the expansion of the Chronicles' version of events to be found in other historical books contains variations that are perplexing to Bible scholars. Barrows has a helpful statement in this connection:

That there are some discrepancies between the books of Samuel and Kings and the books of Chronicles, is generally admitted. These relate, however, mainly to dates, and do not affect the general integrity of the works. But most of the disagreements between the earlier and later histories are only apparent, arising from their brevity, and from the fact that their authors frequently elect from the same reign different events, the one passing by in silence what the other records; or that, where they record the same events, various accompanying circumstances are omitted.[1]

The Years of Bondage

The ten tribes (Israel) as a unit remained in Assyria the land of their captivity, and thus they lost their national existence. However, it is likely that remnants of each of the tribes were preserved through some of their members who attached themselves to Judah in the successive restorations. Also, there were already representatives of the ten tribes among the people of Judah due to the migration of the pious in the time of Jeroboam I. (cf. 2 Chron. 11:16,17). In the light of these facts, it would seem right to consider the people known today as "Jews" as representatives of all of the tribes of Israel. The terms

---

[1]E. P. Barrows, Companion to the Bible (New York: American Tract Society, n.d.), p. 256.

"Israelite" and "Jew" used in this broad sense are thereby interchangeable.

In Babylonia, the captives were not rigorously treated, but were in general considered as colonists. Some of them rose to positions of influence and power. (e.g. Daniel was the third ruler of the Kingdom, and Nehemiah held a position of trust and honor as the king's cupbearer). Notwithstanding, the Jews continued to long to return to their own land, and they rightly interpreted their captivity as God's school of discipline because of their past rebellion. They believed that when the stroke of discipline was fulfilled they could expect to return to their homeland.

In the book of Ezekiel there is reference to the deportation that is associated with Nebuchadnezzar during the reign of Jehoiachin (597 or 596 B.C.). The prophet had been included in the company of those who were deported, although he was permitted to continue his prophetic ministry even in captivity. It is thus that Ezekiel speaks of being by the River Chebar as he received his prophetic vision (cf. Ezk. 1:1). Chebar is apparently a small stream that flows into the Euphrates near Babylon.

The seventy years of the captivity of Judah was also the period of Babylonia's rulership of the world. Babylon fell on the occasion recorded in Daniel 5. The conquest of Babylon was achieved by Darius who was the commander of the army of Cyrus of Media. It is suspected that Darius' success was due to the drunkenness of the guards as they participated in Belshazzar's feast. Archaeological evidence confirms the fact that Babylon was captured virtually without a fight. The population seems to have welcomed the conquerors, apparently preferring the benevolent Cyrus to the despotic Nabonidus.

The fall of Babylon marked the end of the captivity of the Jews, for Cyrus favored them and aided them to return to their own land. While by no means all returned, there were many who did, and thus there were periodic migrations from the lands of captivity to Palestine. Those who remained in the adopted lands were known as the "Dispersion."

The Values of the Captivity

In the sovereign ways and providences of God, even an experience as tragic and bitter as the captivity, had its values:

1. The Jews were almost wholly cured of idolatry. Whatever their faults and failures in later

history, at least they have never nationally returned to idolatry. In general, their Babylonian experience taught them to abhor the worship of idols.

2. The unique circumstances involved in being separated from their land and temple occasioned among the Jews the rise of a new order who became the scribes. While these scholars in a later era confused their mission and came beneath the condemnation of our Lord, in an earlier day they rendered the nation a valuable service. At the outset, the scribes sought to guard and preserve the Scriptures. They produced the Mishna (certain laws which had been received orally from God [purportedly] and never recorded), and the Gemara (a commentary on the Mishna and a compilation of accepted traditions). These two volumes were later combined to form the Talmud.

3. Assembly centers or synagogues were instituted to permit the conducting of Jewish worship and schools even while far from the homeland. The synagogues, which for centuries have been a vital factor in Jewish national spirit, likely would never have developed apart from the unusual circumstances of the Babylonian captivity.

4. The people found time and occasion to occupy themselves with literature. They arduously studied the Old Testament Scriptures and compiled appropriate commentaries as well as some significant secular writings.

5. In a manner reminiscent of the days in Egypt, common isolation and hardship brought common sympathy and a closer relationship between the individuals of the nation. They emerged from captivity both unified and purified. Those who refused to be taught by the captivity simply did not return, and hence such individuals passed from the scene of Biblical history.

A Brief Analysis of the Books of Chronicles

As a means of comparing the books of First and Second Chronicles with the other historical books and with one another, the following brief analysis is proposed:

FIRST CHRONICLES

1. Genealogies and Backgrounds of David
    a. The Patriarchs from Adam to Esau. Descendants of Esau (Ch. 1)

First Chronicles (continued)

> b. The Tribe of Judah until David. David's descendants (Ch. 2:1 to 4:23)

2. The Tribes of Simeon, Reuben and Gad until the Captivity (Ch. 4:24 to 5:26)
3. The Levites (Ch. 6)
4. The Remaining Tribes (Chs. 7, 8)
5. The Inhabitants of Jerusalem (Ch. 9)
6. The Defeat and Death of Saul (Ch. 10)
7. David and His Mighty Men (Chs. 11, 12)
8. David's Victories and Festivals (Chs. 13-16)
9. David Builds the Temple (Chs. 17-22)
10. David's Religious and Civil Officers. His Levites, Priests, Singers, Porters, Treasurers, and His Army and Its Officers (Chs. 23 to 27)
11. David's Last Words. His Death (Chs. 28, 29)

SECOND CHRONICLES

1. Solomon's Prayer and God's Answer (1:1-13)
2. Solomon's Later Power and Wealth (1:14-17)
3. Solomon Builds and Dedicates the Temple (Chs. 2 to 7)
4. The Exploits and Death of Solomon (Chs. 8, 9)
5. The Story of Rehoboam (Chs. 10 to 12)
6. King Abijah and King Asa (Chs. 13 to 16)
7. King Jehoshaphat (Chs. 17 to 20)
8. King Jehoram (Ch. 21)
9. King Ahaziah (Ch. 22)
10. King Joash (Chs. 23, 24)
11. King Amaziah (Ch. 25)
12. King Uzziah (Ch. 26)
13. King Jotham and King Ahaz (Chs. 27, 28)
14. King Hezekiah (Chs. 29 to 32)
15. King Manasseh and King Amon (Ch. 33)
16. King Josiah (Chs. 34, 35)
17. King Jehoahaz (36:1-4)
18. King Jehoiakim (36:5-8)
19. King Jehoiachin (36:9, 10)
20. King Zedekiah (36:11-21)
21. The Return Proclaimed (36:22, 23)

CONTENTS PECULIAR TO CHRONICLES

Among events and details not found elsewhere in the Bible and therefore peculiar to the books of Chronicles are the following:

The names of David's mighty men (1 Chron. 12)
David's preparation for the building of the temple (1 Chron. 22)
The orders, courses, and divisions of the priests and Levites (1 Chron. 23, 26)
The ranks and orders of David's army (1 Chron. 27)
David's address to the national leaders and the offering for the temple (1 Chron. 28, 29)
Rehoboam's fortresses. The migration of priests and Levites from Israel (2 Chron. 11)
Abijah's defeat of Jeroboam I (2 Chron. 13)
Asa's fortification of his kingdom. The defeat of Zerab and the host of Ethiopia (2 Chron. 14)
Asa's suppression of idolatry aided by the ministry of the prophet Azariah (2 Chron. 15)
Hanani's reproof of Asa for his reliance upon Syria instead of upon the Lord (2 Chron. 16)
Jehoshaphat's establishment of military bases in the cities of Judah and Ephraim, his removal of high places and groves, the project of sending forth princes and Levites to teach the people the book of the Law (2 Chron. 17)
Jehoshaphat's rebuke by Jehu for his alliance with the ungodly kings of Israel (2 Chron. 19)
Jehoshaphat's use of a choir to defeat the vast forces of Moab and Ammon (2 Chron. 20)
Jehoram's idolatry and punishment (2 Chron. 21)
Joash' apostasy. The murder of Zechariah, the righteous son of Jehoiada (2 Chron. 24)
Amaziah's preparations for war, his idolatry (2 Chron. 25)
Uzziah's victory over the Philistines and Arabians, his military strength (2 Chron. 26)
Jotham's victory over Ammon (2 Chron. 27)
Hezekiah's reformation, his observance of the Passover, his riches (2 Chron. 29 to 31)
Manasseh's captivity, repentance, and restoration (2 Chron. 33)

9. THE BOOK OF EZRA

The book of Ezra continues the narrative left off by Chronicles and develops the story of the restoration of the nation of Judah to the land of Canaan. The book derives its name from the fact that it records the biography of Ezra in chapters seven to ten. Contemporary with events and personalities described by Ezra were such individuals as: Nehemiah, Esther, Haggai, Zechariah, and Malachi. The book embodies a number of characteristics in common with Chronicles including: a great respect for the Law of God, an interest in temple ritual, an attention to musical groups among the Levites, and the careful enumeration of names of participants in various religious events.

In the Hebrew canon, until the year 1448, the books of Ezra and Nehemiah were counted as one, although their separate names were maintained. The Septuagint recognized the books as separate, and because it included the apocryphal book of Ezra, it designated our canonical book as Second Ezra. Somewhat confusingly, it was for a time the custom in the early Church to recognize our book as First Ezra, and to call what we now call Nehemiah, Second Ezra. However, it appears always to have been the custom in the Church to have separated Ezra from Nehemiah.

The Nature and Theme of the Book

Ezra is a sort of diary or journal report of two restorations of the captive Jews to their own land. Chapters 1 to 6 describe the return under Zerubbabel and Jeshua, chapters 7 to 10 describe the return under Ezra himself. There is a gap of about fifty-eight years between the two sections. Keil writes: "The object and plan of its author must have been to collect only such facts and documents as might show the manner in which the Lord God . . . fulfilled His promise . . . by the deliverance of His people from Babylon, the building of the temple at Jerusalem, and the restoration of the temple worship."[1] The bulk of Ezra is written in Hebrew,

---

[1] C. F. Keil, The Books of Ezra, Nehemiah, and Esther (Edinburgh: T. & T. Clark, 1873), p. 4.

but those portions from 4:8 to 6:18 and 7:12-26 were originally written in Aramaic.

The Authorship of the Book

It is evident that the book was either written or compiled by Ezra himself. The events of the first six chapters, of course, precede Ezra by almost sixty years; hence he would have merely compiled them from existing documents (hence the Aramaic). In chapter 7, as he begins the narrative of his own exploits, he depicts Artaxerxes as addressing him directly (7:14), and in chapter 8 he writes in the first person (8:15). Chapter 10 returns to the third person, apparently to mark the fact that national history, rather than personal exploits, is being described.

The Scope of the Book

The period covered by the book is about eighty years, but the account is not continuous. Chapters 1 to 6 represent the first twenty years of the scope of the book; while chapters 7 to 10 represent only a year or two at the end of the period. There is a gap of about fifty-eight years between the two sections. During the latter section, while Ezra himself ministered to the restored Jews, in China and India the prophets Buddha and Confucius were teaching, and in Greece, the philosopher Socrates.

The Key Phrase of Ezra

The book emphasizes that the events it describes are strictly the outcome of the unfolding word of the Lord. Thus, a key phrase is 1:1 -- "Now in the first year of Cyrus, king of Persia, that the word of the Lord by the mouth of Jeremiah might be fulfilled, the Lord stirred up the spirit of Cyrus." Jeremiah's prophecies had included God's promise: "For thus saith the Lord, That after seventy years be accomplished at Babylon I will visit you and perform my good word toward you, in causing you to return to this place" (Jer. 29:10).

The Value of the Book

Ezra very graphically portrays the faithfulness of God to vindicate His Word; and by corollary he sets forth the absolute necessity of an adherence to the Word of God in all life situations. When the people of God were in right relationship with Him, His Word reached into all avenues of their lives, including the religious, the social, and the civil.

Analysis and Exposition

I. The Return Under Zerubbabel (Chs. 1 - 6)

1. The Edict and Aid of Cyrus (Ch. 1)

Following his conquest of Babylon, Cyrus proceeded to grant freedom to the Israelites. The opening verses of Ezra repeat the closing verses of Second Chronicles in reporting the memorable decree of Cyrus. To a large measure, the decree and subsequent events recorded in this chapter are God's response to the prayers of Daniel (cf. Daniel 9:1-19). Cyrus' edict commissioned the Jews to proceed to rebuild the temple of Jehovah in Jerusalem, and in the process, tacitly conveyed all of the necessary legal rights and authorizations. A tax was prescribed upon those Jews who remained in Babylonia, and these funds, plus such freewill offerings as could be gathered, were given to the emigrants to help them on their way. Cyrus also donated to the returning remnant the gold and silver vessels of the temple that decades before had been confiscated by Judah's conquerors. One tradition holds that Cyrus returned the temple vessels in lieu of gold and silver idols such as existed in pagan religions. Shesbazzar, to whom the temple vessels were committed, is identified as "the prince of Judah." Later, he is known as Zerubbabel.

The releasing of captives and providing finances for their departure was a very unusual procedure for an eastern ruler. It is often suggested that Cyrus' own religious faith made him sympathetic to the Jews. Significantly, he saw Jehovah as "The Lord God of heaven" (v. 2) rather than as "The God of the Jews." For the most part, the Persians were monotheistic Zoroastrians, and they worshipped a god called Ormazd. Whether Cyrus was committed to monotheism remains a matter of scholarly dispute. According to Josephus, Cyrus was impressed by Isaiah's prophecies of a century and a half earlier (Isa. 44:28 - 45:4) and he deliberately sought to fulfil them. An archaeological find known as the Cyrus Cylinder confirms the Biblical account of Cyrus' release of captive peoples. The Cylinder records the words of Cyrus: "All their [i.e. of various lands] inhabitants I collected and restored them to their dwelling places."

2. The Returning Remnant (Ch. 2)

In this chapter, Ezra lists a total of 24,144 family heads or village or town groups who participated in the first restoration. A similar list is found in Nehemiah (Neh. 7:8-38), but he introduces slight variations to arrive at a total of 25,406. The total of all adult individuals, including wives, some servants, and others, was approximately 50,000. Ezra notes (vv. 43-60) that there were 74 Levites included, and more than 650 priests. The majority of those who returned belonged to the tribes of Judah, Benjamin, and Levi, but inasmuch as they offered twelve goats in their sin-offering (6:17), it is evident that the remnant considered themseves as representing all of the twelve tribes. Ironside picturesquely describes the enumeration of this chapter as "a sample-page from the books of eternity . . . a leaf out of God's memorial record."

Neither this Nehemiah (v. 2), nor Mordecai (v. 2), would be those individuals who figure elsewhere in Scripture. The Nethinims were literally "temple-bondsmen" and were those, possibly descendants of the Gibeonites, whom Solomon had assigned to menial tasks in the care of the temple. The return of the "men of Anathoth" (v. 23) vindicated the faith of Jeremiah who seventy years before during the siege of Jerusalem had purchased the field of Anathoth and insisted upon a proper record of the transaction (Jer. 32). The civil leader of the remnant was Zerubbabel, the grandson of Jehoiachin, and a descendant of David; while Jeshua, a hereditary priest, was their spiritual leader. It is noted that Zerubbabel means "a seed in Babel" and the name testifies to the fact that God had His chosen seed even in the midst of Babylon's idolatry. The express task of the initial detachment was to restore the altar of the Lord in Jerusalem. The journey to Jerusalem required about four months and covered about 600 wilderness miles. One assurance of success for the mission was the generosity of the fathers who "gave after their ability unto the treasure of the work."

3. The Building of the Temple Begun (Ch. 3)

After a brief interval to establish daily life in the new land, the immigrants proceeded to fulfil their obligations to God. In the seventh month, of presumably the first year, "the people gathered themselves together as one man to Jerusalem" (v. 1). Acting in vital unity, the people promptly erected an altar, began daily sacrifices, and commemorated the Feast of Tabernacles. Approximately a year and a half later, the temple foundations were laid once more. The restoration of the house of God was thus actually underway. The ceremony was witnessed with mingled joy and mourning; the young men rejoiced, but older men were deeply grieved. The reason for the sorrow

Jerusalem's Hill of Ophel as excavated by archaeologist Kathleen Kenyon. The exposed wall dates to the restoration era, and is known as Nehemiah's Wall.

of the older men is not clearly stated, but perhaps their contemplation of all the tragedy that had occurred in connection with the previous temple caused them to weep. Also, they may have wept in reaction to the miserable circumstances in which they now found themselves. Although it is sometimes suggested that the new foundations may have been pitifully small, it is generally reported in Jewish tradition that the external dimensions of Zerubbabel's temple were not different from those of Solomon's. Oehler suggests that the anonymous Psalms of rejoicing (Psalms 96-99) probably pertained to this period.

4. The Suspension of the Work (Ch. 4)

At this time, a new element was introduced into the history of the Jews. The Samaritans, the racially mixed group of central Palestine, proceeded to apply to Zerubbabel to be allowed to assist with the restoration of the temple. The reply of Zerubbabel, in accord with the counsel of Jeshua, clearly and definitely stated that the Jews would neither accept the help of the Samaritans nor permit their interference. The Jewish leaders recognized that safety and success for their people lay solely in the pathway of separation. The Samaritans had approached with an apparently friendly offer, but Scripture at the very outset designates them "adversaries" (v. 1). The Samaritans were a people of compromise, both racially and religiously, and the system of worship that they represented was schismatic and interwoven with heresy and error. The reaction of the Samaritans to this rejection was an open hostility and determined opposition toward the Jews and towards the project they were attempting.

The Samaritans proceeded with a political maneuver that was contrived to force the Jews to halt the rebuilding of the temple. In reporting these matters, the language of the book of Ezra changes from Hebrew to Aramaic. Thus, the actual transcripts of the correspondence are preserved. The letter from the Samaritans to Artaxerxes, king of Persia, professed grave concern for the interests of the king and alleged that the building program of the Jews would harm these interests. It declared falsely that the Jews were rebuilding the walls of Jerusalem. Artaxerxes was immediately persuaded; he promptly decreed that the Jews were to cease their building project. This suspension, as matters turned out, was to apply for the next sixteen years.

It is possible to infer that the ready submission of the Jews to Artaxerxes' decree was evidence of lack of real enthusiasm for the temple rebuilding project. They had on their side the irrevocable decree of Cyrus, but for one reason or another they chose not to invoke it. The possibility of such spiritual indifference is further corroborated by archaeological investigations of this era. It has been found that during these years the Jews devoted themselves to building elaborate residences and personal dwellings. There is a notable Persian influence in the architecture of this time, which is of course in keeping with the background of the immigrants. Some homes of this era were remarkably "modern" with built in bathrooms and drainage systems.

5. The Building of the Temple Resumed (Ch. 5)

The work of rebuilding the temple was eventually resumed through the ministry of the prophets: Haggai and Zechariah. Haggai exhorted the people: "go up . . . and build the house" and assured them that "the silver is mine and the gold is mine, saith the Lord of hosts." Thus, he urged them to spare no expense in erecting the house of the Lord. Zechariah charged the people with being evil in their indifference to the work of the Lord, and sought to declare to them how mindful God was of them, and what great provision He had made for their future. Through the combined efforts of these two fearless preachers, and in response to a drought which the Lord sent as a punishment, the people were stirred to action, and in 520 B.C. they once more began to build.

As the work progressed, opposition against the Jews once more arose. In order to settle matters, Tatnai, the local governor, compiled a lengthy letter to Darius the king enquiring if permission for the project actually existed. It appears that although this Darius was king of Medo-Persia, he was a different individual from Darius of Daniel, chapter six. While the latter was actually a vice-king under Cyrus, this Darius was probably the successor of Artaxerxes (Xerxes the Great). It is evident that Tatna and his companions believed that their letter would re-

sult in the permanent suspension of the work of the Jews.

6. The Completion and Dedication of the Temple (Ch. 6)

King Darius' search, in response to the letter, fortuitously produced the original decree of Cyrus authorizing the return of the Jews and the rebuilding of their temple. Thus, he replied to Tatnai and his companions: "Let the work of this house of God alone" (v. 7). Darius also authorized that out of customs-tax collections funds be made available to the Jews to help them with their project. Death by hanging was prescribed for anyone who tried to interfere. Scripture reports the response of Tatnai and his associates to the king's decree: "so they did speedily" (v. 13).

In the third day of the month Adar, in the sixth year of King Darius, the temple of Zerubbabel was completed in Jerusalem. Although the ceremonies may have been very simple and humble in comparison with those that had marked the dedication of Solomon's temple, they were nonetheless sincere and meaningful. A spirit of great joy and a sense of general spiritual revival prevailed. The dedication marked the restoration of the leadership and spiritual ministry of the priests, and also the reinstitution of the observance of the Jewish national feasts that related the people to Jehovah.

Darius I (Darius the Great), under whose reign the temple was completed, is the subject of the Rock of Behistun which is a massive mountain sculpture of cuneiform script. This rock stands on the ancient road to Babylon. The story engraved upon the rock concerns Darius' victory over usurping rebels, and his securing the throne. The engraving on the rock is believed to date from about 516 B.C., the same year that Zerubbabel's temple was dedicated to the worship of Jehovah.

II. The Return Under Ezra (Chs. 7-10)

1. The Commission of Ezra (Ch. 7)

In this portion of the book, Ezra, who was of the generation that had survived due to Esther's intercession, begins to describe events in which he personally was involved. Ezra is introduced as a "ready scribe" (v. 6), and as such he is the first of the Biblical order of scribes. In Medo-Persia, his skill won for him a position in the court of King Artaxerxes Longimanus. Also, because he was of the priestly line through Aaron, Levi, and Hilkiah, he would have been among the respected upper class among the exiles. His commission by the king to lead a party of immigrants to Palestine and become the governor of the colony is thus quite understandable. Scripture pointedly notes another vital factor: "the hand of the Lord his God upon him" (v. 6).

The letter of Artaxerxes that precisely set forth the prerogatives and conditions of Ezra's restoration and administration in Palestine is preserved in Scripture. As already noted, this portion of the Old Testament retains the original Aramaic in which the letter was written. Artaxerxes generously contributed to the finances of Ezra's party, and in addition, his letter provided: 1) a nationwide subscription for the immigrants, 2) a contribution of precious metals, 3) equipment and armaments for the temple and court, 4) the right to draw money and provisions from the treasuries in Palestine and Syria, and 5) freedom from taxes for the priests and spiritual leaders. From a human standpoint, it is suggested that the king's interest and generosity were motivated by his concern for a strong state of loyal citizens in Palestine to help to offset threats from Egypt against the Empire.

In his letter, Artaxerxes stressed the term 'freewill' in relation to this return and the gifts of the people to provide for it (vv. 13, 16). The original captivity of the Jews had taken place 130 years previously, and by this time the people in general were comfortably settled in their adopted homes. Artaxerxes removed all legal barriers to the return and did what he could to encourage it, but he was careful to employ no coercion. Conditions in Palestine were far from inviting, and generally the life that was offered was greatly inferior to life in Medo-Persia from the standpoint of natural comforts. Nevertheless, God was interested in the return. Jews who were men of faith no doubt saw a commitment to the restoration as an expression of their love to God and desire to relate rightly to Him.

2. The Journey of Ezra and His Party to Jerusalem (Ch. 8)

The group that Ezra was to lead to Palestine assembled in Babylon and for three days tented beside Ahava's river. The genealogical tables which are given indicate that Ezra recruited 12 families or tribal groups with a total of 1,754 males, or about 6,000 including women and children. Before this group departed, however, Ezra extended an invitation to a colony of Levites to join them. The outcome was an estimated additional 1,000 recruits as 38 Levites and 220 other temple workers (called Nethinim) and their wives and families became part of the caravan. The total party participated in a fast and a spiritual rededication proclaimed by

Figure Fourteen: Palestine during the era of the Restoration (536 to 167 B.C.)

Ezra, and then they began what Ironside called "the march of faith."

From Babylon to Palestine was a distance of more than 500 miles. Ezra's party probably found it necessary to proceed very slowly and to detour frequently, and therefore four months were necessary to complete the journey. Ezra chose not to request a military escort to protect his group, and instead, he proclaimed his trust in God. Nevertheless, he took the precaution of dividing the treasures that they carried among twenty-two of the priests and their helpers. The party arrived safely in Jerusalem in the burning heat of mid-summer, and four days later presented all of the new treasures to the temple authorities to the accompaniment of numerous sacrifices as tokens of joyful worship of God. The existing leaders readily surrendered government to Ezra, but they remained to serve as his deputies.

3. The Prayer of Ezra (Ch. 9)

A critical problem during Ezra's administration was the breakdown of the separation between the Jews and their pagan neighbors. The

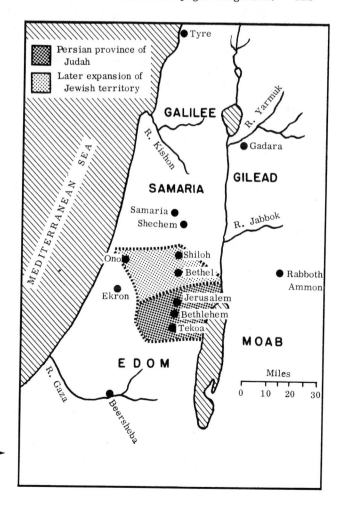

only strength that the Jews possessed lay in their identity with Jehovah, and for them to join with the ungodly was to court ruin. By uniting with their neighbors, particularly in marriage unions, the Jews were confounding their national heritage and committing themselves to manners, customs, and, particularly, religions that separated them from God. In response to this situation, Ezra opened his heart to God in fervent communion. His prayer contains no petition, but by confession, acknowledgment of God's mercy, and the expression of personal surrender, Ezra sought to reestablish himself and his people in the Lord.

4. The Separation of Mixed Marriages (Ch. 10)

When Shechaniah, a Jew involved in a mixed marriage, agreed to put away his pagan wife, the action became a pattern for others, and it provided Ezra with a specific procedure. While personally fasting, he proclaimed a national men's meeting three days later. On that occasion, which was a rainy winter's day, Ezra publicly demanded that all Jews who were married to pagan wives must put them away and repent for the wrong that they had committed. Not only laymen, but priests and Levites were included among the guilty. Officers were appointed to record the separations in proper legal fashion, and a three-month period was designated for its completion. Priests were not only expected to put away their pagan wives, but also to offer an appropriate trespass offering before the Lord.

Those who dismissed their pagan wives under Ezra's reform included: 4 priests of the high-priestly family, 13 other priests, 10 Levites, and 86 laymen. These heart-rending events were the direct outcome of disobedience to God, and even though they offend sentiment, they were necessary in view of the circumstances. It is the very nature of the Law to act without concern for human emotions. Nevertheless, it is proposed that Eastern customs would have softened the severity of these events. Ordinarily, a discarded wife in the East is received back into her family without reproach or disgrace. Probably the ones most hurt were the Jewish men who in spite of better insights had deliberately disobeyed the known will of God and therefore deserved to pay the consequences.

Ezra the scribe continued as a spiritual leader to the Jews for many years to come, and Scripture reports his part in the revival under Nehemiah (cf. Neh. ch. 8). For this reason, Ezra is highly revered by the Jews, and he is known by such titles as "founder of Judaism," or "a second Moses," or "second founder of the Jewish State." He is credited with having collected the Old Testament books to form the canon, and also with organizing the Great Synagogue. This council of Jewish elders later became the Sanhedrin, and in Jesus' time it was the governing body of the Jews insofar as the Romans gave it authority. It is also thought that it was Ezra who was responsible for the organization of local synagogues to serve Jews in their individual communities. Clearly, Ezra's contribution to Judaism was substantial, and probably it is valid to claim that no one, except Moses, accomplished more.

10. THE BOOK OF NEHEMIAH

Between Ezra and Nehemiah there is a short interval of about twelve years. The two books belong together, and as already noted, are joined in the Hebrew Scriptures. The book of Nehemiah is chiefly the prophet's autobiography, although the fortunes of the restored remnant in Palestine are vitally identified with his life. Nehemiah is the last historical book of the Old Testament chronologically.

The Nature and Theme of the Book

The book of Nehemiah is particularly concerned with the account of the erection of the walls of the city of Jerusalem. Although the Jews of the Restoration had been in the land almost a century, they had made no progress in this rebuilding until Nehemiah came on the scene. Nehemiah encouraged both spiritual and practical zeal as the two pillars of substantial progress. When the walls were successfully rebuilt, Nehemiah devoted his efforts to the establishment of civil government in Palestine, and in this realm too, he achieved for the people an enduring legacy.

The Authorship of the Book

There seems to be no reasonable doubt that this book is the work of the man whose name it bears. Though it is true that parts of the book find their origin in other sources; it is also plausible to hold that the whole was compiled and given continuity by Nehemiah. For the most part, the first seven and the last three chapters are written in the first person, and only chapters eight and ten are in the third. This latter would likely be a portion of some other document. The style of Nehemiah resembles that of Chronicles and Ezra, and thus it is clearly established as a genuine document of the age it reports.

A statement in the apocryphal book of 2 Maccabees is of interest: "Nehemiah, founding a library, gathered together the books about the kings and prophets, and the books of David, and the letters of the kings, which had been scattered by war." This statement represents Jewish belief probably a few decades before the time of Christ. It has the authentication of antiquity but not of inspiration.

The Scope of Nehemiah

The events described in Nehemiah represent about twelve years of Jewish history, though the prophet himself continued his ministry for an additional twenty-four years. While it is difficult to reconcile Biblical and secular history, it is proposed to link Nehemiah with the reign of Darius Nothus (424-395 B.C.).

The Key Verses and Key Words

The key verses are found in 1:4 and 6:3 respectively: "And it came to pass, when I heard these words, that I sat down and wept . . . and prayed before the God of heaven," and "I sent messengers unto them saying, I am doing a great work, so that I cannot come down." The key words may be considered to be: "pray" and "work."

The Value of the Book

The book of Nehemiah is an important link in Biblical history. The account of the rebuilding of Jerusalem's walls and the settlement of the city provides the background for historical events in the New Testament era. An important aspect of Nehemiah's history is his concern for the religious and racial purity of the people. In this era, especially, the Jewish people were oriented to their strict racial and religious consciousness that has persisted down to the present. Nehemiah's formula for success in his program is a pattern for any worker for God: work and prayer.

Analysis and Exposition

I. The Building of the Wall of Jerusalem (Chs. 1 - 6)

1. Nehemiah's Sorrow and His Prayer (Ch. 1)

Nehemiah carefully locates the beginning of events in the twentieth year of the reign of Artaxerxes of Persia in the winter palace at Shushan (or Susa). Under that ruler, Nehemiah had risen to the post of cupbearer--a sort of personal stewart or valet. This position would have given Nehemiah frequent contact with the king, and traditionally, cupbearers were in effect doormen to the royal apartment. Thus, he probably held the power of permitting or preventing audiences with the king. No doubt the ruler was aware of the importance of his cupbearer, and he would have recognized that his life was literally in Nehemiah's hand.

A report by Hanani, the brother of Nehemiah, revealed the sorry state of the city of Jerusalem. There is some evidence that the city was in ruins, not only because of the seventh century Babylonian siege, but also because of recent attacks by the Samaritans. Nehemiah's reaction to the news was fourfold: he wept, mourned, fasted, and prayed. The burden of his prayer was that God would vindicate Himself and His promises, and that He would grant prospering mercy to Nehemiah that he might be able to minister to the need. Nehemiah addressed God as "Lord God of heaven," perhaps with the implication that His earthly dwelling place was no longer of consequence. With admirable humility and concern, Nehemiah identified himself with the indifferent colonists: "we have sinned against thee: both I and my father's house have sinned" (v. 6).

2. Nehemiah's Return to Jerusalem (Ch. 2)

Nehemiah had specifically prayed that he might enjoy a favorable interview with the king, but it was four months later that his prayer began to be answered. Even in the midst of the interview, Nehemiah continued his prayer (cf. "So I prayed to the God of heaven" [v. 4]). The king's response was warmly favorable, for not only did he give leave to Nehemiah to participate in the project, but he gave sweeping authorization that in effect placed Nehemiah in the post of governor of the province with all necessary economic and military resources at his command. Nehemiah's return is dated at 444 B.C., and it is inferred that he took with him only an armed escort and no colonists. He likely would have needed two months to reach his destination.

The nighttime survey of the city's ruins by Nehemiah and his men was a careful strategy to avoid the premature disclosure of the plans for rebuilding. Nevertheless, it gave Nehemiah adequate information and understanding, so that shortly thereafter he could announce his intentions. Once more he identified with the people: "Let us build up the wall of Jerusalem, that we be no more a reproach" (v. 17), and in turn, the people wholeheartedly responded: "Let us rise up and build" (v. 18). Not surprisingly, the Samaritan opponents, Sanballat, Tobiah, and Geshem, appeared almost as promptly. Nehemiah rejected their objections and scorn and firmly declared: "Ye have no portion, nor right, nor memorial, in Jerusalem" (v. 20).

3. The Builders of the Wall (Ch. 3)

Even though the rebuilding of the wall was a secular project in contrast to the previous task of rebuilding the temple, the lead was taken by Eliashib the high priest, and the atmosphere throughout was one of faith and prayer. Nehemiah assigned a section of the wall to each of the principal families, and in general he organized the effort on a 'division of labor' basis. A total of 44 family groups or working parties are named in what has been called "God's record of service." This chapter mentions ten of the gates, and two others are mentioned elsewhere (8:16; 12:39), making twelve in all. Basically, Nehemiah assigned families to the construction of the section of the wall nearest their place of residence, and as far as possible he enlisted the participation of men of every social level.

4. External Opposition to the Reconstruction (Ch. 4)

At the outset, the Samaritan opponents limited themselves to contemptuous sneering. However, when it became evident that the walls were definitely being erected, they began a course of armed attack. The leader of these foes was Sanballat who was probably the governor of Samaria; while Tobiah the Ammonite is thought to have been some kind of a stewart in his court. Such overt hostility served to spur the Jews to more intense effort, while at the same time, Nehemiah proceeded to organize an efficient program of civil defence. Apparently, Nehemiah's show of force was sufficient to deter the Samaritans, for no record exists of an actual armed attack, though the Jews would have been ready for it, had it come. This readiness burdened the people with full shifts of guard duty in addition to the full-time work shifts that they were already fulfilling.

5. Nehemiah Deals with Internal Problems (Ch. 5)

The outcome of the extreme poverty of some of the people now came to Nehemiah's attention. There were those who had been forced to surrender title to their lands, vineyards, and houses in order to buy necessary food, or in order to pay the king's tribute. Thus, not only were they in debt, but they now had no means to repay. In some cases, their creditors were taking their children into slavery, and the state of affairs was no better than the bondage in Babylon that they had left. The crucial factor in this instance, however, was that those who were foreclosing mortgages and enslaving children were themselves Jews and therefore the national brethren of the oppressed ones. Nehemiah concluded that such actions were morally wrong, and he called for reforms in the name of proper godliness.

So shamed were the prosperous exploiters by Nehemiah's appeal that they agreed to restore expropriated properties and even to return a portion of the payments that had been collected. Nehemiah vividly demonstrated that anyone who failed to fulfill these reforms would be cast off by the Lord. It seems clear that the issue was not a legitimate business system of loans at interest, but the practice of cruel usury against virtually helpless brothers. Nehemiah's own example of unselfishness in financial matters was an eloquent confirmation of the standards he imposed upon others. In spite of heavy expenses and a large staff to maintain, Nehemiah chose to pay all the costs of his twelve-year administration entirely apart from taxes upon the people.

6. The Completion of the Wall in Spite of Opposition (Ch. 6)

"The rustic tricksters of Samaria" now sought to gain the advantage over Nehemiah by craft; hence, four times they invited him to a meeting. His answer was: "I am doing a great work, so that I cannot come down." When such subtle efforts at apparent conciliation failed, Sanballat proceeded to active intimidation. Thus, through an impressive open letter he attempted to panic Nehemiah into quitting the work. Nehemiah simply repudiated this threat, just as he later rejected the invitation of a false hireling prophet to take secret refuge in the temple. For Nehemiah to have gone into hiding would probably have hurt the morale of the nation, and it would have exposed him directly to his enemies that they might destroy him in secret.

The rebuilding of the walls in the face of vicious opposition in only fifty-two days is an eloquent testimony to the faith and dedication of Nehemiah and his associates. The divine enabling is thus clearly revealed. Nevertheless, the intimation of this portion is that previous mixed marriages still constituted a threat to the nation. Even the rebuilt walls were of no avail against internal treachery. Nehemiah's task in fulfilling the call of God upon his life was not only a struggle with material problems and organization in erecting the wall, but also a struggle in inducing godliness, loyalty, and consistency in the very people he was seeking to help.

II. Religious Revival and the Correction of Abuses (Chs. 6 - 13)

1. The Government and Citizens of the Land (Ch. 7)

Nehemiah now proceeded to appoint associates and deputies for the government of the newly fortified city. Although the walls were designed to exclude, porters (or gate-keepers) were appointed to attend to those who ought to be admitted. Singers and Levites were also appointed, as well as two deputy rulers: Hanani the brother of Nehemiah, and Hananiah. Undoubtedly, spiritual qualifications and not nepotism directed these choices. In administering the city, it was agreed to delay the morning opening of the gates until broad daylight in order the better to thwart any treachery by their foes.

The genealogical data (vv. 7-73) is substantially identical with that of Ezra 2. This was a register of the original 50,000 who returned in the first restoration under Zerubbabel almost a century previous. Discrepancies between the two lists would be accounted for by their different sources (Ezra's was compiled in Babylon, Nehemiah's in Judea), by the varying circumstances of the lapse of years, and by the fact that Jewish custom permitted one individual to be known by more than one name.

2. Revival Under Ezra and Nehemiah (Ch. 8)

At this juncture Ezra the scribe is introduced into Nehemiah's story. He emerges as the minister of the book of the Law of Moses. Scripture describes a national gathering of the people somewhat in the pattern of a modern evangelistic rally. Ezra stood upon a raised platform or pulpit, with the elders at his side, and he proceeded to read, and with the help of the Levites, expound the book of the Law. It is said that this procedure became the origin of the Jewish Targums (an Aramaic translation of the Old Testament Scriptures). The people were moved to Godly sorrow in response to the Word, but the leaders exhorted them to joyfulness. Jehovah was not to be known as a gloomy and morose deity; His worship was to entail joy and gladness.

The practice of dwelling in booths to observe the Feast of Tabernacles had been neglected since the time of Joshua. Thus, as the people learned of the divine plan through the reading of the Law, they undertook to comply. The previous sorrow in God's presence became gladness as with enthusiasm and sincerity the people conformed to the national pattern that God had intended. These events gave new recognition and authority to the Scripture and its canon, and further entrenched the national institutions of Israel under Jehovah. The apocryphal book of 1 Esdras contains a parallel account of this portion of Jewish history, although today's scholars have some difficulty in attempting to reconcile the chronology of Nehemiah and Ezra acting jointly.

3. A Hymn of Praise (Ch. 9)

As increasing heed was paid to the Word of God, the people were led to practice a new measure of spiritual dedication. Hence, on the twenty-fourth day of the revival month Tishri, the people united in a special service of thanksgiving and confession. Events included the reading of the book of the Law, the confession of sin, the worship of Jehovah, and prayer at considerable length. A chorus of Levites led the people in their prayer which sought not so much to move the hand of God as simply to lay before Him their present spiritual state. According to the Septuagint, this prayer was composed by Ezra. It has the distinction of being the longest in the Bible.

The recorded portion of the prayer carefully traces the providences of God toward the nation from its earliest days. The hand of God is humbly recognized, and His patience credited for His willingness to endure when He well might have cast them off. "Yet thou in thy manifold mercies forsookest them not in the wilderness" (v. 19). The consequence of this prayerful review of history was a new national sense of gratitude and obligation to God. "Behold, we are servants this day" (v. 36). So moved were the people, that they responded by agreeing to sign a covenant of wholehearted spiritual dedication.

4. The Covenant and Its Signers (Ch. 10)

All of the chiefs of the people endorsed and signed the covenant. Only Ezra did not sign: he was the one imposing the covenant, and apparently he was not a family head. The people were properly prepared for the signing by the study of the book of the Law and the careful review of their national background. The covenant topics included: 1) the walk in God's Law, 2) maintaining separation from pagan neighbors, 3) Sabbath observance, 4) observance of the Sabbatical years, 5) avoiding usury. Because the imposition of such fundamental standards was new to that generation, this occasion was more properly a "reformation" rather than a "revival." The solemnity of a formal contract was the motivation for faithfulness to what was pledged.

5. Resettlement in Jerusalem (Ch. 11)

At this juncture, the narrative of civil events, which had been interrupted for the account of spiritual revival, is continued. The problem of sufficient population for the city of Jerusalem was solved by assigning every tenth family to reside there. Families were to be chosen by lot. The people agreed to such rather arbitrary direction of their affairs because they saw the outcome as the will of God. The entire population of the nation at this time was probably about 50,000, and therefore, one-tenth was a minimum population to comprise a thriving urban center.

6. The Dedication of the Wall (Ch. 12)

The ceremony of the dedication of the wall may have been delayed with the approval of the Persian court was awaited. In the meantime, a careful directory of the priests and Levites was compiled, and the priests were set into organization. The line of Jeshua is here traced to the time of Jaddua, and according to Josephus, this was the Jaddua who held office in the time of Alexander the Great (early 4th century B.C.). Such a chronology is a problem to Bible scholars, and it is concluded either that Josephus erred or that this portion of the book was written considerably after the time of Nehemiah.

The ceremonial dedication of the wall was conducted in an atmosphere of joy and gladness, with musicians and singers leading the people in worship. The service began with the ceremonial purification of: priests, Levites, the people, the gates, and the wall itself. The worshippers were divided into two groups, and apparently the vocal worship included antiphonal singing or chanting. The occasion marked the reestablishment of voluntary tithes and offerings as the means to support spiritual leaders. The measure of dedication and spiritual interest at this time was complete. "All Israel in the days of Zerubbabel, and in the days of Nehemiah, gave the portions . . . every day his portion" (v. 47).

7. Separation Once More Established (Ch. 13)

It is likely that the events of this chapter took place some time after the dedication of the walls, for they constitute Nehemiah's later recollections. He explains that he did not reside continuously in Jerusalem, but for a time returned to the court of Artaxerxes. During such an absence there was the breakdown of separation, including the episode in which Eliashib the priest provided a chamber in the court of the temple for the use of Tobiah the Ammonite. Nehemiah, upon his return, was greatly displeased with such a flagrant disregard of Biblical standards. He proceeded to cast out all that spoke of Tobiah and to rededicate the chamber to its proper use in the service of Jehovah.

Nehemiah, as already noted, reinstituted the tithe to support the priests and Levites, and he imposed rigorous controls upon Sabbath activity. He sternly denounced all marriages between Jews and their pagan neighbors, and even committed to exile the grandson of Eliashib the priest because this young man married the daughter of Sanballat the Horonite. In general, Nehemiah, firmly and with determination, fulfilled all that he believed to be right, for his sole interest was the eternal favor of Jehovah.

11. THE BOOK OF ESTHER

Although the canon places the book of Esther following Nehemiah, the events of the book actually precede the lifetime of Nehemiah by about thirty years. Humanly speaking, if the deliverance under Esther had not taken place, there never would have been a Nehemiah, nor the restoration he describes.

The Nature and Theme of the Book

The book of Esther is concerned with recounting God's deliverance of His people at a time when physical destruction threatened. The book is primarily patriotic rather than religious. The heroine, Esther, is named fifty-five times, and she easily qualifies for the title: "the most talked about woman of the Bible." The deliverance under Esther is recognized as being just as significant and momentous as that under Moses at the time of the Passover. To this day, the Jews read the book of Esther on the occasion of their festivals, and they value its record of the origin of the Feast of Purim.

A noteworthy peculiarity of Esther is that nowhere in the book is the name of God mentioned, nor is there any reference to prayer. A possible explanation is that the book was abstracted from official Persian court records which would deliberately omit references to Jewish religious beliefs and practices. Evangelicals are unlikely to be impressed with the claim that God's name is four times spelled out in acrostic form in the Hebrew original. Adeney calls the effort to discern the name of God in the book by this means "fantastic trifling." A more conventional approach is Matthew Henry's comment: "If the name of God is not there, His finger is."

The Authorship of the Book

It is evident that the author had a thorough and intimate knowledge of the details that the narrative relates. Even the servants are personally named, and there are many references to the practices and usages of the Persian court. The reference to the chronicles of the kings of Media and Persia in that order implies a date of writing approxi-

mately contemporary with the events of this book. Even critical scholars who report: "inaccuracies, exaggerations, and inconsistencies" have to admit that the author was well informed about the Persian court and manners and customs of that era.

The one contemporary who best qualifies as author according to the facts of the situation is Mordecai. This choice was endorsed by Josephus, and it has the precedents of Ezra, Nehemiah, and Daniel who similarly wrote of events in which they personally figured in the Persian court. Additional support for this claim derives from within the book: "And Mordecai wrote these things, and sent letters unto all the Jews that were in all the provinces" (9:20). While this literary effort by Mordecai may not have been the actual book, it is considered that what was done at that time may well have been the basis of the actual historical record.

The Scope of the Book

The events of the book of Esther are estimated to have extended over a twelve-year period. At least some scholars hold that the events of the book bridge a portion of the gap between the sixth and seventh chapters of Ezra.

The Key Verse

Since the book is concerned with the unfolding providences of God, a suitable key verse is 4:14c "Who knoweth whether thou art come to the kingdom for such a time as this?"

The Value of the Book

The book of Esther provides the Jews with an account of the origin of their observance of the Feast of Purim. Since this religious festival, which is observed in mid-March, has no authorization in the Law, it is necessary that this be found in history. So effectively does the book of Esther communicate its message of Jewish backgrounds that among traditional Jews it became the custom to encourage children and youths to jeer and stamp their feet at every mention of the hated Haman during the reading of the book at Purim. Though there is a possibility that a feast with similar associations was already being held in Persia, it is evident that the Jews totally "Judaized" the occasion in the same way that the Christians "Christianized" various winter solstice celebrations to constitute Christmas. It is clear that the claim of a Persian Feast of Purim in no way detracts from the merits of the Bible account, nor the accuracy of its facts.

In its message of the overruling providence of God, the book of Esther communicates significantly to Christian believers. God is seen acting to extend protecting care to His covenant people that He might uphold His promises that Messiah should be born to the seed of Abraham. Almost no one today would support Martin Luther in his criticism of this book. Luther classed Esther with the Apocrypha and of these books declared: "I wish they did not exist at all; for they Judaize too much and have much heathen perverseness." To a generation far-removed from the problems of Luther's day, the book of Esther stands approved among the masterpieces of sacred literature and it constitutes a portion of God's legacy to His people.

Analysis and Exposition

I. The Jews Threatened (Chs. 1 - 7)

1. Queen Vashti's Downfall (Ch. 1)

The great feast given by Ahasuerus on this occasion is thought to have been a planning meeting in preparation for military campaigns against Greece. If so, it culminated in the battles of: Artemisium, Thermophylae, and Salamis. The extended duration of the feast not only demonstrated the grandeur of the kingdom, but it served the practical purpose of permitting the appearance of princes and nobles on a rotation basis so as not to disturb unduly the administration of the state. The Persians are known to have been inordinately fond of sumptuous banquets, and history records gatherings of perhaps 15,000 guests amidst lavish surroundings and provisions. Such gatherings freely provided entertainment as well as food.

In the episode recorded in this chapter, Queen Vashti appears to have acted virtuously in her refusal to appear before the king and his drunken guests. Nevertheless, the king paid heed to Memucan, a councillor, who held that Vashti's example must not be permitted to stand. He held that Vashti, by her actions, did not rightly fill the role of the leading woman of the empire. Thus, Vashti was deposed, and an edict sent forth throughout the empire affirming that wives must honor their husbands. Adeney

notes that Ahasuerus' decree would change nothing for the typical husband and wife, and that its only significance was that "the poor silly king . . . was advertising his domestic troubles to the world." The traditions of the Medes and Persians provided that once a royal pronouncement was made, it was totally unalterable, and therefore even if Ahasuerus later had second thoughts about his queen, he could not undo what he had done.

2. Esther Becomes Queen (Ch. 3)

As Ahasuerus sought for a replacement for Queen Vashti, the beautiful young Esther eventually came to his attention. Scripture implies that Esther largely rejected conventional adornments, and she relied simply upon her natural charms to impress the king. Her strategy was wholly successful, so that the "king loved Esther above all the women, and . . . he set the royal crown upon her head, and made her queen" (v. 20). It is noted (1:3 and 2:16) that there was a four-year interval between these events and those of the previous chapter, and it is assumed that Ahasuerus had occupied the time in his battles against Greece. History records that King Xerxes returned to Susa in defeat after four years of warfare against Greece, and that he promptly married Amestris. Such parallels appear to be more than mere coincidence in interpreting and identifying the Biblical story.

Esther's guardian, Mordecai, the nephew of her father maintained close contact in spite of her exaltation. His daily visits may have been in conjunction with his conduct of official duties on behalf of the king (cf. v. 21). Thus, Mordecai was in a position to intervene when he discovered two of the court staff plotting to murder their king. One plausible theory holds that these men were seeking to avenge the rejection of Vashti. Through Mordecai's report the plotters were brought to justice. The event was subsequently recorded in the royal annals where it became a vital strand in the unfolding story of the book. In the meantime, Esther appears to have remained wholly unspoiled in spite of her exaltation, although her ancestry was concealed from those around her (v. 10).

3. The Plot of Haman (Ch. 3)

Haman's appointment as chief minister (or vizier) was evidence of the high regard in which he was held by the king and his court. Nevertheless, Mordecai, perhaps because of religious scruples against honoring a human leader, refused to render the expected homage. Because Haman was motivated by intense personal conceit, he magnified the issues out of all reasonable proportions. Thereby, Haman proceeded by subtle craftiness to persuade Ahasuerus to pass a decree proclaiming the annihilation of the Jews. The king apparently failed to recognize the far-ranging consequences of his decree, and he believed that he was merely taking steps to free his kingdom of a troublesome minority group. If Haman was a descendant of Agag the Amalekite (cf. 1 Sam. 15:33), as seems to be indicated (v. 1), then the feud between Haman and Mordecai was simply a personal perpetuation of a centuries-long conflict.

The procedure of Haman in casting Pur (lots) was common among the Medo-Persians and their peers when they desired guidance in important decisions. By this means, Haman determined what he believed would be the best day for the destruction of the Israelites. The reward that Haman offered Ahasuerus for the privilege of destroying the Israelites has been computed to be equivalent to as much as twenty million dollars in today's values. No doubt Haman expected to obtain such a vast sum from the property which he would confiscate from his victims. The ruthless callousness of the heart of Haman is revealed in his actions following the issuing of the decree: "And the king and Haman sat down to drink" (v. 15).

4. The Reaction of the Jews (Ch. 4)

The Jews reacted to the decree by universal lamentation, with mourning, fasting, weeping, and wailing. The fact that they had a full year to contemplate their fate would only have served to aggravate its horror. Mordecai conspicuously joined the mourners, and he refused to put off his sackcloth even though Esther sent him other clothing. Apparently, only Mordecai was aware that the lovely queen, being a Jewess, was included in the decree. He saw her, humanly speaking, as the nation's sole hope in their hour of peril.

At Mordecai's urging, Esther agreed to attempt to intercede on behalf of her people. Mordecai had entreated her: "Who knoweth whether thou art come to the kingdom for such a time as this?" (v. 14). Esther courageously responded: "So will I go in unto the king, which is not according to the law: and if I perish, I perish" (v. 16). In requesting the three-day fast, Esther almost surely understood that she was summoning divine aid. She saw herself embarking upon a mission that she was willing to place above her own comfort and well being, and even her life itself. Even though she was a great queen, Esther remained responsive to the needs of her people and obedient to her guardian.

5. The Intercession of Esther (Ch. 5)

Fortunately for Esther, the king extended his sceptre toward her when she appeared in his presence, and her life was spared. The king's gesture also, at least tacitly, implied his preliminary approval upon her petition, whatever it might be. In tactful restraint, Esther asked only that the king and Haman attend a banquet. And even when her guests came, Esther simply renewed her invitation for a second banquet. The book of Esther effectively illustrates the principle of the vital role of wise and skillful human participants in the unfolding plan of the eternal God.

Haman was greatly delighted to share the queen's hospitality, but afterward his delight went from him when he once more confronted the unresponsive Mordecai. In the pattern of a man reacting to an obsession, Haman recounted his privileges to his family and friends and then reported: "All this availeth me nothing, so long as I see Mordecai the Jew sitting at the king's gate" (v. 13). Upon the advice of his wife, Zeresh, and perhaps as a practical therapy, Haman proceeded to arrange the erection of a towering gallows upon which he hoped Mordecai would soon be hung.

6. Haman Exalts Mordecai (Ch. 6)

The king's sleeplessness and his consequent perusal of the court records clearly reveals the providential intervention of God. Someone has remarked that the reading of the book of records of the chronicles was "the strangest soporific ever sought." It was thus that the king was reminded of the assassination attempt upon him and he thereby sought to honor Mordecai. The king's procedure in asking the advice of a court attendant and then following it precisely was typical of the Persian court. Haman's conceit on this occasion glaringly shows through, for he could conceive of no other than himself whom the king would desire to honor. The resulting consternation and seething frustration of Haman when he found himself commissioned to honor Mordecai is one of literature's all time ironies. The sudden change of status no doubt reassured Mordecai that the hand of God was upon him.

Scripture specifically notes the wisdom of Haman's associates in regard to these matters: "Then said his wise men and Zeresh his wife unto him, If Mordecai be of the seed of the Jews . . . thou shalt not prevail against him, but shalt surely fall before him" (v. 13). Wise men must recognize that God's hand is upon the Jewish people and no attempt to destroy them as a nation can ever succeed. Haman was to learn this lesson at the cost of his own life, just as every other satanically inspired schemer of subsequent generations.

7. The Final Banquet. Haman Hanged (Ch. 7)

At her second banquet, Esther finally made known her plight to Ahasuerus. Having been won over by her lovely presence and generosity, as well as by the episode of the past night, Ahasuerus readily endorsed the cause of Esther. The cowardly and unseemly conduct of Haman at this time led to his speedy execution on the very gallows he had prepared for Mordecai. Haman is an outstanding example of the wicked man who is caught in his own trap. There is some historical basis for considering that the gallows of Persian times would simply be a pointed stake upon which the victim was impaled.

II. The Jews Delivered (Chs. 8 - 10)

1. The Second Decree of the King (Ch. 8)

Upon Haman's death, King Ahasuerus proceeded to bestow upon Esther, and she in turn upon Mordecai, not only the possessions of Haman, but his administrative authority as well. Thus, Mordecai came into possession of the king's signet ring. The customs of that day provided that a king would validate official documents by impressing the design of his signet ring into the wax seal upon the document. To possess the king's signet was to share at the highest level in the administration of the land. Although the Persians believed in the deity of their rulers and held that no royal decree could be rescinded, Mordecai was thus empowered to do what he could to deliver the Jews from their original sentence.

At the specific instruction of King Ahasuerus, Mordecai prepared an official decree to provide for the survival of the Jews. On the date of their intended fate, they were to be permitted to gather together in armed bands and were to be free to protect themselves and to avenge their enemies as they saw fit. As this decree reached the Jewish communities, bitter mourning promptly changed to gleeful joy, and the effect has been compared to the announcement of salvation to condemned sinners. Mordecai left the royal court clothed in the festive garments of state, and throughout the provinces many were so greatly impressed that they became Jewish proselytes.

2. The Massacre of the Enemies of the Jews (Ch. 9)

Not only did the Jews successfully protect themselves on the announced day of doom, but they succeeded in waging offensive warfare and were able to destroy a large number of their enemies. In the provinces, the Jews spent the thirteenth of Adar fighting and the fourteenth resting; in the capital city of Shushan they spent both the thirteenth and fourteenth fighting and only on the fifteenth did they rest. In the second day of battle in Shushan the Jews destroyed an additional 300 of their enemies and they displayed the bodies of the ten sons of Haman upon a gallows. Apparently a total of 75,000 militaristic enemies of the Jews were slain, although no booty was taken. Through this chain of rather drastic events, the Jews were assured freedom from molestation and national peace for years to come.

3. Mordecai, the Prime Minister (Ch. 10)

The greatness of Ahasuerus and the Persian Empire simply enhanced the status of Mordecai in his role as prime minister. Both in word and in deed, during very dark days, Mordecai had sought only the good and the prosperity of his people. His hopes, and what surely had been his prayers, were vindicated and he is thus set forth as a great deliverer of his people. That this pious man of God should have risen to so important a place in a gentile empire is indeed testimony to the mysterious ways of God. In the unfolding of the divine plan of the ages, the finger of God constantly touches those of His choice to fill an essential role, and it is clear that Esther, and Mordecai with her, were just such chosen ones.

Some preaching values and lessons from the book of Esther are as follows: 1) The quality of grace is illustrated in Mordecai's adoption of the orphaned Esther, 2) The king's sleepless night, on the eve of Esther's second banquet, illustrates the uniqueness of God's providences, 3) Just as Esther came to the kingdom for a time of crisis, so God has a specific plan for each believer in his own lifetime, 4) The amazing power of everyday virtue, faithfulness, trust, and perseverance is illustrated both in the life of Esther and of Mordecai.

BIBLIOGRAPHY

Adeney, Walter F. Ezra, Nehemiah, and Esther. London: Hodder and Stoughton, 1893.

Aglen, A. Lessons in Old Testament History. New York: Arnold, n.d.

Angus, Joseph. The Bible Handbook (rev. by Samuel Green). Grand Rapids: Zondervan Publishing House, 1952.

Barrows, E.P. Companion to the Bible. New York: American Tract Society, n.d.

Blaikie, W.G. The First Book of Samuel. New York: Hodder and Stoughton, n.d.

_____. A Manual of Bible History. New York: Thomas Nelson and Sons, n.d.

Bodie, Mary M. Meditations on Ruth and Esther. Kansas City: Grace and Glory, 1926.

Booth, Osborne. The Chosen People. St. Louis: The Bethany Press, 1959.

Braley, Edith R. A Neglected Era. New York: E.P. Dutton Company, 1922.

Bruce, F.F. Israel and the Nations. Grand Rapids: Wm. B. Eerdmans Co., 1963.

Culler, Arthur J. Creative Religious Literature. New York: The Macmillan Company, 1930.

Deane, William J. David, His Life and Times. New York: Fleming Revell Co., n.d.

_____. Joshua, His Life and Times. New York: Fleming Revell Co., n.d.

_____. Samuel and Saul. New York: Fleming Revell Co., n.d.

DeHaan, Martin R., The Romance of Redemption. Grand Rapids: Zondervan Publishing House, 1958.

Douglas, George C. The Book of Judges. Edinburgh: T. & T. Clark, n.d.

Elder, John. Prophets, Idols and Diggers. New York: Bobbs-Merrill, 1960.

Farrar, F.W. Solomon, His Life and Times. New York: Fleming Revell Co., n.d.

Finegan, Jack. Light From the Ancient Past. Princeton: Princeton University Press, 1946.

Fuller, Charles E. Ruth: A Life of Love and Loyalty. Westwood: Fleming H. Revell Co., 1959.

Grollenberg, L.H. Shorter Atlas of the Bible. New York: Thomas Nelson and Sons, 1959.

Halley, Henry H. Pocket Bible Handbook. Chicago: Henry H. Halley, 1944.

Henderson, Archibald. Palestine. Edinburgh: T. & T. Clark, n.d.

Hester, Hubert I. The Heart of Hebrew History. Liberty: William Jewell Press, 1949.

Ironside, Harry A. Notes on the Book of Nehemiah. New York: Loizeaux Brothers, 1913.

_____. Ezra, Nehemiah and Esther. Neptune: Loizeaux Brothers Inc., 1941.

Jamieson, Fausset, and Brown. A Commentary on the Whole Bible. Grand Rapids: Zondervan Publishing House, n.d.

Jensen, Joseph. God's Word to Israel. Boston: Allyn and Bacon, 1968.

Keil, C.F. The Books of Ezra, Nehemiah, and Esther. Edinburgh: T. & T. Clark, 1873.

_____. The Books of the Kings. Edinburgh: T. & T. Clark, 1872.

Kern, M.E. The Distribution of the Races. College View: International Publishing Assoc., 1907.

Knapp, C. The Kings of Judah. New York: Loizeaux Brothers, n.d.

Lang, John M. Gideon and the Judges. New York: Fleming Revell Co., n.d.

LaSor, William Sanford. Great Personalities of the Old Testament. Westwood: Fleming H. Revell Co., 1959.

Lee, Robert. The Outlined Bible. London: Pickering and Inglis, n.d.

Macartney, C.E. Great Women of the Bible. New York: Abingdon-Cokesbury, 1942.

BIBLIOGRAPHY

Maclear, G. F. Old Testament History. London: Macmillan, 1879.

Manley, G. T. The New Bible Handbook. Chicago: The Inter-Varsity Christian Fellowship, 1948.

Marston, Charles. The Bible Comes Alive. London: Eyre and Spottiswoode, 1937.

Muir, James C. His Truth Endureth. Philadelphia: National Publishing Co., 1937.

New Biblical Atlas. London: The Religious Tract Society, n. d.

Newell, William R. Old Testament Studies. Chicago: Moody Press, 1950.

Oehler, Gustave F. Theology of the Old Testament. (rev. by George E. Day). Grand Rapids: Zondervan Publishing House, n. d.

Pearlman, Myer. Through the Bible Book by Book. Old Testament: Law and History. Springfield: Gospel Publishing House, 1935.

Price, Ira M. The Monuments and the Old Testament. Philadelphia: The Judson Press, 1925.

Raven, John H. Old Testament Introduction. New York: Fleming Revell Co., 1910.

Rawlinson, George. Ezra and Nehemiah. New York: Fleming Revell Co., n. d.

_____. The Kings of Israel and Judah. New York: Fleming Revell Co., n. d.

Ridout, Samuel. Judges and Ruth. New York: Loizeaux Brothers, 1958.

Robertson, James et al. Book by Book. London: Isbister and Company, n. d.

Sampey, John R. The Heart of the Old Testament. Nashville: Broadman Press, 1922.

Sayce, A. H. The Races of the Old Testament. London: Religious Tract Society, n. d.

Thiele, Edwin R. The Mysterious Numbers of the Hebrew Kings. Grand Rapids: Wm. B. Eerdmans Publishing Co., 1965.

Thompson, J. A. Archaeology and the Old Testament. Grand Rapids: Wm. B. Eerdmans Publishing Co., 1959.

Thomson, W. M. The Land and the Book. London: Thomas Nelson and Sons, 1886.

Unger, Merrill F. Introductory Guide to the Old Testament. Grand Rapids: Zondervan Publishing House, 1951.

_____. Unger's Bible Dictionary. Chicago: Moody Press, 1957.

Watts, J. Wash. A Survey of Old Testament Teaching. (Vol. I). Nashville: Broadman Press, 1947.

White, Edward J. The Law in the Scripture. St. Louis: Thomas Law Book Company, 1935.

White, Wilbert W. Old Testament Records, Poems and Addresses. New York: Young Men's Christian Association, 1900.

Winter, Williard W. Studies in Samuel. Joplin: College Press, 1967.

Wright and Filson. Historical Atlas to the Bible. Philadelphia: Westminster Press, 1946.

Wright, G. Ernest. Biblical Archaeology. Philadelphia: The Westminster Press, 1962.

APPENDICES

ONE: FALSE DEITIES OF THE OLD TESTAMENT ERA

It should be recognized that generalizations about any religious system do not necessarily apply at all times and places. There appear to have been "denominations" of ancient pagan systems, just as there are of modern religions. Thus, not all that was true of a particular system was necessarily the case on a local and individual basis. Gods and goddesses that figure in the Old Testament narrative include the following:

ASHTORETH: This goddess was chief of the female deities of the Canaanitish tribes, and she may be identified with: Ishtar, Astarte, Anath, Asherah, and Anat. In later times, the concepts and characteristics of Ashtoreth merged with those of: Venus, Aphrodite, Diana, and Artemis. In strict usage, the form Ashtoreth is singular; Ashtaroth is plural and is used as a generic name for any religious system involving female deities. It is doubtful whether this distinction is always observed. References to Ashtoreth (or Ashtaroth) include: Jud. 2:13, 10:6; 1 Sam. 7:3, 12:10, 31:10; 1 Ki. 11:5, 11:33; 2 Ki. 23:13. References to groves where the worship of Ashtaroth was conducted include: 1 Ki. 15:13, 18:19; 2 Ki. 21:7, 23:4.

In general, Ashtoreth was considered as combining the role of a fertile mother with that of a bloodthirsty goddess of war. Images and representations of Ashtoreth are always of a nude woman, and Palestinian archaeology has produced more statues and statuettes of this type than that of any other place in the world. In many instances, temples and groves of Ashtoreth were simply centers of prostitution and vice, and "worship" rites included the unrestrained expression of sex. Typically, this religion demanded the surrender of virginity by its young female followers. In some contexts, Ashtoreth (perhaps under a variant name) was seen as the wife or mistress of Baal. Tyre and Sidon, as well as Abram's home city of Ur, were among the centers given to the worship of Ashtoreth.

BAAL: This name served as the generic identification of local or regional male deities that were the counterpart of Ashtoreth. In general, Baal (plural Baalim) was the god representing the prosperity of agriculture and the fruitfulness of domestic animals. The name means "master." As the chief active deity in the pagan system, Baal represented the cycle of the seasons with birth and growth in the springtime, culminating in the harvest of the summer and fall. In many cases, the religion of Baal was associated with that of Ashtoreth, and temples to each were built side by side. Since Baal concerned agriculture, groves and similar worship centers, including high places or hilltops, were set apart for his worship conveniently adjacent to fields and pastures.

Involved in worshipping Baal were such practices as: kissing the image, cutting one's body with a knife, sacrifice of children by fire, communal meals, the sacrifice of animals, licentious dances, and various forms of prostitution. The temples and high places often provided private rooms for so-called "sacred" prostitution, and both male and female prostitutes served the religion. It was held that the worshipper, by engaging in sexual ceremonies, could promote the fertility of the cosmos by a sort of sympathetic magic. The cult fostered homosexuals (called "sodomites" or "dogs"), and such abnormalities as sex relationships with animals. Backsliders in Israel periodically were attracted into Baalism by its open licentiousness, its dances, and its banquets.

CHEMOSH: Although Chemosh was known particularly as the national god of the Moabites, worship of Chemosh was the practice of a number of nations in Old Testament times. In general, Chemosh was considered to be the sun god, and he was worshipped as king of his people. The Ammonitish god Milcom or Molech (also known as: Moloch, Malcam) was similar or identical to Chemosh. A particular characteristic of this religion was the practice of sacrificing living infants by fire as the supreme act of worship. Solomon foolishly built an altar to Chemosh, and this abomination desecrated Israel's capital for three centuries. (cf. 1 Ki. 11:7).

DAGON: Although originally the god of Mesopotamia, this god was adopted by the Philistines, and they considered him the chief god and the father of Baal. Dagon is represented with the body of a fish and the head of a human. He was considered to be identified with the life-giving effect of water in its contribution to the success of agricultural harvests.

TAMMUZ: One aspect of Ezekiel's vision concerning the causes of the divine wrath upon the nation involved prophetic insight into the fact of worship to Tammuz being conducted in the temple of Jehovah in Jerusalem. In many aspects, Tammuz appears as a Syrian or Phoenician counterpart of Baal, and the traditions and associations were similar. Among his worshippers, Tammuz was considered responsible for the fertility of vegetation and the unfailing supply of subterranean water in wells.

Babylonian legends told of the death of Tammuz in the fall of each year and his resurrection with the advent of new life and growth in the spring. In the Babylonian calendar, the name Tammuz was given to the month that marked the beginning of spring.

TWO: QUESTIONS AND PROJECTS

ONE: THE BOOK OF JOSHUA

1. Does God today exalt Christian leaders as He exalted Joshua? (4:14).
2. Can you satisfactorily justify the utter destruction of the Canaanites by Israel?
3. Prepare a paper on recent archaeological activities and findings concerning Jericho.
4. Comment on the procedure of the Israelites in imposing tribute upon the Canaanites instead of destroying them as they had been instructed.
5. When Joshua captured a Canaanite city he would "devote" it. What does this mean?
6. How would you explain the possession of Phinehas (24:33) when Scripture declares that priests had no possessions?
7. List the names of each of the cities of refuge and give the meaning of each name.
8. How do you account for the fact that the Gibeonites were the only Canaanitish tribe to make an effort to obtain a covenant from Israel?
9. Why had Moses apparently permitted the Passover and circumcision to be neglected during the wilderness wanderings?
10. Some have claimed that the two and one-half tribes that stayed east of Jordan were characterized by lack of spiritual concern. What is your opinion.
11. List five (or more) spiritual lessons derived from the book of Joshua.

TWO: THE BOOK OF JUDGES

1. Someone has said of Ehud: "His courage, patriotism, and faith are commendable, but his means of gaining his goal are not." What is your reaction to this criticism?
2. How would you justify Jael's murder of Sisera?
3. Explain the expression "a fleece test." Comment on the practice of some Christians to seek signs from God.
4. Make a study of idolatry under Gideon. What was the nature of the ephod and of the accompanying religious exercises?
5. It has been said of Gideon: "He refused the kingship, but wanted the priesthood." Comment on this charge. (8:22-27).
6. Comment on the spiritual validity of making a bargain with the Lord such as Jephthah's vow: "If thou shalt without fail deliver . . ." (11:30). What about determining the will of God by chance: "Whatsoever cometh forth of the doors of my house to meet me" (11:31)?
7. Comment on the exact nature of Jephthah's vow.
8. List and discuss spiritual lessons from the life of Samson.
9. Report on the appearances of angels in Judges and the significance of their ministry.
10. What does the book of Judges reveal concerning the heart of man?
11. What does the book reveal concerning the longsuffering of God?

THREE: THE BOOK OF RUTH

1. How would you justify Naomi's advice to Ruth to return to Moab when Naomi knew that Moab was a land of idolatry?
2. Prepare a genealogical chart in as much completeness as possible showing the relationship of Ruth to Christ.
3. Compare the ceremony of the loosed shoe as prescribed in Deuteronomy 25 and as observed in Ruth 4. How do you explain differences?
4. Prepare a character sketch of Naomi.
5. Compare and contrast the lives and backgrounds of: Rebekah, Rahab, and Ruth.

FOUR: THE BOOK OF FIRST SAMUEL

1. Prepare a report on the lives and persons of the prophets Nathan and Gad.
2. Why was the "word of the Lord precious in those days" (3:1)?
3. Prepare an enlarged map of David's wanderings, showing by dotted line his journeys from place to place.
4. When had Israel been delivered into the hand of the king of Moab? (12:9).
5. Justify Israel's destruction of all the Amalekites, including women and children. (15:3).
6. Comment on the apparent non-fulfillment of the promises of Saul in 17:25.
7. Did David really have the right to request provisions from Nabal? (Ch. 25).
8. Comment on the witch of Endor. Did she really bring up Samuel? Did God intervene? Was the whole performance an illusion?
9. What lessons could a Christian learn from the story of Saul's downfall?
10. Write a paper on the topic: "The Ineffectual Penitence of King Saul."

11. Study and report on the subject of "Anointing" as it is practiced in this book.
12. How would you account for the fact that both Eli and Samuel had wicked and unworthy sons?

FIVE: THE BOOK OF SECOND SAMUEL

1. How would you reconcile the account of the death of Saul as reported in 1 Samuel with the story of the Amalekite in 2 Samuel?
2. Explain the reason for Uzzah's death in the incident of the transport of the ark.
3. Prepare a full report on the Davidic Covenant.
4. Report on the conduct of worship in the tabernacle and at the altar during David's time.
5. In your opinion, how would the word of the Lord have come to Nathan? (7:3).
6. How would you reconcile David's sins with God's estimate of him in 1 Sam. 13:14 and Acts 13:22?
7. What is your reaction to the deliberate lie told by the woman to protect the priest's sons on their way to report to the exiled David? (17:20).
8. In his later treatment, was David fair to Mephibosheth? (19:25-30).
9. Trace the seven instances in the books of Joshua through 2 Samuel when an altar to Jehovah was erected.
10. Write a paper: "Why I would like to have lived under King David's rule." [If you prefer, you may tell why not.]

SIX: THE BOOK OF FIRST KINGS

1. What claim had Adonijah to the throne? Why did David disregard this claim?
2. What may have been some reasons why Abiathar supported Adonijah?
3. Report on the Lord's appearances to Solomon.
4. Comment on the purpose of the visit of the Queen of Sheba to Solomon.
5. Prepare a sketch that you believe suitably interprets the ground plan of Solomon's temple in the light of Scripture.
6. Comment on the polygamy of David and Solomon.
7. Report on King Solomon's mines.
8. Was the "old prophet in Bethel" (13:11-32) actually a true prophet of Jehovah or was he an imposter?
9. Trace the effects of Jeroboam's golden calves upon the history of the Israelites.
10. Inasmuch as Asa won a smashing victory over Zerah, how may we account for his fear and lack of wisdom in response to Baasha's growing strength? (cf. Jer. 41:9).
11. Comment on the discouragement of Elijah. What lessons does this event teach the Christian?

12. How would you account for the presence of the seemingly godly prophet Obadiah in the court of Ahab? (18:3-16).
13. Compare and contrast the person and ministry of Elijah with the person and ministry of John the Baptist.

SEVEN: THE BOOK OF SECOND KINGS

1. Discuss the effort to raise the Shunammite's son by means of Elisha's staff. What significance attaches to the failure of the effort?
2. Report on archaeological findings pertaining to Hezekiah's pool and conduit. (20:20).
3. Trace the exploits of Jeremiah during the era of 2 Kings.
4. How do you account for the fact that although Scripture presents Elisha so favorably and explicitly, it was Elijah who appeared with Christ on the Mount of Transfiguration?
5. How do you account for the apparent discrepancy wherein 2 Ki. 15:30 declares that Hoshea began his reign in Jotham's twentieth year, while 2 Ki. 17:1 says it was in Ahaz' twelfth year?
6. Prepare a report on the Moabite Stone.
7. Gather and report information concerning the city of Selah. (14:7).
8. Discuss the "minstrel" mentioned in this book in his effect upon a prophet. (3:15).
9. If God healed Hezekiah, what was the purpose of the poultice of figs? (20:7).
10. Report on the prayers of Second Kings.
11. Report on the person and ministry of the non-writing prophets during this period.

EIGHT: THE BOOKS OF CHRONICLES

1. Select one or more of the historical reports peculiar to Chronicles and develop it in detail.
2. Trace and describe four great religious revivals which took place in Judah during the time of the monarchy.

NINE: THE BOOK OF EZRA

1. How do you account for the differences in totals between Ezra and Nehemiah in reporting the various enumerations? (e.g. Ezra 2, Neh. 7).
2. Discuss further the action of Ezra in dissolving the mixed marriages. Can you defend such a procedure?
3. What is your opinion of the old men who wept on the occasion of the laying of the foundation of the temple?
4. Prepare a character sketch and appraisal of the life and ministry of Ezra.
5. Investigate and report on the order of the scribes.
6. Report further information on the Nethinim.

TEN: THE BOOK OF NEHEMIAH

1. Investigate and report on life in the Persian court during this era.
2. Compile a list of the various schemes of the Samaritans in their efforts to hinder the work on the walls.
3. Prepare a character sketch and overall appraisal of Nehemiah.
4. Comment on the belief of the Jews that the will of God was communicated by casting lots.
5. The list of covenant signers in chapter 10 omits the name of the high priest. Is there any significance or explanation of this?
6. Compile a list of spiritual and practical lessons taught in the book of Nehemiah.
7. Prepare a list of noteworthy verses in Nehemiah: Gospel texts, promises, devotional texts, and unique texts.

ELEVEN: THE BOOK OF ESTHER

1. Report on the meaning of proper names: Esther, Mordecai, Ahasuerus, Haman.
2. Adeney wrote: "Esther is not a Madonna, . . . the heroine of the Jews does not reach the Christian ideal of womanhood." Comment on this statement.
3. Ironside is very critical of Esther for concealing her national ancestry and marrying a Gentile even though he was a king. Would you agree?
4. Would you judge that Vashti refused to appear before her husband and his guests out of modesty or was it some other motive?
5. In speaking to Esther of the impending destruction, Mordecai declared: "Think not with thyself that thou shalt escape in the king's house." Would not the concealment of Esther's national background have saved her?

INDEX

Abdon	20	Ahimaaz	52,53	Athaliah	78-80
Abi	86	Ahimelech	39,40	Azariah (Uzziah)	82,83
Abiah	31	Ahinoam	41,50	Baal	9,18,19,70,79,80,89
Abiathar	40,59,60	Ahithophel	50,52	Baanah	47
Abigail	41	Ai	5,6,15	Baasha	68
Abijah (Abijam) of Judah	68	Allenby	34	Babylon	87,89,91,104
Abijah son of Jeroboam	67	altar	11,12,71,84,89,98	Balkis	64
Abimelech	18	Amalekites	16,34,44,45	Barak	17,18
Abinadab	48	Amasa	54	Barzillai	53,59
Abishag	58-60	Amaziah	81,82	Bathsheba	50,52,59
Abishai	49,53,55	Amestris	108	Battle of Carchemish	89
Abner	46,47	Ammonites	16,19,33,49,50,84,89	Battle of Haran	89
Absalom	50-53,59	Amnon	50,51	Beersheba	71
Achan	5	Amon	88	Belshazzar	95
Achish	39,42-44	Amorites	7,22,30	Benaiah	60
Achsah	16	amphictyony	14	Ben-hadad	71,72,78,81,82
Adoni-bezek	15	Anakim	8,38	Benjamin	16,22
Adonijah	58,59	angel	15,20	Bethel	6,15,31,66,67,76,89
Adullam	39	Aramaic	86,100	Bethlehem	25,36
Agag	34,36	Araunah	56	Beth-shan	10,44,51
Ahab	70-74,80	ark	29,39,48,63	Beth-shemesh	30,82
Ahasuerus	108-110	Artaxerxes	100-103	Boaz	24-26,62
Ahaz	84	Asa	68	brazen serpent	86
Ahaziah (Israel)	73,75,76	Asahel	46	Caleb	9,15,16
Ahaziah (Judah)	78,80	Ashtoreth	44,68,70,71	Canaanites	4,15,30
Ahijah the prophet	66-69	Assyrians	81,83,89	captivity	84,90,91,95

chariots	8,10,15	
Cherethites	59	
Cherith	70	
Chilion	25	
Christophany	4	
choir	48,74	
chronology	13,61,90,92	
cities of refuge	10	
Cyrus	97,98,100	
Dagon	10,21,29,44	
Dan	21,22,66,69	
Darius	95,100	
David	36-60	
Davidic Covenant	49,63	
Dead Sea Scrolls	40	
Debir	16	
Deborah and Barak	17	
Delilah	21	
deportation	90	
destruction of Canaanites	8,9	
Doeg	39,40,44	
Ebal and Gerizim	6	
Ebenezer	30	
Edom	82	
Egypt	49,91	
Ehud	16	
Ekron	30	
Elah	69	
Eleazar	12,28,29	
Eli	28,29	
Eliashib	104	
Elijah	70,71,76,94	
Elimelech	25	
Elisha	71,74,76-81,94	
Elon	20	
emerods	30	
Engedi	40	
Enrogel	53	
ephod	40	
Ephraim	10,20	
Esdraelon	9,17,42	
Esther	100,107-110	
Etam	21	
Evil-merodach	91	
evil spirit	36	
Ezekiel	89,95	
Ezion-geber	49,64,74,83	
Ezra	93,97,100-102,105	
fable	19	
fasting	34	
Feast of New Moon	39	
Feast of Purim	107,109	
Feast of Tabernacles	67,98,105	
foxes	21	
Gaal	19	
Gad	40	
Gath	30,39,42,49	
Gebal	61	
Gedaliah	91	

Gehazi	77	
Geshur	51,52	
Gezer	48,64	
Gibeah	32,33	
Gibeon	6,48,54,60,63,98	
Gideon	18	
Gihon	47	
Gilboa	44	
Gilead	83,84	
Gilgal	3,10,31,33,77	
gleaning	25	
Goliath	37,38	
Great Passover	85	
Hadad	65	
Haggai	100	
hail	8,17	
Haman	108-110	
Hannah	28	
Hanani	68	
Hanun	49	
Hareth	40	
Hazael	78,80,81	
Hazor	8,17	
Hebiru	6	
Hebron	46,52	
Hercules	21	
Hexateuch	1	
Hezekiah	84-87	
Hiel	5,70	
high place	32	
Hiram the king	48,61,64	
Hiram the builder	62	
Hittites	15	
Hivites	7	
Hophni and Phinehas	29	
Horeb, cave of	71	
Hoshea	84	
houghing of horses	8	
Huldah	88	
Hushai	52,53	
Isaiah	87	
Ibzan	20	
Icabod	29	
Ijon	69	
Ishbi-benob	48,55	
Ish-bosheth	34,46,47	
Ishmael	91	
Ittai	52,53	
Jabesh-gilead	22,44	
Jabin of Hazor	8,17	
Jachin	62	
Jair	19	
Jebusites	7,9,10,15	
Jehoash	(see Joash)	
Jehoahaz	80,81,89	
Jehoiachin	90,91,98	
Jehoiada	80,81	
Jehoiakim	89,90	
Jehonadab	80	

Jehoram	(see Joram)	
Jehoshaphat	72-77	
Jehu son of Nimshi	79,80,83	
Jehu son of Hanani	69	
Jephthah	19,20	
Jeremiah	58,75,89,90,91,98	
Jericho	3-6,16,70,76	
Jerusalem	47,49,53,67,82,	
	86,91,98,104,106	
Jeroboam I	65,66	
Jeroboam II	82,83	
Jeshua	85,99,106	
Jesse	36	
Jesus Christ	2,27,39,41,49,58	
Joab	46,47,50,52,53,56,59,60	
jewels of gold	30	
Jews	94	
Jezebel	70,72,79,80	
Jezreel	71,79	
Joash (Jehoash) of Israel	81,82	
Joash (Jehoash) of Judah	80,81	
Joel	31,81	
Johanan	91	
Jonathan the priest	52,53	
Jonathan, Saul's son		
	33,34,38,39,41,49	
Joram (Jehoram) of Israel		
	72,74,77-80	
Joram (Jehoram) of Judah		
	74,78	
Joseph	12	
Joshua	1-12	
Josiah	88,89	
Jotham	19,83,84	
Karkar, Battle of	74	
Keilah	40	
Kenites	15	
Kethubhim	23,93	
king	45	
Kirjath-jearim	30,48	
Kirjath-sepher	10,15,16,18	
Lachish	82,86	
Laish	22	
Lamentations	91	
laver	61,62	
Lehi	21	
leprosy	77,78,83	
levirate law	25	
Levites	9,11,21,48,66,98	
	101,102,105,106	
Lo-debar	49	
Lord of Hosts	28	
Luz	15	
Mahlon	25	
Manasseh	87	
Manoah	20	
Maon	40	
Megiddo	44,64,80	
memorial	3,12	

Menahem	83
Mephibosheth	47, 49, 52, 54
Mesha	77
Methegammah	49
Micah	21
Micaiah	72, 73
Michal	38, 46, 48
Midianites	18
milk cows	30
Millo	19, 48
mixed marriages	102, 105, 106
Mizpeh	30-32, 40
Moab	16, 40, 49, 75, 76, 89
Moabite Stone	70
Molech	9, 20
monarchy requested	31
Mordecai	107-109
Naaman	77
Nabal	41
Nablus	85
Nabonidus	95
Naboth	72, 79
Nadab	68
Naioth	39
Naomi	25
Nathan	45, 50, 59
navy	64, 74
Nebuchadnezzar	89-91
Necho	89
necromancy	42
Nehemiah	103-106
Nethinims	98
Nisroch	86
Nob	31, 39, 48
Northern Confederacy	8
Obadiah	77
Obed	26
Obed-edom	48
Omri	70
Ophir	64
Orpah	24, 25
Othniel	10, 15, 16
Paran	41
Passover	4, 89
Pekah	83, 84
Pekahiah	83
Pelethites	59
Pentateuch	1, 2
Penuel	67
Perizzites	15
Phaltiel	46
Philistines	8, 9, 16, 19, 20, 21, 29, 30, 33, 34, 39, 40, 42, 44, 48, 54
Pool of Gibeon	46
Pool of Siloam	87
prayer	27, 106
priests	3, 67, 98, 102
prism of Sennacherib	86
Pul	83
Queen of Sheba	64
Rabbath-Ammon	49, 50
Rab-shakeh	86
Rahab	3, 5, 6,
Ramah	31, 32, 39, 41, 68
Ramoth-gilead	72, 79
Rechab	47
Rehoboam	66-68
repentance of God	36
Reuben	2
Rezon	65
Rezin	84
Rizpah	54
Rock of Behistun	100
Ruth	23-26, 40
sacrifices	63
Samaria	70, 78, 81, 84, 89, 104
Samaritans	85, 99, 100, 104
Samson	20, 21
Samuel	13, 27-33, 35, 41
Sanballat	104
Sargon II	85
Saul	6, 22, 29, 32-44
school of the prophets	31, 39
scribes	18
Sela-hammahlekoth	40
Sennacherib	86, 87
Shallum	83
Shalmaneser V	74, 84
Shamgar	16
Sheba	54
Shechem	12, 18, 19
Shechaniah	102
shewbread	39
Shibboleth	20
Shiloh	3, 10, 22, 28, 29, 30, 31, 67
Shimei	52, 54, 59
Shishak	67
Shobi	53
Shunammite	78
Shunem	77
Shushan (Susa)	108, 110
Sihon	2
Sisera	17
So	84
Solomon	50, 59-66
Sorek	21
Southern Confederacy	6-8
spies	3, 15, 49
syncretism	85
Syria	49, 71, 72, 78, 81, 84, 89
tabernacle	3, 10, 29, 32, 39, 48
Tamar	50
Tarshish	64
Tatnai	100
Tel el Amarna	6
temple	48, 56, 61-63, 79, 81, 84, 86, 91, 98-100
ten tribes	94
teraphim	22, 38
Thebez	19
theocracy	12
theophany	15
thunder	30
Tibni	70
Tiglath-pileser	83, 84
Timnath-serah	10, 12
Tiphsah	83
Tirzah	67, 69, 70
Tobiah	104, 106
Tola	19
Two and one-half tribes	2, 3, 9, 11
Tyre	48
Uriah	50, 55
Urim and Thummin	40
Uzzah	48
Vashti the Queen	108
vow of Jephthah	19
well of Bethlehem	48, 56
witch of Endor	42
Xerxes	108
Zachariah	83
Zadok	48, 60, 61
Zarephath	71
Zebul	19
Zechariah	81, 100
Zedekiah	90, 91, 98
Zelophehad	10
Zerah	68
Zeresh	109
Zerubbabel	85, 98-100
Ziba	52, 54
Ziklag	42, 44, 46
Zimri	69
Zion	47, 48
Ziph	40